MARKETING PRACTICES IN THE TV SET INDUSTRY

MARKETING PRACTICES IN THE TV SET INDUSTRY

BY

ALFRED R. OXENFELDT

COLUMBIA UNIVERSITY PRESS

NEW YORK AND LONDON

1964

Alfred R. Oxenfeldt is Professor of Marketing at the Graduate School of Business, Columbia University.

COPYRIGHT © 1964 COLUMBIA UNIVERSITY PRESS
LIBRARY OF CONGRESS CATALOG CARD NUMBER: 64-15449
MANUFACTURED IN THE UNITED STATES OF AMERICA

To the memory of my mother Minnie Koff Oxenfeldt

PREFACE

This study is based mainly on information that I collected by interviewing many persons associated with the television set industry. Included among them were several company presidents, many vice-presidents of marketing, several vice-presidents of engineering, members of top management in the financial and control function, and a very large number of executives representing middle-marketing management; interviewed also were several journalists and editors representing the trade press, members of the industry trade association and some executives in firms that are suppliers to television set manufacturers. Several of the individuals from whom information was obtained no longer are associated with the industry; even more are now working for different set producers; a few have died.

These interviews were made mainly during the period 1959 to 1962. This study therefore represents a moving picture rather than a snap-shot of a major and modern industry. The reader should be alert to the time dimension: conditions that were observed in 1959 may have changed by now—though it has been sobering to find upon a revisit to a firm that practices, procedures and concepts were just as they had been more than two years before. It would nevertheless be an error to take what is said here as a description of conditions existing on the day this book is published. It would have been impossible to update information on one point without allowing other information to become more out of date. If the particular time to which a statement applies is relevant, it will be given.

The personal interview is mainly the research instrument of the journalist and clinician and has received little use in business and economics investigations. Properly used, it is a powerful device for obtaining information, but one cannot measure its accuracy or insure uniformity of procedure. Despite these serious limitations, there is no escape from heavy reliance upon this research technique. No other sources reveal what this study seeks to investigate.

To minimize the inherent weakness of personal interviews as a tool for obtaining accurate information, the following steps were employed in most cases. After a member of the industry was interviewed, I sent him a summary of the discussion for review and correction. Persons interviewed often added to what they had said during the interview. Occasionally, considerable correspondence followed to clarify or elaborate matters discussed in person. Not infrequently the persons interviewed asked that specific things they said be kept in the strictest confidence. Unfortunately in many cases they did not respond at all for reasons that can only be conjectured.

The chief measure employed to guard against error due to heavy reliance upon information obtained from personal interviews was an elaborate system of cross-checks. Different persons in the same firm were asked similar questions; persons employed by other firms and by trade journals were interviewed about matters that seemed sensitive or where the information obtained did not seem complete or accurate. In this process many bits of information were discarded or changed their shape dramatically. The reader, nevertheless, would be naive to assume that everything said here is accurate and all interpretations valid. The nature of industrial life is too complex and too shrouded in secrecy to permit complete accuracy, despite the great efforts that were made to achieve it.

Some information of considerable interest was collected that has not been used here. Although many persons spoke quite frankly and honestly to me, they nevertheless, understandably, reserved the right to censor some information. Possession of this censored information was invaluable, even though it could not be cited directly.

Every student of business practice—and every reader of this book—should recognize the difference between what executives *actually do* and what they *believe they do*; both are often different from what they *say they do*. This difference, which is wide in many cases, sometimes leads to the deception of the investigator without conscious attempt to deceive. Regrettably, there are some who, for a variety of

Preface

reasons that they consider sufficient, consciously conceal information or misrepresent the facts. Although careful checking has permitted the elimination of some such errors, it is unlikely that all have been caught.

Some of the information on which this study draws was collected for a different purpose. In 1954, I began an investigation into the factors accounting for variations in the market success of individual television set producers.[1] Information was gathered for that study by personal interviews with executives, trade association officials and members of the trade press in the TV set industry. Also, I consulted published sources.

Before the present study was initiated, I participated in a series of meetings with members of the television set industry, persons interested in distribution and members of the Columbia University faculty[2] which investigated the distribution practices and costs in the industry. Detailed minutes of these meetings were prepared, and they represent a valuable source of information.

This study was financed primarily by the Edward Filene Goodwill Foundation. The section dealing with the marketing functions of television set dealers (Chapter VII) draws heavily upon research into the nature of retail competition in the sale of television sets that was made possible by a grant from the Sperry & Hutchinson Research Fund. I wish to acknowledge my great debt and sincere gratitude to both sponsors for providing me with an opportunity to study a major industry in depth. This study unquestionably represents the richest single learning experience of my career—as well as the most frustrating.

A handful of individuals associated with the television set industry helped me over the many years that this study was in preparation. For several reasons, I shall not name them; they already know of my profound gratitude. This study would truly have been impossible without their help. My thanks also go to my research assistants during the period that I was engaged on this study: Sidney Bloom, Eric

---

[1] The results of that study are summarized in an article by the author entitled "Scientific Marketing: Ideal and Ordeal" in the *Harvard Business Review*, March–April, 1961.

[2] This group composed the "University Seminar on the Economics of Distribution."

Kisch and Mrs. Dorothy Cohen. In addition, I am deeply indebted to Misses Carol Fortin and Grace Epps for diligence far beyond the call of duty in typing the manuscript through its many drafts.

I am obliged to record a lack of cooperation of many persons in the television set industry which multiplied the difficulties of completing this study. Their failure to cooperate changed this study from fundamentally an economic one into something resembling a case for a private eye. They too shall remain unnamed. However, let those who would attempt a behind-the-scenes picture of any industry provide in their time and money budgets for the enormous costs of widespread noncooperation from members of that industry.

Rockville Centre, New York, 1963   A.R.O.

CONTENTS

I	Introduction	1
II	Parties Involved in the Television Set Industry	15
III	Internal Distributive Activities of Manufacturers	38
IV	Manufacturers' Activities Related to Distributors	89
V	Other Marketing Activities of Manufacturers	128
VI	The Role of the Distributor	143
VII	Distributive Activities of Dealers	179
VIII	Appraisal of Individual Marketing Activities	213
IX	Summary and Conclusions	232
	Index	277

TABLES

1	Television Sets Available, December 1938	10
2	Television Sets Available, July 1939	11
3	Division of the Retail Television Sales Dollar, 1962	17
4	Estimated Cost Breakdown for Major Manufacturers, 1953 and 1961	17
5	Costs of a Table Model Television Receiver, 1959	22
6	Distributor Organizations for Seven Large Manufacturers, 1962	26
7	Retailer Gains from Up-Selling, Based on One Manufacturer's 1960 Price List	59
8	Composition of Advertising Outlays	61
9	Variations in Outlays for National Advertising Media	71
10	Market Shares of a Large Television Set Manufacturer	90
11	Cost of Major Appliance Distributors, 1959	150
12	Estimated Distributors' Costs on Television Set Sales, 1962	151
13	Outlets Classified by Product Category, 1960, 1961 and 1962	181
14	Outlets Classified by Annual Sales Volume, 1960, 1961 and 1962	181
15	Location of Outlets According to Region, 1960, 1961 and 1962	182
16	Location of Outlets Classified by City Size, 1960, 1961 and 1962	182
17	Costs of Appliance and Radio Dealers, 1947–59	187
18	Operating Costs of a Small Chain of Television Set Dealers, 1962	188

CHARTS

1	Development of Television	8
2	Marketing Activities	15
3	Marketing Functions Performed by Large Television Set Manufacturers	39
4	Competition in the Television Set Industry	244

MARKETING PRACTICES IN THE TV SET INDUSTRY

Chapter I

INTRODUCTION

Marketing is no small potato! Not only is it already large, it also is a rapidly growing form of economic activity. Moreover, the economy's production activities depend upon and are conditioned by the marketing process. Marketing arrangements and practices, which include all activities involved in getting a product from the end of the production line into the hands of the customer, are changing rapidly. They also are one of the less openly and candidly discussed phases of business; indeed, information about many marketing activities is closely guarded even in firms that regularly conduct escorted tours of strangers through their production facilities. As a consequence most people remain relatively uninformed about marketing.

Out of ignorance, many businessmen and consumers may favor certain costly marketing activities that injure their own economic interest. If this is correct, then an opportunity to improve their situation is being lost simply because we know so little—as well as because of indifference. This study is intended to serve as a pilot effort that should facilitate similar studies of other industries. Although ostensibly the television set industry is its subject, it mainly seeks out standards, concepts and criteria that would assist in describing, understanding, appraising and improving marketing arrangements in all sectors of the economy.

If this book errs, it consciously does so by being overly critical and raising doubts, rather than by finding silver linings and extenuating circumstances or by inventing rationalizations. Study of economic arrangements is only partly intended to satisfy curiosity about the world in which we live; it can also serve to point the way to improvement. Certainly there is nothing sacred in the way we distribute goods. People, at least those who are not personally engaged in distribution, should be objective about these matters and welcome all opportunities for improvement. Unfortunately, such is far from the case; discussions of the merits of advertising, for example, arouse about as much emotion as do debates about civil liberties. If some business practices have become sacred cows, then this study frankly seeks their desanctification.

One should consider whether it is even possible to appraise economic activities? Do we know enough to be able to judge what is "good" and what is "bad"? And, if we find that something helps one segment of the population but is harmful to another, how can we reach a verdict? Can we apply and give specific content to "the greatest good for the greatest number"? Are all groups equally "deserving"? Should the interests of businessmen be held as vital as those of consumers? Should the prosperous consumer be considered as deserving as the poor?

One is tempted to pass over vexing problems of this sort, for they have no demonstrably "correct" answer. But these issues will not go away. By refusing to deal with them we make everything immune to criticism and change. To pass by such matters is not taking a passive or neutral position; rather, it condones just about everything that man can devise, including some fiendish as well as magnificent works. There is no place to hide from the necessity of making value judgments. Although no individual can make value judgments for everyone, he can help others by showing what is involved in his own judgment and how he has reasoned his way to a conclusion on a particular issue.

The preceding paragraphs may suggest that, in modern vernacular, this is an "angry" book. Actually, only a few sections deal with controversial matters, and even these are comparatively mild. For the most part, this study is descriptive and factual. Probably social appraisal has not been stressed as much as would have been desirable, but no one who reads this book will escape the conclusion that there is much to ponder and some serious questions to be raised about prevailing marketing arrangements.

It is disturbing to find that the evidence on which many writers base their conclusions about our business system is shallow and unreliable. There are very few "professional" studies of the operation of individual business enterprises or industries that deal with basic economic forces and their probable consequences. True, one can read about the American business system in some novels and also in the sometimes even more fictional accounts that appear in magazines dedicated to glamorizing business executives. Many of the questions discussed here, however, rarely are covered in the existing literature; when they are discussed they are barely recognizable as the same. Direct contact with the business world has presented the author with many surprises for which a reading of the literature of business did not prepare him.

What are the sources for learning about marketing arrangements and our business system in general? First, there are the writings of economists and political scientists. Ordinarily these writers discuss the business system in broad terms and deal with the degree of competitiveness among firms and the various forms that competition takes, the nature and severity of general economic fluctuations, the growth patterns of the total economy and of individual sectors, and the like. They tell little or nothing—indeed, they do not claim to—about the nature and behavior of firms and executives which might then serve as bases for explaining the operation of the total business system. They eschew the analysis of individual firms and primarily discuss industries and even broader categories of enterprise. Economists and political scientists perhaps should not be criticized for their failure to treat individual firms in detail, for that sphere has been largely reserved (wrongly, it seems to this author) to the specialist in "business" or "management."

A second source of information is the kind of novel which discusses the internal politics of a large corporation. Included in this group is the classic nonfictional study by Mr. William Whyte, *The Organization Man*. These writings sometimes are referred to as the "Executive Suite" literature, and include a novel with that title, among a large number of others. A reading of some of these novels suggests that they are not entirely fictional. However, these authors are not equipped either by their personal experience or researches to know what happens in business. Moreover, one must expect—and indeed demand—that a novelist take some liberty with the facts.

The trade press is another source. Each industry has one or more periodicals which discuss current developments in the trade and present a wide variety of personal details and sometimes inside stories about what is going on. Often one finds some juicy and valuable nuggets here, along with some erroneous reports. Very few reports, whether accurate or not, can be found about the workings of individual firms in the areas that are discussed here, however.

An additional source of information about the way the business system operates may be described as "business practice materials." These represent studies made specifically for the purpose of explaining how businessmen perform certain functions. Notable among the sources are the studies made by the National Industrial Conference Board and the American Management Association. Of a similar nature are businessmen's statements before a wide variety of business groups in executive training courses about the way their company handles the specific matters under discussion. These studies suffer from a strong tendency to present executives' actions in the most favorable light possible. A similar source are "business cases," prepared primarily for use in training of executives. Cases vary in their quality and depth, but often give a fairly realistic picture of the position in which many businessmen find themselves and how they perceive their situation; they tell rather less about what businessmen actually do.

One also learns about our business system from law-suits. These include both private litigation, in the course of which much information that would otherwise be hidden from the public is made available and, law-suits instituted by government. When the latter are intended to stop or punish business for actions taken in a market place, they sometimes are extremely illuminating.

Hearings held by Congressional committees investigating business practices represent another source of information. Even before the beginning of the twentieth century, the United States Congress has sporadically investigated business behavior—especially in sensitive areas like the financing of business, pricing and advertising. Outstanding among these investigations was the Temporary National Economic Committee hearings (between 1938 and 1941) which culminated in the publication of roughly 80 volumes of hearings and reports. Recent investigations by the late Senator Estes Kefauver and others into prices of farm and pharmaceutical products and "payola" also give some insights into the way our business system occasionally operates.

Introduction

Clearly there *is* information about business. The questions we must ask about this information are: How much reliable information exists about the nature of current marketing arrangements? How representative is this information? How currently descriptive is this information—that is, is it already out of date? Is this information internally consistent or does it contradict other information available?

It would be almost impossible to evaluate the available information about the business system piece by piece. After my experience in preparing this case study, I must conclude that the nature of our business system is mysterious even to most people who specialize both in business practice and in the teaching of business. Business specialists as a group seem to rely upon a caricature of the business system which they treat as if it were empirically derived.

We have a great deal to learn about the things that businessmen do and the consequences of their actions. The information available is limited in scope and highly unrepresentative. It is in many cases extremely inaccurate, but it is impossible to tell in advance which accounts are accurate and which are not, and most of the information available is far out of date. The business system and the methods of operation employed by business executives have changed drastically over the last 15 years. Nevertheless, most of what we believe to be true of the American business system is based upon writings published before the Second World War.

Let us assume that our business system should be fully and widely understood. What is it essential to understand? Our goal is to discover its true nature, to understand its social and economic effects, to appraise its efficiency and to uncover defects that are remediable.

Any industry study is highly selective, of necessity. Accordingly, some matters are discussed in the following chapters that could have been passed over altogether, while others that might have been discussed in detail are only touched upon lightly. No reliable guides or frameworks exist by which one can assess the importance, relevance and interrelationships of various aspects of an industry's distribution arrangements. This state of affairs betokens a basic deficiency in our understanding of the business system.

Some frameworks, or "models," do underlie all industry studies. Most of them reflect the market models developed by economic theorists. Undoubtedly the most widely used is related to the concept of "competition." Industries are described and analyzed mainly with the aim of assessing the degree to which they are competitive. More specifically, these studies concentrate on the number of firms in the industry and their changes over a period of time; their size, location, degree of vertical integration; the ease with which newcomers can enter the industry; the extent to which customers view the offerings of rival firms to be similar; the nature and extent of cost variations with changes in volume of output; and the like. One could discuss these topics in depth and still fail to cover most of the subjects that occupy most of the following pages. Although the aspects of industry singled out by price theory are pertinent for some purposes, they do not give an illuminating picture of the nature and behavior of an industry. To have organized information about the television set industry around the economic theorist's model would not have satisfied the major objective of this study, which was to probe the true nature of the business and to explain how it really does work. Until that is done, one runs the risk that models developed "in the armchair" are likely to omit important, and perhaps critical, variables.

There are other models that might have been employed to structure a description of the television set industry. One may be termed a "functional" model. Its use would call for an identification of the different functions performed by the parties involved in the industry. More specifically, it would have required a description of the different types of "utility" created by persons and institutions associated with the industry. Ordinarily such studies also identify the institutions that create the different types of utility and indicate their cost as a proportion of the final sales with a vital difference. No assumption was made here that the activities in which parties to the industry engaged do yield "utility;" room was left for the conclusion that some activities render a net social disservice. Nevertheless it is pertinent to inquire into the service rendered to the ultimate consumer or to other members of the distribution system as a result of activities performed by each party to the industry.

A historical framework might also have been employed to describe this industry. In particular, the concept of an industry "life cycle" might have been used to organize the information gathered. Such a model would have put emphasis upon the changes that have taken place since the inception of commercial television set production, mainly in an effort to understand the developmental processes at work in industry. (One brief study endeavors to sketch the life-cycle of the television set industry,[1] and that approach also seems to find little room for description of the activities in which the various parties to an industry's distribution system are engaged.)

Another historical framework that could have been used to organize the material presented here would call for a review of basic economic trends. These could have been sought in many aspects of the industry, including: industry structure, costs, bargaining power, geographic location, business size, price line of product, expenditures by individual cost categories, technology, etc. The trends at work in an industry surely are of interest, but hardly in and of themselves. The study of any institution inevitably touches upon trends—either to explain the conditions that prevail or to forecast the direction in which they will change. Consequently, references to trends in the television set industry were made in passing at several points in the following pages.

Actually, this study of the television set industry was relatively unstructured almost to the very end. The author was determined to allow the information collected to dictate his choice of framework as much as possible because, as explained, frameworks traditionally employed in industry studies do not require all of the information about an industry's activities that one must possess to understand it thoroughly. In particular, I tried to discover the framework used by top executives in the industry itself to describe and interpret its operations. The result represents a decidedly nontraditional structure, which puts heaviest emphasis on a description of the "what" and the "how" and the "why" of business practice.

The present patterns of distribution in the television set industry can be understood fully only if one is familiar with the birth of the product and its technological development. Accordingly, this chronology sketches the history of television from its early laboratory stage, through the period of commercial sale of the first home re-

[1] Arch Patton, "Top Management's Stake in a Product's Life Cycle," *The Management Review*, June 1959.

ceivers, and up to the complex market situation that prevailed at mid-century:[2]

CHART 1
DEVELOPMENT OF TELEVISION

1873 A chance observation was made of the reactions of selenium to exposure to light.
1884 Paul Nipkow, in Germany, used selenium to create a mechanical "scanner," achieving primitive television with the transmission of crude images.
1906 In the United States, Lee De Forest perfected a three-element amplifier tube.
1907 In Russia, Boris Rosing patented a cathode ray tube to receive impulses from a scanner.
1911 A. A. Campbell-Swinton, in England, foresaw the uses of Rosing's tube for both transmitting and receiving.
1925 In the United States, C. Francis Jenkins achieved the projection of a silhouette.
1926 In England, John L. Baird arranged "the first true television broadcast" for 40 members of the Royal Institute. As a result, the British Broadcasting Company decided to support the development of the art.
1927 An image of Secretary of Commerce Herbert Hoover was transmitted from Washington to New York.
1928 J. L. Baird accomplished short-wave transoceanic transmission of images.
1930 Baird in England and Allan B. DuMont in the United States achieved dual transmission of sight and sound.
1931 Theater demonstrations of television in New York, London, Berlin, Paris and Stockholm.
1930s Dr. Vladimir Zworykin, a pupil of Boris Rosing, working first at Westinghouse and later at R.C.A. greatly improved electronic scanning and reception.

Regular home broadcasting and the commercial sale of receivers got under way first in England. In 1933, mirror-drum type sets were

[2] The following historical material has been drawn from many sources. Foremost among them are Orrin E. Dunlap, Jr., *Radio and Television Almanac* (New York, Harper & Brothers, 1951); O. E. Dunlap, Jr., *The Future of Television* (Rev. ed., New York, Harper & Brothers, 1947); Lenox R. Luhr, *Television Broadcasting* (1940); S. A. Mosley and H. J. Barton-Chapple, *Television—Today and Tomorrow* (New York, Pitman Publishing Co., 1940); and Lee De Forest, *Television—Today and Tomorrow* (New York, Dial Press, 1942).

offered for sale; they received the 180 line transmissions being offered four evenings a week by the British Broadcasting Company. No American company undertook the commercial sale of home receivers until the spring of 1938, and that effort was abortive, despite the fact that both the National Broadcasting Company and the Columbia Broadcasting System operated experimental television stations in New York City as early as 1931.

The commercial sale of television sets in the United States was strongly influenced by two factors: the role of the Federal Communications Commission and the outbreak of the Second World War. The F.C.C. clearly possessed the authority and responsibility to establish transmission standards for television and thus had the power to determine the nature of receivers that could receive those transmissions. Moreover, until the Commission established transmission standards (chiefly by dictating the number of "lines" that were to be transmitted per inch of picture received on a screen), manufacturers could not know what kinds of receivers to manufacture and consumers would take great risks in the purchase of any particular version of a television set. As late as May 24, 1939, the F.C.C. announced that it was "firmly of the opinion that it would be hazardous to both the best interests of the industry and the public to attempt by administrative fiat to freeze the art at this stage of its development." In November of the same year, the television committee of the F.C.C. restated this viewpoint, in a report which stated, "extensive developments are yet to be accomplished before the public can be informed that television broadcasting is a dependable service."

The United States became involved in the Second World War at about the time when the F.C.C. finally had established transmission standards at 525 lines and 30 frames and had allotted new frequencies for telecasting. As a result of wartime material and manpower shortages, production of television sets was banned.

Despite these two factors, which delayed the commercial sale and home use of television, the industry did have a brief pre-war history. Television sets were offered for sale in the United States for the first time in April 1938, at Piser's Furniture Store in the Bronx. At that time, approximately 4,000 sweating customers jammed into the store to witness a demonstration of the two sets offered by Communications Systems, Inc., and announced to sell for $125 (3-inch screen) and $250 (5-inch screen). By December 1938, five manufacturers had announced their sets.

TABLE 1
TELEVISION SETS AVAILABLE, DECEMBER 1938

Company	Size of Screen (in inches)	Price Range (in dollars)
American Television Corp.	3 and 5	125–395
Andrea Radio Corp.	*	175–595
DuMont	14	395–445
General Electric	5, 9, 12	175–600
R.C.A.	5, 9, 12	175–600

* Data not available.

At Macy's in May of 1939, four makes of sets were available: Andrea, DuMont, R.C.A. and Westinghouse. The makes of sets either available or "announced" by July 1939 are shown in Table 2. It indicates that fourteen companies had begun or at least made serious plans to begin commercial production before the end of 1939.

Indeed, by December of 1939, eight manufacturers had produced 5,000 sets. Of these, 800 were sold in the New York area. Prices ranged from just under $200 for 5-inch screens, to around $600 for 9-inch screens. By April of 1940, some 3,000 sets had been sold. Most sets were used for demonstration purposes by retailers in a few large cities.

Very few sets were sold for home use before production was stopped by government controls. Most estimates place the number at 10,000. About twice that number had been produced, but about half were used for demonstration or for testing by the producing companies and their executives.

For most practical purposes, commercial television started in the United States after the Second World War. However, the hiatus between 1941 and 1946 was not without major effect on the development of the industry. During this period, many important technological developments took place primarily because of the growth of a wartime electronics industry. Also, a few firms acquired

Introduction

TABLE 2
TELEVISION SETS AVAILABLE, JULY 1939

Company	No. of Models	Size of Tube (in inches)	Retail Price (in dollars)
American Television Corp.	3	5	185–395
Andrea Radio Corp.	2	5–12	190–350
Crosley	2–4	Announced for August	
DuMont	2	5	190–600
Farnsworth	2–4	Announced for the Fall	
General Electric	5	5–12	195–1000
International Television	1–3	Announced for December	
Majestic	1	5	*
Majestic (Kit)	1	5	125
Philco	6	5–9	200–425
Pilot	3	9–12	250–425
R.C.A.	4	5–12	150–600
Stewart-Warner	1	9	600
Stromberg-Carlson	1	9	575
Westinghouse	3	5–12	200–600
Zenith	None for sale, but some for loan		

* Data not available.
SOURCE: *The Annalist*, August 17, 1939, p. 207.

personnel, technical know-how and manufacturing facilities as a result of their participation in the production of military electronic products. These companies were, understandably, mainly those firms that had produced radios before the war. They emerged from the war possessing physical, personnel, financial and technological resources required to embark on the commercial production and sale of television sets. Complete newcomers were at an extreme disadvantage compared with these firms—more so than usually is the case in a new industry. (The enormous demand for sets kept this relative disadvantage from resulting in losses until several years later, when competition became fairly severe.) In other words, the links between the post-war television set industry and the pre-war radio industry and the war-time electronic activity were very strong. These interrelations go far toward explaining the number and identity of the firms that have been successful in this industry.

The production of television sets grew spectacularly following the war, though it took manufacturers more time to attain high volume production than had been anticipated. From an output of little more than 175,000 sets in 1947, almost 7½ million units were produced in 1950. Output exceeded that level only twice—in 1955 and 1963. The number of firms engaged in set manufacturing increased steeply also—even after production started to decline. Among the producers in business in 1950 (which was before the major shakeout began) were a substantial number that were new to the major appliance industry. However, among those that occupied a significant share of the market in 1963, not a single firm was new to the radio or major appliance business.

The links between the television industry after the war and the pre-war radio industry are nowhere clearer than in distribution. The major, established manufacturers, unlike the newcomers, did not need to devote their main energies to the creation of a dealer structure. The new product did require sales training and product information work, but these firms had previously established channels along which to move. By and large, the distributors who sold television sets after the war also sold radio sets and other major appliances—and had done so before the war also. It was "natural" and probably wise for television set manufacturers who had established distribution channels handling somewhat related products and calling on the kinds of retailers that were anxious to sell television sets (department stores, electrical appliance dealers, etc.) to sell their television sets in the same way. Given the hunger of consumers for the new product, the established distributors were anxious to obtain supplies of it. Thus there was strong mutual interest on the part of manufacturers and distributors to use the same channels established for radio and major appliances to distribute television sets also.

Firms new to the industry were in a very different position, however. Their problems and attempts at a solution are suggested by the following account of DuMont's experience. This firm was a bold newcomer, one that tried to speed up the commercial sale of television sets before the war. It was, indeed, the first company to place a full line of sets on the market after the war. Its display to prospective dealers in May of 1946 beat R.C.A. to a public showroom by several weeks. DuMont believed that speed was essential if it were to attain a sizable share of the national market. Unlike those companies that had already built up distribution-dealer organizations through their radio or appliance business, DuMont was starting virtually from scratch. (Philco in 1947, for example, had 27,000 radio dealers on which to build its television distribution. When Admiral made its bid for a large share of the television market, in 1949, it could count heavily on its strong organization of 81 distributors, including 5 factory branches which could be used to test sales and merchandising plans, and 36,000 dealers—at least one in every county in the United States.)

DuMont's television set division adopted a policy of highly selective distribution to match the company's quality product and class-conscious, "snob-appeal" advertising. Dealers were sought among the more successful radio merchandisers who displayed enthusiasm for television's future.

DuMont was determined that its television line would be the main source of its distributor's income; consequently, radio experience was not required of a distributor. New organizations, preferably with a name appeal were sought: e.g., Sid Luckman in Chicago, Bob Hope in Hollywood. Despite a few misfortunes, DuMont sales and profits mounted. By 1949, it had become one of the fastest growing television set manufacturers with perhaps the best profit position in the industry. Of a total industry sales volume of 810,000 sets in 1948, Dumont's share was 2.6 percent. (The company was unable to build more sets than this at the time.) In 1949, with total sales up to 2,948,000 sets, DuMont's share exactly doubled. (R.C.A. during the same period dropped from a 42.6 percent position to 19.7, and Philco fell from 16.6 percent to 7.2. However, Admiral and G.E., making their first real bids, jumped from shares of 1.9 percent each to 11 percent and 7.5 percent, respectively.)

By July of 1950, DuMont had acquired 2,600 dealers and 36 distributors. On sales of $50 million in 1950 there was a heartening profit of $3 million; nevertheless, this position was not maintained. In 1951's glutted market, DuMont's sales fell sharply and the year's loss was a resounding $4,500,000. With Zenith and Motorola joining R.C.A., Philco, Admiral and G.E. in carving out the biggest slices of the market, DuMont was hard put to maintain its place in the picture. Thereafter the company gradually lost position. In 1958, DuMont sold its television division to Emerson.

DuMont's experience was different in degree but not in kind from that of other aspirant television set producers that entered the industry without a history of performance in the major appliance business. Such large and talented firms as C.B.S., Stewart-Warner, Stromberg-Carlson and Hoffman Electronics were compelled to leave the business, and in every case inability to secure strong distributor representation seems to have been a major cause.

It thus appears that, from the standpoint of distribution structure and practices, the television set industry is a direct lineal descendent of the major appliance business. No unusual experiments were made with new methods of distribution, except for the development of the service company and the service contract. For a few years, distribution of television sets was unusual in one other respect. During the period 1947 to 1951, approximately, an incredibly wide and diverse array of retail trades offered sets for sale. Just about any retailer who could persuade a distributor or one of his salesmen to provide him with sets was delighted to take on the item. Such unlikely trades as beauty parlors, gasoline stations, hardware stores, and cleaners and pressers were retailers of television sets for a while in some communities. That situation was relatively brief. By about 1954, a very clear distribution structure for television sets emerged, despite the great turnover among manufacturers. Most manufacturers were selling directly to distributors, who resold to retailers. A small number sold directly to retailers, and one (Sears-Roebuck) was essentially selling directly to the consumer. This state of affairs very closely paralleled the condition that prevailed in the distribution of other major appliances at that time.

Chapter II

PARTIES INVOLVED IN THE TELEVISION SET INDUSTRY

It scarcely need be mentioned that each of the chief participants in the industry structure performs his functions, and indeed selects them, in awareness of the existence and typical behavior of the other participants. Also, there are contractual relationships, informal understandings and a long history of business dealings among them which permit each one to fit himself into the total structure. The combination of mutual awareness, contractual arrangements and markets on which they buy and sell to one another create what might be called a "system" in which they all play a part. The cast of characters includes suppliers of components, television set manufacturers, distributors, retailers, servicemen, consumers and government. The marketing activities that might be performed by these parties to the system are shown in the following chart.

CHART 2
MARKETING ACTIVITIES

I. Physical distribution
   A. Transportation
   B. Warehousing
   C. Refrigeration
   D. Insurance
   E. Materials handling
II. Services to facilitate the purchase act
   A. To make purchase easier or faster or more "successful"
      1. Assembly (assortment building)
      2. Provision of information
      3. Display and opportunity for product examination
      4. Provision for credit accomodation
      5. Delivery

        6. Return privileges
        7. Provision of pleasant and comfortable purchase surroundings
    B. To provide special post-purchase services and facilities
        1. Alteration
        2. Repair service and guarantees
III. Persuasive activities
    A. Competitive (noninformative) advertising
    B. Nonsubstantive product improvement outlays (including research and development)
    C. Personal selling, other than that needed to facilitate purchase
IV. Product and service improvement: research and development of substantive product features
V. Planning, organization and control (of the foregoing types of activity)
    A. Market research
    B. Distribution cost accounting
    C. Planning, budgeting, etc.
    D. Collection of cost and sales information
    E. Sales forecasting

One method of identifying and measuring the contributions of the various groups involved in set distribution is to follow the customer's expenditure after it leaves his hands. Consider the average dollar spent for an average television set at retail: Who ultimately receives how much for rendering what service? How much goes for distribution and how much for production? And, of the distribution portion, what share is paid to manufacturers, distributors and retailers? Also, in any year, what proportion of expenditures goes for new sets, what share for repair parts and how much for servicemen?

However carefully compiled and precisely stated, this type of information suffers from grave limitations. At best, it represents an average for the entire industry and does not describe the situation of any single firm. In view of the wide differences among firms, the system of weighting used to compile the average would influence the result strongly. In addition, the data presented here are imprecise on other scores. In the first place, they were not derived directly from accounting records, but represent estimates prepared on the basis of discussion with executives for several manufacturers who were familiar with their firm's cost studies over a period of many years. Also, the data are strongly affected by arbitrary cost allocations among different products (in multiproduct firms) and as between present and future costs (the last mainly involving the allocation of charges for depreciation, research and advertising). Despite these genuine limitations, the data to be reviewed probably do accurately indicate general orders of magnitude. They even more accurately describe what members of top management believe to be the situation and on both scores provide a useful backdrop for a description of the various groups involved in the industry.

TABLE 3

DIVISION OF THE RETAIL TELEVISION SALES DOLLAR, 1962

	Percent of Retail Net Sales
Manufacturer	60.5
Distributor	13.0
Retailer	21.0
Excise tax	5.5

TABLE 4

ESTIMATED COST BREAKDOWN FOR MAJOR MANUFACTURERS, 1953 AND 1961

Item of Cost	Percentage 1953	1961
Federal excise tax	9.10	9.0
Cooperative advertising	1.35	1.35
Other advertising and promotion	4.00	4.50
Product engineering	2.00	2.00
Parts warranty	2.00	.50
Direct production	66.00	67.50
Selling effort, direct	.67	1.25
Service effort	.50	.50
Merchandising, product planning	1.25	1.50
General and administrative, research, profit, profit sharing, traffic, federal income tax, etc.	13.13 *	11.90 *
Gross revenue	100.00	100.00

* This figure has been adjusted to get a total for all expenses and profit equal to 100 percent rather than determined directly. The magnitude of the differences among individual companies is suggested by the fact that Zenith's profits, alone, exceeded the percentage shown here for the entire item, "General and administrative, research, profit . . . etc."

Table 3 indicates that the manufacturer receives about two-thirds of every retail dollar. Part of what he gets—roughly five and one-half cents—represents excise tax which he must pay to the federal government. The distributor receives about 13 cents and the retailer 21 cents of every dollar. These figures represent rough averages composed of amounts that vary considerably from set to set.

Table 4 examines the 66 cents received by the manufacturer to determine for what purposes they are spent. Here we bump into another figure of approximately 66 cents, which represents the part of every dollar received by the manufacturer that he must spend to produce a television set. (The proportion of a manufacturer's costs required to pay for production has increased modestly between 1953 and 1961, as the table indicates.) Excise tax amounts to roughly 9 cents of every sales dollar and the balance is composed of many relatively small costs to cover engineering, selling, transportation and management activities.

Although not presented here, an analysis of the manufacturing costs incurred to produce a set shows labor costs account for about ten percent of the total, and about 75 percent goes for materials and components. The balance represents charges to factory overhead.

Modern industry has moved a long way from the independent artisan who took crude raw materials and turned them into finished products which he sold to a customer. Nowadays a very large number of people and business firms combine their resources and talents to produce and distribute every product. In addition, the government either participates actively or influences the behavior of those persons engaged in the industry. The main participants in the television set industry will be described briefly, starting with those who are most remote from the consumer: suppliers of components. Even the largest manufacturers depend heavily upon other firms for major set components, though their dependency varies widely. The most costly items purchased by most manufacturers are cabinets, picture tubes and tuners. The average set has well over a hundred different parts, almost every one of which costs only a small sum.

The most vertically integrated or self-contained firms in the television set industry are R.C.A., Sylvania and General Electric. These companies are important suppliers of various items for the entire industry; nevertheless they buy approximately two-thirds of their television set components, measured by value, from independent suppliers.

Television suppliers are extremely varied in size. Viewing tubes are produced by eight firms, all quite large. Three major independent producers of tuners sell to the industry, and each one represents a substantial business in its own right. (Three set makers make most of their own tuners.) On the other hand, cabinets are made mainly by small firms, as is almost every other component that enters into a set. Moreover, if one looks behind the suppliers of viewing tubes and tuners, he finds many suppliers of components to these firms, most of which again are quite small. The National Credit Office publishes an Electronic Marketing Directory; its "Electronic Components Section" in 1962 included over 146 pages, each listing an average of 18 plant locations. Even if a minority of the listings represent firms selling to television set manufacturers, the number of suppliers listed in that directory (which may not be complete) is well over a thousand. In terms of employment and value added, it is these firms rather than the firms typically regarded as television set producers that compose the major part of the industry.

Many of the components of television sets are similar to those used in radios and other types of electronic equipment. The suppliers of most television set components have operated for a long time as suppliers to the radio industry and still derive a large share of their income from outside the television industry. Components for military equipment represent an important market for most of them.

From its inception, television was able to draw upon the resources of established industries for most of its components. Since its suppliers also serve other large industries, their fortunes have never depended solely upon the level of the activity of the television set industry. Moreover, producers of components ordinarily sell to several set manufacturers rather than to one, so the sales of most of them are more dependent upon total television sales than the sales of any single producer.

The chief economic interests of suppliers to television set producers are fairly obvious: they gain from a strong and steady market for sets, for an important portion of their sales varies directly with television set sales; they desire a relatively high price for their wares; their interests are furthered by stable or gradually rising prices for their output to avoid loss from unforseen price declines; they hope for stability of manufacturer's product specifications; they desire consistency of customer relationships; they hope that the manufacturers of television sets will relieve them of the burden of technological change. These objectives can be translated into a desire for large unit sales at profitable prices, low costs of production and sale and a minimum of risk—the hopes of all businessmen.

From this list of objectives, it is easy to deduce the point at which their aims are in harmony with those of set manufacturers. They know that their sales of television components depend upon the set manufacturers' ability to sell to consumers, for suppliers make virtually no efforts to spur set sales.[1] Consequently they share manufacturers' interest in a large and steady market. Like all businessmen they desire an "orderly market"—stable prices, little variation in unit sales, except for orderly growth, and little shifting about of customers.

They are in conflict with set manufacturers mainly over price. They gain from a high price for their wares, while the set manufacturer wants to buy at a low price. Many suppliers are apprehensive lest their biggest customers decide to produce the item for themselves; they know that many of them possess the financial resources and technological know-how to do so.

Most suppliers are affected by the sales volume of the entire industry, rather than by the sales of a single brand of set. Moreover, they would appear to be mainly affected by the unit sales, rather than the profitability, of the set manufacturers. It is not clear whether set manufacturers try (and succeed when they do try) to pass along to suppliers any pressure on price that is exerted on them. Price pressure is often quite contagious.

Only one industry supplying television set producers has tried to appeal directly to the ultimate consumer, and then only sporadically. That is the viewing tube industry, which sells to the ultimate consumers—at least for replacement purposes. Almost all sales are ac-

---

[1] One outstanding exception was the development of the "new-shaped" 19- and 23-inch viewing tube, for whose introduction Corning Glass is responsible. That company's motive for making the change was consciously and explicitly to spur set sales.

tually made to television servicemen, who will install the tube for the set owner. A few tube manufacturers have attempted to create consumer preference for their brand. Not infrequently, a set manufacturer will base his sales appeal on the color, size or shape of tube—but will do so largely at his own expense.

Television set manufacturing is one part of the electronics industry, which in 1958 was the fifth largest manufacturing group in the United States. This industry in 1961 achieved aggregate sales of $7.9 billion and was composed of approximately 1,500 equipment manufacturers and major assemblers, 2,400 component manufacturers, and 700 producers of switches, wire and other electronic hardware. Of the $7.9 billion of sales by the electronics industry, $686 million (or less than 7 percent) was accounted for by factory billings of television receivers.[2] In 1950 manufacturers' billings for television sets were over $1.3 billion.

Measured by total income to manufacturers, the television set industry has been declining. Paradoxically, most of the individual firms engaged in the production of sets have grown larger. The decline in total dollars received by manufacturers between 1950, when it reached its peak, and in 1962, when it was down by over 30 percent, was more than offset by the drop in the number of firms that produced sets. In 1950 the number of manufacturers was more than double the 22 that operated in 1962. The growth in the size of some firms, even while the size of the industry is declining, led one executive to describe the industry as "cannibalistic" because some firms feed off the others.

In 1962 there were 22 "recognized" producers of entertainment-type television sets. This number remained after a period of substantial attrition, during which many small and some fairly large and well-known companies left the business or were forced to merge—or to otherwise alter their corporate structure—due to financial difficulties. Manufacturers of sets vary in total business size, degree of integration, volume of television set business and location.

Television set manufacturers are basically assemblers, as are many other firms that are usually regarded as manufacturers. The extent to which they merely pass along the components they purchase from others and the extent to which they add value to the product is sug-

[2] Electronic Industries Association *Fact Book* for 1962.

gested by the following table. It shows the manufacturing costs for a widely sold and not untypical model of set. These have been divided into material costs, labor and overhead (factory).

TABLE 5
COSTS OF A TABLE MODEL TELEVISION RECEIVER, 1959

	Materials	Labor	Overhead	Total
Chassis	$33.85	$3.20	$4.67	$41.72
R. F. Unit	7.40	1.11	1.62	10.13
Kenescope	20.83			20.83
Speaker (8″)	1.46			1.46
Instrument assembly	10.17	1.14	1.66	12.97
Cabinet (Masonite)	17.04			17.04
Packing	1.87			1.87
Materials and handling	3.06			3.06
Efficiency standard	95.68	5.45	7.95	109.08
Manufacturing variance	.86	.55		1.41
Build-up and change-over		.33	.48	.81
Cabinet rework		.14	.20	.34
Recovery standard	$96.54	$6.47	$8.63	$111.64

As Table 5 indicates, about 87 percent of total manufacturing costs are composed of materials cost and less than 6 percent consists of payments for direct labor; the balance consists of factory overhead. Thus, only a small part of the total value of a set represents production effort contributed by the manufacturer. On the other hand, manufacturers do add substantial value to the product by their marketing efforts. Specifically, a set that involved production costs of $111.64 would be sold (and in fact this one was sold) to distributors for approximately $200 and listed at retail for $319.

The goals pursued by an organization necessarily are a blend; some reflect the directions in which the organization, as such, must move in order to flourish, and some represent the paths along which influential members of the organization would like to move for personal reasons. It is impossible to describe these goals for any specific firm, for they are always complex and some are unconscious. Also, there appear to be substantial differences in the blend of goals that individual firms pursue.

This is scarcely an appropriate place to discuss business objectives in depth. Considerable interest has been shown in this subject of late, but relatively little is known about it still. General agreement can be found for the proposition that profitability, security (that is, avoidance of serious loss and freedom from great risk of loss) and growth are the clearest and most compelling objectives of most firms.

The manner in which any firm—or television set manufacturer in particular—seeks to increase its profitability, to gain security and and achieve growth depends heavily on the circumstances in which it finds itself. For example, the manufacturer who is vertically integrated to a high degree may feel particularly strong pressures to achieve high sales volume; firms with strong financial resources can adopt courses of behavior that are more daring than can others whose resources are thin; also, they can wait longer before taking drastic action, if they experience financial difficulty.

Although the objectives of set manufacturers cannot be discussed in specific terms, it is possible to indicate many of the goals that the manufacturers pursue, the conditions that they fear most and the respects in which their interests sometimes conflict with those of suppliers, distributors, retailers and consumers. The conscious and explicit goals are very strongly oriented around unit sales. More than anything else, they apparently strive to enlarge their sales volume—and especially their proportion of the industry's total sales. Claims of being "first" have been made between 1955 and 1963 by R.C.A. (which has occupied first position more than any other firm to date), Zenith (which had been sixth in 1956 but rose to first in 1959–60 and is there still) and General Electric (which occupied a relatively minor position until it introduced the 14-inch portable in 1955 and took first place in unit sales for a few weeks). The emphasis that manufacturers place on sales volume may be consistent with their desire to increase profits, for they rarely will *knowingly* take business "at a loss." Unfortunately, with many, market penetration apparently has become an end in itself. Consequently, manufacturers may sometimes adopt measures which raise market shares but reduce profits in the long run.[3]

---

[3] For a detailed discussion of the mistaken use of market share measurements illustrated primarily by the television set manufacturing industry, see A. R. Oxenfeldt, "How to Use Market Share Measurements," *Harvard Business Review*, Jan.–Feb., 1959.

Television set manufacturers pursue a variety of sub-goals which add to their sales and profits. These are goals that underlie most specific operating decisions. The following list, while long, is surely not complete: Low prices for labor and supplies purchased from others; high manufacturing productivity; high prices for their output (from distributors); low, but adequate, margins for those who resell the product; strong consumers' preferences for their own brand, a relatively short "line"—few models; strong sales support from retailers; low turnover among distributors and dealers; high obsolescence rate on product; high productivity of sales promotion effort. Listed this way, the manufacturer's goals seem to involve some outright conflicts; certainly they call for many delicate balances. He wants a high price from his own customers but wants a low price to be charged to the ultimate customer. He wants strong sales support from retailers but wants to pay them very little for their services. The manner in which balance is defined and sought and the extent to which it is achieved is discussed in the following chapters.

One does not ordinarily think of manufacturers as being heavily engaged in distribution activities. Their very designation implies that they produce something and rely upon others to sell it. That impression is patently false. Manufacturers require customers for their own output, whom they must find for themselves. It is a rare manufacturer indeed in any industry that produces solely to order and makes no effort to obtain orders.

In the television industry, as in many others, manufacturers are no more concerned with sales to their own customers than with sales to their customers' customers. Most of all, perhaps, they are concerned with sales to their customers' customers' customers. Specifically, manufacturers are engaged in many activities to win and retain good distributors; manufacturers also, through their distributors, assist in selling to retailers; one of their largest marketing costs—consumer advertising—is intended to increase their retailers' sales to ultimate customers.

The distribution activities of manufacturers will be described in detail in subsequent chapters. What has been said already shows profound interdependence of many members of the industry, even though they may operate as independent businessmen and despite their conflicting interests. The manufacturer depends upon a very large number of suppliers, some large and some small, for most of the components of the product he sells; he depends upon those to whom he sells directly (distributors) to be able to resell his output to others. They in turn must find retailers to sell what they purchased from the manufacturer. Unless ultimate consumers buy the product, parts suppliers, the manufacturer, the distributor and the retailer all will founder. This harmony of interests in "pushing goods out of the end of the distribution channel" explains why manufacturers and distributors acitvely help their customers to resell their merchandise.

Distributors of television sets will be discussed here in two parts: the first describes the structure of major appliance distribution. The second discusses functions, fears and aspirations of major appliance distributors.

As already indicated, 22 firms manufactured sets in 1963. In size and mode of distribution they vary enormously. Several sell virtually their entire output under a private (retailer) label, and the retailer performs most of the functions carried out by "regular" distributors. Similarly, a few of the 22 are really very small local producers, who essentially assemble components and special cabinets to order for customers willing to pay heavily to gratify their special desires. These firms generally manufacture, distribute, retail and service their output —frequently from a single location. One major (Magnavox) and one minor (Curtis Mathes) manufacturer sell directly to independent retailers and can be said to have no distributors. (Magnavox does conduct operations at some locations that strongly resemble factory-owned branches.) Sears-Roebuck, which owns Warwick and Pacific Mercury, combines production and retail sale of television sets under a single ownership.

The following discussion refers to the trade through which the largest firms, all manufacturers of sets that sell in at least one third of the United States, sell most of their output. These firms include: R.C.A., Zenith, General Electric, Philco, Admiral, Motorola, Sylvania, Westinghouse, and Emerson-Dumont. A subsequent section describes the distribution arrangements of other producers such as Sears, Magnavox, Muntz, and Packard-Bell, whose distribution arrangements depart from the usual distribution pattern.

The major manufacturers of television sets have different numbers of distributors. In part, the differences are accounted for by variations in the number of markets in which they try to sell their product, with a few not seeking national distribution. (In particular, Emerson-Dumont and Packard-Bell mainly confine their sales efforts to metropolitan centers and then mainly to those in their own section of the nation.) To some extent, the differences are accounted for by the availability to them of qualified distributors. Company policy and historical accident also figure in determining the number of distributors of each brand.

TABLE 6
DISTRIBUTOR ORGANIZATIONS FOR SEVEN LARGE MANUFACTURERS, 1962

Company	Distributor Outlets	Distributor Headquarters	Factory Branches Headquarters	Depots
Admiral	84	80	15	0
General Electric	80	37	25	31
Motorola	91	84	1	0
Philco	96	70	18	6
R.C.A. (Whirlpool)	88	70	14	1
Westinghouse	85	50	29	35
Zenith	84	78	2	0

In 1962, the manufacturers of television sets with the largest number of distributor outlets (both headquarters and depots) were Philco with 96 and Motorola with 91.[4] General Electric with 80 had the fewest distributor outlets. If one counts only headquarters—locations where top management is present and where administrative functions are performed, the differences among these seven manufacturers are far greater. Motorola has 84 headquarters, whereas General Electric has only 37. The manufacturers differ greatly in their policies with respect to factory branches. Motorola has only one, whereas General Electric and Westinghouse have 56 and 64 respectively, if one counts depots as well as headquarters.

Several references have been made already to the distinction between independent and factory-owned distributorships. One of the

[4] Many manufacturers were reluctant to divulge this information, for reasons that are very difficult to fathom.

burning issues with the industry, almost from its inception, is whether to sell through independent distributors or to establish factory branches. The considerations involved in this issue will be discussed presently. The present balance between independent distributorships and factory branches might well change markedly, but few in the industry are confident that they know the direction, speed, and magnitude of the change.

No major television set manufacturer that sells through distributors currently distributes exclusively through either factory branches or independents. General Electric is moving toward factory branches as a basic policy but has not arrived at that goal. At the opposite extreme is Motorola, which operates only one factory branch, in Chicago. In the very largest metropolitan markets one mainly finds factory branches. (R.C.A.'s distributor in New York City is an outstanding exception, as is the Motorola distributor in all big cities except Chicago). A vague pattern emerges outside these markets; independent distributorships are used in the least competitive markets and especially in medium size and small ones. Exceptions to this generalization are fairly numerous, however.

A later section discusses the differences between independent and factory-owned distributors and the forces favoring one over the other. This section simply describes the situation without interpretation.

Almost every television set distributor sells only one brand of television set—though he may handle other appliances for different manufacturers. (He could, theoretically, handle these other appliances for a rival manufacturer who also has a line of television set, though such cases are rare.) In any territory, only one firm is distributor for the brand of a given manufacturer. He possesses an "exclusive franchise" in fact, if not *de jure,* and enjoys territorial exclusivity. Exclusive distribution has been attacked by the antitrust regulatory authorities and has created considerable apprehension and confusion, but the realities remain unaffected. Exclusive distributorships are virtually universal in the major appliance business and almost nonexistent in food, furniture, building materials and in most other lines. The rationale for this system and its consequences are discussed in Chapter VI.

Some distributors who handle television sets carry a full line of major appliances, including radios, hi-fi, refrigerators, stoves, washing machines, dryers, freezers and air conditioners, together with many minor appliances such as fans, toasters, vacuum cleaners, etc. Others limit their offerings to only a few kinds of major appliances. Many distributors of television sets handle also some products that are not appliances. There is a general tendency for distributors in the largest markets to handle the smallest number of items. Distributors in small territories must carry many products to attain a potential volume of business sufficient to "cover overhead and yield a profit." The smaller the sales of a given brand of television set, the larger the number of other products that the distributor usually is obliged to handle.

Independent distributors, in general, have objectives very similar to those of manufacturers themselves: they want to pay low prices and receive high ones; they want stable markets and prices; they wish to have security of supply and enjoy the loyalty of their customers. The independent television set distributor has more specific desires and fears. He wants the franchise for a line that consumers consider high in quality and one that enjoys strong sales support from the manufacturer and retailers. The distributor knows that a design failure by the manufacturer will hurt his sales—even though he is in no way responsible for the error. Also, he recognizes his partial dependence upon the manufacturer for creating brand acceptance among retailers and consumers, by national sales efforts.

The distributor's hopes and fears revolve around his franchise. A good franchise—a brand that is in strong demand in his area and a territory that represents a large potential market—is very valuable. Consequently, a distributor of such a brand will be anxious to keep his franchise and to retain all of his present territory. His overwhelming fear is that he will lose his franchise and either find himself out of the business of distributing television sets altogether or forced to handle weak brands. Another major fear is that the manufacturer will sell directly to his largest retail customers.

In several ways, the distributor is caught in the middle between the manufacturer and retailers. He is required to represent both parties and therefore gets involved in their conflicts as well as his own. Disputes between manufacturers and retailers in which distributors often become involved concern the size of margins of profit, servicing of sets in need of repair and payments for advertising. In addition, difficulties sometimes arise about the adequacy of inventories of repair parts and fast-moving models.

Excellent independent distributors are hard to find and difficult to keep. It is even harder to obtain a good distributor franchise. Consequently, the mutual dependence of the distributor and the manufacturer is incomplete and unequal; their economic interests conflict on several points. Conflict of interest arises over margins and, perhaps even more, over the sales quotas that most manufacturers establish for their distributors. In the past, some manufacturers never had any warehouse space and just shipped their output directly to distributors as the sets were completed by the factory. At some times, this practice resulted in what distributors viewed as "ramming sets down our throats." Also, manufacturers have sometimes dictated the particular models that distributors were to purchase. In addition, manufacturers want distributors to sell to some dealers that distributors turn down on grounds of weak financial standing. Then, too, most manufacturers want their distributors to conduct vigorous and ingenious (and often costly) sales promotions in an effort to spur sales volume—even at the expense of their profit margins.

If one views the structure of the television industry in broad terms, the distributor performs the following functions: He physically transports the product closer to the consumer. He stores it until the retailer from whom the consumer buys wants to purchase it. He seeks out retailers who are equipped to sell the product efficiently, and he "services" these retailers. He services sets in support of the manufacturer's warranty. He transmits information from the manufacturer to the retailer—mainly about the special sales features and the servicing of his product. He provides credit accommodations for retailers in need of such assistance. He provides advice and guidance to retailers with respect to the display and advertising of the manufacturer's output. He actually contributes funds toward retailers' advertising of the product. He provides information and advice to the manufacturer. In performing these functions, the distributor can be regarded as the manufacturer's agent—doing for the manufacturer what the manufacturer could not do so well for himself, or that he has good reasons for not doing. Also, the distributor invests his own financial resources in the enterprise, thus reducing the manufacturer's capital requirements.

Every distributor at some time believes that the manufacturer is taking advantage of him. Conversely, the manufacturer will feel that his distributors are letting him down at times. The strong mutual dependence that exists between manufacturers and distributors makes their relations highly personal and often emotional.

Independent distributors vary structurally in many respects; some are large, others are small; some serve territories which extend over wide areas, while others are confined almost entirely to a single metropolitan area; some carry a wide line of appliances, while others carry only a few; some carry the output of only a single manufacturer, while other distributors put together a line including several different brands of product. These structural differences influence the mode of a distributor's operations, and it is impossible to generalize about all of them on any score. The generalizations advanced above consequently have numerous exceptions. They, nevertheless, should clarify the position of the independent distributor within the total structure of the television set industry.

On the other hand, there is the factory-owned distributor. Although the so-called "factory branch" represents a division of the manufacturer's business, it almost always functions like an independent distributor. Common ownership does not prevent conflicts of financial interest between the branch and the factory. Since branch managers are usually accountable for the profits of their branches, conflicts arise that are not basically different from those arising between the manufacturer and the independent distributor. The difference between independent distributors and factory branches in mode of operation will be discussed presently. The reader should note, for now, that a separate variety of distributor exists and differs from the independent distributor in ownership, rather than in function.

With the functions of distributors thus understood, we can now examine the job of the television dealer. Sets are sold at retail by approximately 65,000 to 80,000 different retailers. These retailers vary from gas stations to large department stores; the retail trade that sells the largest number of sets are appliance stores—stores that carry radios, refrigerators, stoves, electric washers, etc.

Due to the almost infinite variety of retail trades that carry television sets, few generalizations apply equally to all of them. A crucial fact is that a very large majority of retailers carry more than one brand of television set—the average probably lies between four and five. Some retailers carry only a single brand. Generally they are small stores located in small communities; but Sears-Roebuck stores also offer only one brand.

Much that was said about independent distributors applies quite as well to retailers—except for the factor of exclusiveness. The dealer usually carries particular lines of sets because they are in active demand—at least among his customers; he therefore fears the loss of these lines. Conversely, good dealers are hard to find, and distributors (and manufacturers) are extremely anxious to retain dealers that "do a good job for them."

Conflict again centers around margins. If distributors attempt to assign quotas to dealers, these quotas frequently become a source of grievance. Dissension sometimes arises, also, over the prominence of display that the dealer accords the manufacturer's brand. Distributors may feel that competing brands are given too much prominence and too favorable a position on the selling floor.

The manufacturer and distributor are strongly affected by a retailer's basic business philosophy. If he elects a policy of "good margin and modest volume," the manufacturer and distributor may end up with small sales and low profits. The manufacturer and distributor desire most a retailer who will, by aggressiveness and ingenious operation, increase unit sales at the expense of rival brands. One can easily imagine cases where such a business policy would not be best for the retailer himself.

If one takes a broad economic view of the industry, the function of the retailer is to bring merchandise to the point where the consumer finds it convenient to make his purchase. At this point, the retailer displays it, provides information about alternatives to facilitate choice, informs the consumer of the availability and price of the product, possibly extends him credit or assists him in obtaining credit from other sources, and gives him an opportunity to examine the offerings of many manufacturers. In addition, the retailer can serve customers by making it possible for them to purchase quickly and comfortably;

he may make the act of purchase almost fun instead of an unpleasant chore.

Most television servicemen are small, independent enterpreneurs who repair television sets as well as radios and phonographs; an increasing number also sell the types of instruments that they service. In some cases, they are employees of large television manufacturers, appliance distributors, or a large retailer. Service is provided at all three levels of the industry—by the manufacturer, distributor and retailer. However, resources devoted to service are not remotely equal at these three stages; distributors provide most of the service on sets while they are under "warranty." The total amount and division of service outlays varies from manufacturer to manufacturer.

The functions performed by the serviceman are not easily classified as either production or distribution. Since service considerations figure prominently in consumers' television purchases, it is treated here as part of the marketing process.

Service has exerted an important effect upon television set sales, marketing arrangements and market shares. Indeed, many persons attribute the dominant market position of R.C.A. in the industry, at least up until 1958, to its provision of service in the early years after the Second World War—even though a special and substantial fee was charged. The rise of Zenith to first position in sales is attributed by many in the industry to the fact that servicemen, especially those of limited skills, find it the easiest national brand to repair. Even in 1963, and especially in connection with the purchase of color television, anxieties about repair costs influence the purchase of television sets. Persons who desire a second or third television set probably are especially concerned about the cost of keeping several sets in repair.

Servicemen influence distribution because prospective customers frequently consult them about product quality. In addition, servicemen in the employ of retailers who sell several brands exert a strong effect on sales, for they alert their retailer-employer to any sets that do, or are likely to, give trouble. The retailer, in order to minimize service costs and to avoid consumer ill-will, will generally discourage customers from buying brands that their servicemen criticize. As a result of close ties between some servicemen and retailers, sets of poor design are hard to sell, even before customers have trouble with them.

Parties Involved in the Industry

According to the traditional view, the consumer has no place in industry structure. Indeed, he is the beneficiary of the services performed by businessmen. This view ignores the important respects in which consumers do perform functions similar to those carried out by retailers for compensation. Also, it leads to a faulty understanding of some new types of distribution—like self-service stores and discount houses—which shift some distribution activities from the retailer to the consumer.

Consumers of television sets perform very different functions according to where they make their purchase. Some actually take the set from the retailer's premises to their home and make the initial installation. Especially is this true of portable sets that are purchased from discount houses. Consumers inevitably participate in the repair and service function, for they must select the person to call and decide when to call him if the set fails to perform satisfactorily. Some consumers make repairs themselves, especially when the difficulty is a tube failure. This last group of consumers also may perform the function of storing a supply of repair parts.

Much is made of the point that consumers dictate what shall be produced. The concept of "consumer sovereignty" is employed to indicate that the consumers play the same role in our economy that the economic planner plays in economies based on detailed economic planning. Others say much the same thing when they point out that the consumer tells the manufacturer what to produce. Sometimes he gives this advice by participating in consumer surveys; mainly, he performs this function whenever he makes a purchase. Thus, it is possible to regard the expression of choice by consumers as an economic service, though this view of the matter seems forced.

The consumer can, similarly, produce "time utility." He does this whenever he holds stocks of goods for future consumption. He does the equivalent when he waits for the product to be delivered on occasions when the retailer is unable to provide it immediately. The willingness of customers to wait, and the very act of waiting, reduces the inventories that retailers must carry and thereby lowers their costs. (Moreover, it may permit delivery to be made from the local warehouse of the distributor directly to the premises of the consumer, without passing through the hands of the retailers.) This waiting function of consumers is quite parallel to the function performed by retailers when they keep inventories on hand in order to provide the consumer with goods at the moment he desires them.

The rise of the discount house, which has been as great in the sale of television sets as anywhere, has resulted in an increase in the distributive functions performed by consumers. Since most discount houses and many of the retailers who compete with them directly charge extra for delivery, the consumer has an incentive to make delivery himself. Although no reliable study has been made on this matter, it appears that a substantial proportion of all television set purchases are delivered to the home from the retailer's premises by the consumer. Partly as a consequence of the discount house's growth, also, it appears that the placing of an order for future delivery has grown. Consequently, the consumer is producing more time utility now than in the past. Also, since sets, in an increased proportion, are now being purchased as replacements, many consumers render an economic service by connecting the set to the outside aerial. As indicated, moreover, set repair by the householder has grown substantially.

We must consider the objectives and fears of consumers, as well as those of other participants in the television set industry.[5] The consumer mainly wishes a wide choice, convenience, confidence in the seller's statements and good value.

Consumers tastes and requirements vary, and they often do not know what features they want in a product until they have seen many alternatives. On the other hand, many consumers are bewildered by an extremely broad selection and may eventually buy a less suitable purchase than if they had been offered fewer choices. Accordingly it appears that consumers want a wide but limited variety of products. Consumers' wishes for wide choice conflicts with the economic interest of producers very often.

Every manufacturer, consciously or unconsciously, tries to strike a balance between making products that are easy to sell and making products that are easy to produce. To make his products easy to sell,

[5] A consumer survey was conducted in Philadelphia during 1962, which was concerned entirely with television set purchase. It is one of many sources upon which this discussion rests. See David J. Rachman, Robert J. Robichaud and Henry Gomez, *The Consumer's Image of the Television Retailer.*

he must adapt each unit to the specialized needs and whims of individual consumers; this course leads to heavy costs of production. On the other hand, a producer who seeks to keep production costs to a minimum will keep his output uniform and will find that his offerings are not what most of his customers want. Accordingly, to sell his uniform output, he would be forced to make strong efforts and heavy outlays to persuade customers to accept something different from what they want. This route leads to heavy *sales* costs in order to achieve low costs of *production*.

In almost all industries, and certainly in the television set industry, manufacturers limit the alternatives they offer consumers. Partly, they are limited by the fact that they know of and control only a few special product features while their competitors know and control others; mainly, however, they are limited in their offerings by the high cost of producing a large number of different models and styles and by the heavy costs to distributors and retailers of handling a very broad line of products. Strong financial sanctions thus limit manufacturers' offerings. Within these cost constraints, producers try to offer their customer a wide choice, for by so doing they are able to hold down their sales costs.

In addition to a wide variety, the consumer wants many things that come under the heading of "convenience." Included are such things as courteous treatment by sales personnel, near-by and readily accessible retail shops, speedy service, free and speedy delivery, special wrapping, credit accommodations, air conditioning, wide aisles, opportunity to examine the product, freedom from intimidation by salespeople, return privileges, etc.

The average consumer seems most fearful that his ignorance will be exploited by the retailer. His apprehension probably is due as much to the personal embarrassment that would result from making a mistake and being outsmarted by someone else as from the financial loss caused by unwise expenditure. Especially in the case of the television set, which requires an unusual level of technical competence to make a wise selection, the consumer is likely to feel insecure and vulnerable. Accordingly, he may be especially anxious to be able to trust the manufacturer's claims and the retailer's statements. However, he is likely to be suspicious of them because he recognizes how poorly he is equipped to protect himself—and he suspects that the retailer knows and is willing to exploit that fact.

There is a strong bias on the part of consumers to describe what they want from a purchase almost exclusively in terms of the quality and price of the product. They rarely talk about comfort, convenience, credit accommodation, broad assortments and pleasure in shopping. This bias is even stronger among those who speak for the consumer. They view his interest as being served if, and only if, he gets the "highest quality of product at the lowest price"; the service component of every purchase generally is ignored.

To judge by consumer behavior, on the other hand, very substantial consideration is given to service. And, much as he may deny it, the consumer is consciously or unconsciously influenced by advertising, salesmen's skill, attractive displays, and the like. All of these, perhaps more than product quality, combine on occasion to give consumers a feeling of importance or of self-indulgence. It may well be such feelings, more than the use of a physical product, that the consumer seeks from his purchase. Certainly, as his level of consumption rises, he increasingly seeks to gratify general desires—such as those for status, self-importance, activity for its own sake—rather than to fill specific needs.

We turn now to the role of the government in this industry. It is common in discussion to shift from the "proper role" for government to its "actual role." [6] Since the gap between these two is often regrettably large, each will be discussed separately.

In a free enterprise system, government theoretically is an umpire who ensures that all groups within an industry play fair and according to the rules of the game. It basically enforces contracts and law and order. The character of the game and its outcome is to be determined by the participants and, in particular, by their industriousness and skill. Wherever the contestants seem to be unfairly matched or one or more gang up on the others, the government is to step in and ensure that everyone sticks to the rules.

---

[6] An interesting discussion of who can best define the public interest is presented in an interview with Dean Courtney Brown of the Graduate School of Business, Columbia University. See *Nation's Business*, June 1962, pp. 70ff.

One bumps into the government at many points in analyzing the economics of the television set industry. It digs its hands deeply into the pockets of everyone in the industry in its role of tax collector. In addition to all of the usual property and payroll taxes, the federal government collects ten percent excise tax from the manufacturer who, though he passes it along, apparently does not want to call it to the attention of the ultimate consumer. As already discussed in the review of the industry's early development, the government determined at what technological stage of development television sets were to be offered for commercial sale. It regulates the number and quality of telecasts; it also establishes the standards which determine the quality of picture that is transmitted and received at the present time. The hand of the government is also seen in the nature of the industry's price structure. Exercise of the legal power to establish resale prices in some states and the great care that most television set manufacturers take to avoid even the appearance of price discrimination all reflect government influence.

One might well ask whether government, judged by what it has done in this industry, represents the bystander and referee concept described above, or whether it has taken an active position. If the latter, have its actions been motivated by a desire to protect the consumers' interests, or has it yielded to the pressures of some particular labor or business group? Or, has government represented a wholly independent and special interest in itself—one that represents neither consumer, labor nor industry?

Many have charged government with seeking to perpetuate itself, even when government is not needed. They have suggested government is afflicted with an irrepressible propensity to grow and add functions—solely in the interest of expanding government control. At several later points brief reference will be made to the activities of government. No exhaustive analysis will be made of its activities here, however—even though one can only hope to understand and define free enterprise by analyzing the role of government in specific industry contexts.

Chapter III

INTERNAL DISTRIBUTIVE ACTIVITIES OF MANUFACTURERS

The notion that manufacturers make items and turn them over to others for distribution is less than a half-truth. Manufacturers of television sets and most branded consumers' products actively create markets among both resellers and ultimate consumers and also engage in many other forms of distribution.

Distributive functions are shared differently among manufacturers and resellers in most industries than they were several decades ago. Also, and partly as a result, the relative bargaining power of manufacturers, distributors and retailers has shifted. Manufacturers of consumer's goods increasingly influence, and occasionally dictate, the actions of independent businessmen who resell their product. Significant exceptions can be found to this generalization; in foods, in some "white goods" (appliances like refrigerators, ranges, washing machines, dryers), a few powerful distributors and retailers perform increased marketing functions and exercise great market power. Specifically, large national chains of supermarkets, mail-order houses, and department stores have created consumer acceptance for their private brands and have persuaded consumers that whatever merchandise they sell is of assured quality. By these means, they have "liberated" themselves from dependence on national brands and obeisance to manufacturers; they now are able to dominate many manufacturers.

To understand fully any industry which depends upon resellers, one must study the balance of power among manufacturers and resellers and the manner in which they divide the functions that must be performed. The main consequences of the present balance of power in the television set industry and the results of possible shifts in that

Manufacturers' Distributive Activities

balance will be considered elsewhere. The relative bargaining power of the manufacturer, distributor and retailer exerts a major influence on the complexion and cost of distribution.[1]

Although every manufacturer performs many distributive functions, some engage much more actively in distribution than others. Individual firms, moreover, perform their distributive functions in different ways. Consequently, no single list will describe all companies accurately. The following list applies to the major television set producers: R.C.A., Zenith, General Electric, Motorola, Admiral, Philco and Sylvania. Smaller manufacturers, those selling "private brands" or selling direct to retailers, do fewer things and do them differently. These distributive activities are classified according to whether they are internal to the manufacturer, relate to his dealings with distributors, with retailers, with ultimate consumers, with suppliers or with servicemen.

CHART 3
MARKETING FUNCTIONS PERFORMED BY LARGE TELEVISION SET MANUFACTURERS

I. Internal distributive activities
   A. Formulation of marketing programs and policies
      1. Pricing
      2. Advertising
   B. Selection of product designs and level of product quality
   C. Determination of a model "line" and "mix"
   D. Production scheduling and forecasting
II. Activities relating to distributors
   A. Management of independent distributors
      1. Distributor selection
      2. Distributor servicing
      3. Motivation and control of distributor performance
      4. Distributor development
      5. Communication of product information
      6. Provision of financial accommodation
   B. Management of factory branches

---

[1] In a highly original and penetrating (though possibly incorrect) article published in 1940, Craig and Gabler argued that distributor domination of industry was probable and would yield substantial economies. See D. R. Craig and W. K. Gabler, "The Competitive Struggle for Market Control," *The Annals of the American Academy of Political and Social Science*, May 1940.

CHART 3 (*continued*)

III. Activities relating to retailers
   A. Training of dealer salesmen and transmission of product information
   B. Aids to distributors to persuade or to assist retailers
   C. "Direct" sales to large retailers
   D. Provision of financial accommodation
IV. Activities relating to ultimate consumers
   A. Direct consumer advertising
   B. Product guarantees and servicing
V. Activities relating to suppliers
   A. Product design
   B. Advertising of key components
VI. Activities relating to servicemen
   A. Advertising
   B. Training

This chapter and the two that follow discuss most of the foregoing functions. Chart 3 is not, however, an exact outline of the discussion to follow.

It is difficult, and somewhat artificial, to separate a manufacturer's distributive activities into those that are internal and those that are external. However "internal" an activity may appear, it almost always is carried on under the influence and in full awareness of "outside" circumstances. For example, cost accounting activities may seem clearly internal, but even they usually are dictated by the requirements of government and stockholders—and above all, by the desire to keep costs in line with those of (outside) competitors. Similarly, all other distributive activities reflect an awareness of the probable reactions of potential customers and competitors. And, when "internal" distributive activities are exposed to customer review, they may be revised. Accordingly, the activities described here as "internal" differ only in degree from those discussed in subsequent sections.

Internal distributive activities are those that take place within the firm and do not require direct collaboration or negotiation with outside parties. Foremost among them are the formulation of marketing programs and policies, the selection of product designs, the definition of a line of models and its "mix," and production scheduling and forecasting.

Formulation of Marketing Programs and Policies

The so-called "New Marketing Concept"[2] has greatly broadened the scope of marketing activities in the United States generally. Many activities heretofore autonomous are now brought together in the marketing division of many firms; also, the need to coordinate and "balance" these many activities is now widely recognized. These changes have altered the fundamental character of marketing action in the nation's largest companies. It has changed from several independent and autonomous activities into more of a team effort, with each team member carrying out assignments which reenforce the effectiveness of the others.

To put this changed conception of the marketing function into effect requires effective planning and control. Coordination and balance, by their very definition, demand conscious efforts to fit together the activities of many people to attain maximum effectiveness. The logic of the "New Marketing Concept" demands the use of market plans.

Even without this new concept of marketing, one would expect that planning of marketing activities would be standard operating procedure. Top marketing executives are "managers" rather than "doers": they direct and work through other people, and only a small part of their job involves actually performing some nonsupervisory business action. As such, planning presumably is at the very top of their list of duties. Textbooks in marketing have dutifully stressed the importance

---

[2] This represents a series of notions that were originally set forth in 1951–52 by the top marketing staff of General Electric and were later explained and sold to the business community by other organizations—mainly consulting firms that specialized in the marketing sphere. Not all persons who have discussed the "New Marketing Concept" refer to the same bundle of notions; however, they almost all agree on the following:
1. Businesses should be customer, rather than product, oriented.
2. Firms should pursue profits rather than volume goals.
3. All of a firm's activities that concern the customer should be placed under the direction of a vice-president of marketing. These activities include at least the following: marketing research, product planning, advertising, customer service, personal selling and marketing administration (concerned mainly with planning).
4. A firm's operations should be guided by a long-range marketing plan.

of planning, but they do not tell how effective marketing planning might be accomplished. Possibly for that reason, until quite recently businesses in this country did very little detailed and explicit planning outside the manufacturing sphere.

The primary purpose of this discussion of television marketing planning is to describe rather than to preach. Some preaching is inescapable, it seems, when dealing with a practice, like planning, that businessmen admit is essential and yet rarely find the time to do. Some may find the following discussion critical in tone. I wish to state emphatically that the caliber of executive talent I have observed in the television set industry certainly is as high as in any of the others with which I have had direct personal experience. Many factors beyond intelligence and logic must dictate what executives do and how they do it. Methods that appear defective may nevertheless be the best that are feasible, because such matters as personalities, speed and cost cannot be ignored in concrete business situations.

It is helpful to explain the steps involved in "total" or "rigorous" planning in order to describe the kind of marketing planning carried on in the television set industry. Recognize at the outset that few managements would be wise to incur the money costs and other costs involved in very thorough, rigorous marketing planning. The proper degree of rigor in marketing planning will vary from firm to firm and from time to time. Just how thoroughly to plan represents a critical management decision.

A marketing plan is not different in basic concept from any other type: it represents a current set of decisions about future actions or "a predetermined course of action." A thorough plan contains at least these six essential parts: a statement of objectives (both ultimate and intervening objectives); a review of recent pertinent developments (sometimes termed a "situation analysis"); a forecast of relevant conditions during the planning period; an assessment of the firm's resources and opportunities; a selection from among alternatives of the actions by which the firm will employ its resources to attain its main objectives; and assignments to individuals for the execution of the necessary activities, setting time schedules and specific "controls" against which performance might be measured. These parts of a total plan are composed of sub-parts, in turn.

Manufacturers' Distributive Activities

Management specialists are not unanimous about the ingredients of a thorough plan. The foregoing description should nevertheless serve as a point of reference to facilitate a description of the planning activities of television set manufacturers.

Every manufacturer, however small and backward, has plans, policies and objectives. They are not necessarily conscious or stable or consistent; only rarely are they fully explicit and in writing with their underlying rationale fully explained. Increasingly, firms in the television set industry are formalizing their planning procedures and stating them in writing. Almost every top marketing executive in television who was asked stated that his company currently prepares a comprehensive marketing plan. One company president stated that his firm had had no comprehensive marketing plan up to that time but was going to produce its first one that year (1961). The chief exception was the president of one of the smaller companies who said, "It is impossible to plan in this industry. You've got to be able to change on a dime. What others tell you about their plans is just plain baloney." It does appear that the largest producers do, in fact, prepare annually a document, or a group of fairly independent documents, which represents a marketing plan, although frequently it is called by a different name.

These planning documents vary enormously in size, content and quality, however. Some are simply annual budget requests for the coming year. Others spell out in considerable detail the activities that the marketing division contemplates for the year ahead in all spheres of marketing, including, in addition to the obvious, such matters as research and development, distributor changes and the like. Although very dissimilar, the marketing plans that are prepared by the large manufacturers (judging only by those that the author has seen or discussed in depth) all deal primarily with two matters: target sales and planned financial outlays. None of them represents a "total" or "thorough" plan, as that term has been defined here. Very few attempt to implement the goal of a balanced marketing effort. The separate sections of the plans prepared—when they are composed of sub-plans for the individual marketing spheres—appear to be prepared independently of one another and simply bound together in the same document.

In one large television set manufacturing firm, the major document that governs operations in marketing apparently is basically a "control document." It sets down the company's operating targets for 16 "control points." If there is a total marketing plan (and I do not know that there is), it almost certainly has not been coordinated with their control document. That company, like others, prepares a series of planning documents for individual marketing activities which together compose a marketing plan.

Every television set producer has a financial budget of some kind; the advertising group in almost every company prepares a written plan and program (largely at the insistence of and mainly drawn up by the advertising agency); also, the firm is likely to prepare an annual schedule of sales promotions—inspired to a large extent by the needs of the advertising program. Occasionally, and quite independently of a total plan, programs are prepared in the marketing division for the addition and change of distributors and the training and recruitment of salesmen. These documents generally are uncoordinated. They do possess the virtue of being in writing so that they can be scrutinized by others. They represent a potentially effective communication device. Moreover, top management may review them to insure their mutual consistency.

Thus it appears that most top marketing managements in the industry do not hold the view that the marketing function consists of many activities related to the customer that must be balanced and coordinated by a single head. Individual marketing activities—such as pricing, advertising, product development, distributor management and marketing research—are often conducted as quite independent and unrelated activities. This is because the people who prepare marketing plans for television set manufacturers do not consider that all marketing activities must be coordinated and balanced and do not employ a procedure that could achieve such a result.

The caliber of plans prepared by many set manufacturers is affected by other circumstances. A few executives stated in confidence that they sometimes are powerless to express their opinions with complete candor and to use the power that ostensibly is theirs. Consequently, even the few firms that seem to employ effective procedures and to adopt an enlightened view toward planning may produce poor plans because actual procedures and concepts differ from what is supposed to take place. More serious, a high level marketing executive in two different firms admitted that they do not even know for sure what is formally correct planning procedure for their firms. They follow what they believe to be regular practice, but they would not even know where to go to learn their firm's planning procedure. It has become customary in many television set firms (and others, no doubt) to treat planning manuals as uncomfortable new shoes; they are kicked off when they begin to pinch and the comfortable old slippers are put on again.

Finally, the plans prepared in some firms are quickly filed away in a drawer, literally, not to be examined even once during the period covered by the plan, because top management apparently does not "stick to the plan." "If the top brass is going to ignore the plan, why should I be concerned with its contents?" is one statement made to the author. This executive said that he was not even sure that he could find a copy of the plan currently in effect. He searched his desk drawers and did produce the document, but he said that he had not even looked at it after it reached his desk, except to see what it contained with respect to his own activity. His final comment was, "Plans are a sort of a joke around here."

The following instance suggests the degree of planning done and the use made of the planning document in one large manufacturing company. Around 1959 this firm took the first steps in the direction of formalized planning of its marketing activities. The impetus came from the appointment of a new vice-president for finance. Under his urging and direction, this company each year prepares a statement of "Objectives and Goals." These are set down at the corporate level by very top management after informal discussions among themselves. There is no upward planning—from the lower echelons of management to the top—involved in this process.

The "Objectives and Goals" statements prepared by this firm are extremely broad and general. One executive, after reading some statements from the then current "Objectives and Goals," stated, "How ambiguous can you get?" The statements he had read certainly justified that comment. One wonders whether and how "Objectives and Goals" influences actual marketing policy and behavior. One executive stated that the "Objectives and Goals" of the preceding year had included a statement referring directly to his operation. He accordingly prepared a program to carry out the stated objective. When it was submitted to top management, he was told that no funds had been allocated for that purpose. He no longer had any interest in reading "Objectives and Goals." Top management may have been trying a few "dry runs" with its new planning arrangements before putting them into effect. If so, in the process they may have created difficulties to be overcome in the future.

One obtains a clearer notion of a typical television set producer's annual marketing plan if he examines the headings of a specific plan for a recent year prepared by a major manufacturer. They were as follows:

1. General distribution and financial plans
2. National advertising plans
3. Cooperative advertising plans
4. Sales promotion plans
5. Service plans

These five sections apply to all of this manufacturer's consumer products. The plan then continues with a discussion of the merchandising plans and volume forecasts for individual products. The following subjects were covered in the merchandising plan section for television sets during the same year:

1. Television trends and their effect
2. Size of tubes and trends in tube size
3. Price thoughts
4. Ideas on how our company should distribute
5. Trends in sales of consoles

The total section dealing with television sets occupied only about six pages of the full report.

The two most vital portions of marketing plans are those discussing objectives and financial budgets. These two plan-ingredients are fairly similar from company to company. They also dominate the rest of the plan and exert great influence upon the industry's operations generally. Management specialists identify several levels of a firm's objectives. To arrive logically at specific operating targets for any planning period, a firm should derive each level of objective from the

Manufacturers' Distributive Activities

higher levels. The various levels of objectives that can be distinguished are: (1) the firm's "credo" (which represents top management's broad business philosophy), (2) long-term objectives (which usually concern such matters as profitability, growth and financial security), (3) short-term objectives (which might deal with rate of profit, cash position, distribution ratio, number of distributors, etc.), (4) operating targets (specific numerical goals to be reached during the planning period), and (5) intervening objectives (which will be explained presently). In drawing up marketing plans it is not always necessary to make all of these distinctions, but usually most of them apply.

The marketing plans of most television set producers set forth only a single level of objective—operating targets. Executives who discussed this matter with the author stated that they "took for granted" that all persons concerned understood the firm's credo and long-term objectives; also they hinted that a frank statement of the firm's objectives could be a possible source of embarrassment if put into print. The notion of "intervening objectives" is relatively new and requires some explanation. Business specialists have emphasized the importance of a firm's having a clear "customer target" or a "specific niche in the market." Both phrases refer to a vital intervening objective—namely, the type of customer to which the business will direct its appeals for patronage. Many marketing specialists consider the firm's "customer targets" its most essential objective. (Another important intervening variable for most firms is the "brand image.") A strong effort was made to determine if the major set producers have a clearly defined set of customer targets—whether spelled out in their marketing plans or not. The results were clear: most large producers try to sell to everybody. Some believe that "with the large number of models in our line, everyone should be able to find a set of please him."

If one examines the marketing plans of most manufacturers, one finds that they start by setting forth a sales target for the period covered by the plan. It is usually stated as a share of market and as an absolute unit volume of sales, though some firms use one or the other. The usual marketing plan does not explain how the sales target was determined. Executives questioned on this point indicated that top management usually "dictates" the company's sales target and requires its executives to meet them. The process by which sales targets are set in one company is suggested by the term that was used during a discussion about planning with an executive in that firm—"setting sales targets by temper tantrum." Another high-level executive in a large firm explained that before accepting employment with that firm he had attended a meeting of their top executive committee and watched it throw out a plan with which it had been presented, with the statement, "You've go to get a larger share of the market than your plan calls for." This executive told the company president that he wanted it understood that if he joined the firm he would not "expect" to have any of his plans rejected unless the committee could tell him how to draw up a better plan. He said that he could not understand how an executive who had labored over a plan could allow the committee to arbitrarily change its operating targets. Until the time of that interview, at least, he had had no reason to complain about that committee's reaction to the plans he submitted to it.

One would expect a planner to establish sales targets only after exploring the programs that management could devise. Once the best of alternative programs was selected, presumably management would forecast their consequences under the conditions that are expected to prevail. Those forecasts would become their sales targets. In short, one would expect sales targets to be the result of planning rather than the starting point for planning. In the television set industry, the reverse is the case—as it is in most other industries with which the author has had experience.

Top executives in this industry are enormously preoccupied with market shares. Almost always, their sales targets are expressed as a share of total industry unit sales. In evaluations of other companies, executives rarely refer to their profitability; rather, they describe them by their "market penetration." The great importance attached to market share goals in television set companies' marketing plans, and the forces that influence those goals, help to explain some puzzling things about the industry's general performance.

One finds in almost every set producer (and in other industries as well, no doubt) the assumption that every firm will increase its share of total industry sales during the forthcoming planning period. This assumption probably stems from the following sources. First is a

Manufacturers' Distributive Activities

presumption of growing strength that may simply reflect human vanity. This presumption is often combined with what is here termed a "New Year's Resolution Syndrome." When management draws up a marketing program for the forthcoming year, it almost always lists some things to do that were not done during the current year. Or, it makes provision to do the same things more effectively. To do otherwise would be interpreted by those reviewing the plans as symptoms of decadence and failure. The entire focus and feeling of a marketing program for the future is progress and advance. Consequently, it is natural to project an increase in the firm's market share.

A fairly common and an effective managerial control device also explains why firms generally assume that their market share will grow. This device consists of picking out the ten or twenty local markets in which the company's market share is lowest and then providing for special efforts to pull them up to the average. Simple arithmetic shows that the firm's national market share would rise if this were done, and usually quite substantially.

Despite these two apparently reasonable bases for expecting any single firm's market share to rise, it is quite clear that the combined shares of all firms cannot exceed 100 percent. Consequently, one finds a paradoxical situation: producers may accurately estimate total industry sales during the planning period but collectively expect to sell substantially more than that amount. Some, or all, will therefore be frustrated. One consequence of this situation is a tendency for manufacturers to produce more than they can sell at prevailing prices. The result is an overhang of merchandise that leads to "deals" and strong sales promotions that either reduce price or inflate sales costs. Perhaps the main reason that this industry, which produces a glamorous and revolutionary new product, has made relatively small profits is the tendency of each company to overestimate its sales.

Preoccupation with market shares has other adverse consequences on occasions. Specifically, it may lead firms to sacrifice profits, as the following case illustrates. Although not completely verified, the story has been carefully checked and found consistent with all available evidence. The chief executive of one large television set producer directed management to reach a position of "not worse than second" in the industry within a specified period. In order to attain this goal, which apparently carried with it no expense or profit constraints, the firm introduced a dramatically new model at a price below the costs that some of its competitors would sustain to produce it; it purchased several costly television programs, which gave the firm advertising costs much higher than almost any other producer could support; it employed a variety of sales promotions and made price deals—all of which added up to greater volume at lower profits. However, the company was successful in achieving its sales goal. Indeed, for a few weeks, it claimed to have reached first position in total unit sales.

As the story continues, this executive some time later told his management that he now wanted them to achieve the target rate of profit that the television set division had traditionally set itself. Thereupon, the sales of that division declined to roughly the same relative position it had occupied before the crash program was undertaken.

The financial budget is a time-honored feature of large businesses the world over. Top management must know how much money its operations will require in the future; all those responsible for expenditures must therefore submit estimates of their financial needs. To prepare such estimates logically, one must first decide on the activities that would best further the firm's objectives and then estimate their cost. A budget request implies a consciously selected activity plan. However, to all outward appearances, budget requests generally precede and dictate the activities that are carried out by television set producers. It appears that only after an executive has been told how much money he can spend does he proceed to map out his activities for the following year. Some manufacturers escape the logical necessity of starting with an activity plan either by assigning sums to different departments on the basis of "standard" percentages of past, or estimated, or "standard" sales, or by cutting back the requests of all divisions by the same proportion.

The manufacturers that require a program of activities to be submitted in conjunction with their budget requests make it possible to match "means" against the "ends" they are to achieve. If marketing executives spell out their goals and the activities by which they hope to achieve them, others can assess their budgetary requests.

Management of at least one large television set manufacturer explicitly uses the annual marketing program as the basis for allocation of funds. Even in this case, however, the company's marketing program falls very far short of being a rigorous and detailed document. It is detailed only where it is necessary to justify a new activity or the expenditure of much larger amounts than were spent in the past. For the most part, this firm's marketing program reads as if it were prepared by someone who, though he would be paid by the word, found the task unpleasant and delayed its preparation until the deadline was upon him.

The importance of budget requests in business is obvious. They determine the allocation of efforts and funds within the enterprise and thereby almost dictate the firm's activities and emphasis; consequently they strongly affect its total performance. Not only are they crucial, they are also fascinating because they are so heavily overlain with taboos and empty gesturing. This key document could only by strange coincidence perform effectively the function it is intended to accomplish.

By some almost mysterious process, the adjudication machinery of the firm shaves, trims and slashes the bloated budgetary requests of its various departments and leaves each one with a sum it can spend during the period covered by the plan. In practice, deviations from this figure are fairly common. For example, most producers will cut back their marketing research and advertising outlays promptly when sales decline throughout the industry. If the research and development department should turn up something very special, the budget may be revised completely to "push" the new item or product feature. On the other hand, it appears that the budget is rarely revised because it was discovered that Mr. A. was modest in his budget requests while Mr. B. was not.

The budgetary process apparently is complicated by the different outlooks possessed by sales and finance executives. The former are very optimistic in their forecasts of sales and prices, whereas the latter usually are extremely conservative. It seems that in some companies the finance executives go along with the budgets prepared by the sales department in order to bolster their morale, while at the same time compiling a more realistic budget of their own.

If there is any principle governing the allocation of funds among activities and divisions, it apparently is to depart as little as possible from last year's division of funds. Many pressures compel firms to shift expenditures very gradually. In the first place, there clearly is a strong desire to retain the people already on the payroll—and preferably in their current jobs. Any request for a big increase in outlays generally implies that the funds will have to be taken away from another activity; the company would be forced to drop staff and cut back an activity which theretofore was—rightly or wrongly—regarded as essential. To cut it back for next year raises questions about why it was carried on at the higher level this year.

The foregoing remarks about budgets should *not* be considered a body of reliable conclusions based upon a close analysis of the procedures and decisions of television set manfacturers. These observations might well represent profound misinterpretations of what actually happens. However, they were submitted to several marketing executives in the firms and were accepted as fundamentally accurate descriptions of what happens in their firms. But then, even they might not correctly interpret what actually takes place.

Although top marketing management in the television industry started to plan rather late, compared to some other industries, marketing planning is developing rapidly in many companies. In an industry as volatile as this one, planning is incredibly difficult—enough to discourage any but the most determined from even trying. In this industry, plans drawn up in August are necessarily out of date by January, when they are to go into effect. It is therefore the rule that plans are modified, often substantially, after they have been adopted but before they have gone into effect.

Despite these difficulties, several executives gave overwhelming credit to better over-all planning and coordination in explaining a substantial improvement in their individual firm's market position. Among the things achieved by better planning was the fact that "the company no longer advertised products that would not even be built for two months or so." Most spoke highly of the benefits to lower-level executives from participating in the planning process, even if their plans never were used.

Long-range planning does not show good results, judging from the industry's experience. In the first place, some top marketing executives just refuse to plan ahead as far as five years. Three years is as far as most are prepared to go. In the second place, those marketing executives who had prepared long-range plans who reexamined them several years later said, in one way or another, that they represented a "lot of wishful thinking." One executive who says that he discussed the matter with others in the industry reported that this situation was general. "You just cannot find a hard-headed, conservative marketing plan," he said. "Marketing executives are naturally optimistic."

The most ambitious marketing programs prepared include the firm's plans for adding, dropping and developing distributors; executive and salesmen training programs; geographic areas to be cultivated very intensively and special promotion programs. Some specify new product features, style changes, and changes in the number of models to be included in the line. Where a special advertising program is contemplated, it often is described in great detail. Almost always, some comments are included with respect to prices to be charged.

It is impossible to consider all issues discussed in the most ambitious marketing programs prepared by TV set manufacturers. Two essential ingredients—pricing and advertising—will be discussed briefly. As will become immediately apparent, these subjects are vastly complicated. Moreover, it is virtually impossible to separate planning from execution. Consequently, the following discussion is fairly general and covers all phases of manufacturers' pricing and advertising activities.

PRICING TELEVISION SETS

Top executives are unanimous in the opinion that this industry places undue emphasis on price. One prominent executive who was commenting on an early draft of the foregoing discussion of planning said that at points the tone seemed excessively critical. He went on, "I do not want to imply that executives in this industry are very smart. In fact, I think they are downright stupid." Asked why he condemned executives in the industry so harshly, he said, "They only know how to sell with price." This viewpoint, always expressed with great emotion and usually in pungent vocabulary, was stated to the author in virtually every company he visited. Price clearly is the jugular vein of this industry and a constant preoccupation of its major executives.

The importance of price in this industry has little to do with the intelligence of its executives. As a group, they certainly are not less competent or intelligent than those in other industries. The importance of price simply reflects the nature of the market in which they sell their merchandise—rivalry is very keen. The most intelligent businessman operating in a highly competitive market will do less well than a fool who is able to collude with his rivals or who enjoys great market power. In addition, emphasis upon price is found not only at the manufacturing level; if anything, it is even greater among distributors and retailers.

Decisions about price usually are the responsibility of the product planning officer. In some companies he is called the "Product Manager for Television" or the "Television Product Sales Manager." This executive is responsible for deciding how many and what models are to be offered and for suggesting a specific price for each model. The unusual considerations that dominate their pricing decisions are: there should be fairly narrow price gaps between individual models in the line; these price differences should be justifiable by *perceptible* "step-up" features; the gross and net profit on the entire line should meet a predetermined target percentage. This last consideration requires a sales and profit margin forecast by individual model. Some planners tell of going through their cost-sales-profits plans up to 50 times before arriving at their final decisions.

Everyone in the industry agrees that consumers obtain excellent value when they buy sets and that price competition is extremely keen. However, intensity of competition is a relative matter. It appears that price competition is even greater on white goods (refrigerators, washers, ironers, stoves, etc.) than on television sets. One executive whose firm handles both "brown" and white goods stated that "prices of television sets are at a pretty good level, and thus hold an umbrella over marginal operators; in the white goods trades, on the other hand, prices are so low that no small producer can make a profit."

On occasion, manufacturers do communicate with one another about matters of price, but not in ways to be confused with attempts to collude. One executive spoke of calling a competitor that had just introduced a new model at a price substantially below those then prevailing. The company introducing this low-priced set was frequently quoted in the press as committing itself to dampen price competition and to help introduce sanity into the industry. As this executive told the story, he called someone in that company and asked, "What are you doing with that $——— portable? You are killing us with it." His friend said, "I don't know what you're complaining about. We're making a good profit on that set." The executive who originated the call responded, "That's all I want to know." He got some of his engineers together and in two weeks found out how that set could be produced at a profit.

Although one finds almost universal criticism of executives in this industry because of their heavy reliance upon price as a competitive weapon, there are a few heretics. One volunteered that, "Maybe television sets *should* be sold mainly on the basis of price." He expressed determination to put his company in a position that would enanble it to thrive in a price-competitive environment.

Analysis of the price lists of many manufacturers and a probing of the thinking of persons responsible for pricing discloses that prices for televisions set have the following characteristics:

1. Models are offered that cover a very broad range of prices. Ordinarily the most expensive set in a line costs distributors, retailers and consumers at least twice as much as the least expensive.

2. Every manufacturer includes one or more "promotional models," which usually carry a suggested retail list price that is considerably lower than the other models of that general class. Occasionally no retail price is suggested for some or all models, the distributor and retailer being left free to charge what they choose.

3. On "promotional models" the manufacturer, distributor and retailer all accept a lower percentage unit profit than they obtain from nonpromotional models. The difference in *suggested* margins for distributors and retailers between promotional and other models is very often considerable. (The *actual* margins probably differ much less because there is less room to cut prices on the promotional models.)

4. Manufacturers simplify charges for transportation greatly by hav-

ing only a few price zones. A few small manufacturers charge all distributors the same delivered price everywhere in the nation. Almost all others have two zones and sell on an F.O.B. basis.

5. The largest manufacturers include models at prices only a relatively small step away from other models. Consequently, a consumer can buy a model at almost any price he wants to pay, within a 10 or 15 dollar range. Manufacturers like to have models within two or three dollars of one another at distributor cost.

6. Despite the prevalence of many models and fairly small price jumps, there apparently are some "price-line" feelings reflected in the retail prices suggested by the major manufacturers. The $199, $249 and $299 prices seem to be favorites—though not the only ones. Because of discounts at retail, however, these prices may be among the most unusual prices ever paid by consumers.

7. In the television industry at present, the excise tax is buried so that the final consumer rarely knows it even exists and the retailer rarely knows its size.

8. Charges for service and installation are not handled in a uniform manner by retailers.

9. Increasingly, manufacturers are invoking "fair trade legislation" in order to gain control over the price charged at retail.

10. "Suggested retail prices" are not set by all manufacturers any more. The present trend is for manufacturers to allow distributors and retailers to set prices for themselves—a common practice in the white goods industries.

11. Manufacturers often make price changes without altering their price sheets, in efforts to stimulate sales—especially of those models which have been moving slowly.

12. Whenever manufacturers add components or circuits to a "basic set," they believe the retailer price should be increased far more than proportionately. Some say that suggested retail price should rise approximately $3 for every $1 increase in the manufacturer's direct costs.

13. Promotional models account for only a relatively small proportion of sales—5 percent or less for most manufacturers—though the proportion appears to be rising gradually.

14. Many manufacturers handle large retail accounts in a special

Manufacturers' Distributive Activities

manner. They are charged only slightly more than the distributor's price and designated "Associate Distributors."

15. Occasionally a large retailer will be given a few models that are not offered to other retailers in his area to free him from direct price comparison and to ameliorate competition. At one time, the number of such special models increased almost without limit, causing great problems to the manufacturing department. At present, major manufacturers make about four or five special models, each one of which is sold exclusively to one dealer per major market.

16. Most manufacturers find that their profits spurt sharply during periods of increased sales. This rise is far greater than can be explained by economies of large-scale production. The chief explanation seems to be that special deals decline or disappear at such times. Special deals clearly make important inroads into manufacturers' profits most of the time.

17. Manufacturers recognize that the addition of a model to their line could have the effect of diverting their own sales of other models rather than from competitors. To avoid this result, ordinarily they will not add a new model unless they can incorporate a substantially new product feature or remove it sufficiently in price from their present models to tap a new stratum of demand.

18. Many distributors, perhaps at the behest of manufacturers, have recently begun to set "minimum prices" to govern retail prices on some or all of their sets. These minima are almost always below the suggested list price, but above the levels to which retail prices sometimes sink. It is too early to tell how effectively distributors as a group will enforce these minimum prices.

19. The late winter and early spring generally are characterized by "dumps" as manufacturers try to clean up their inventories of merchandise that will be superseded by new models announced early in June. Price reductions are very common during this period, though some companies do not employ price promotions until they have exhausted all other methods of stimulating sales.

One wants to know many things about these statements about television set prices—assuming that they are accurate and apply to most manufacturers. First and foremost, how did each come to pass?

This question is not difficult because the industry's pricing arrangements simply exhibit the characteristics of other major appliance prices. None of these features is new or unique. Second, what are the consequences of the more unusual of these price characteristics? This question is extremely difficult, and the following paragraphs only sketch some possible lines of cause and effect for a few important characteristics of major appliance prices.

What is the effect of including promotional models in a line? To the extent that they are sold—which is to a surprisingly small degree—they increase the number of people financially able to acquire the product. Indeed, promotional models seem to involve "private subsidies" to those who buy them. It is not simple to determine who pays the subsidy. One might think that the manufacturer, distributor and retailer together pay the subsidy by accepting lower-than-average margins on those models. However, they do so because they believe the use of promotional models enables them to sell other models at larger margins. By accepting the low margin on promotional models the manufacturer, distributor and retailer obtain something in addition to sales—namely, "traffic"—which gives them an opportunity to deliver their sales message directly to more customers. It could be argued that the subsidy is paid mainly by purchasers of nonpromotional models that carry a margin above the average. Serious exception can be taken to this view also, for these sets "turn over" slowly. They are truly more costly to sell than promotional sets. Difficulty in locating the customers who pay the subsidy suggests that subsidy is absent.

The relatively high charge made for additions to the "basic set" is another significant feature of pricing. (See Table 7) In the first place, this procedure requires consumers to pay far more for additions of desired features than the cost to the manufacturer and his resellers of making those additions. Consequently, the consumption of these features may be unduly limited; that is, many more people would obtain these features if they were required to pay only the added cost to the manufacturer, distributor and retailer plus a modest profit for each. An unusual and perhaps unfortunate situation has thus been created. Designers are well aware of the rule of thumb that each dollar added to manufacturing costs means at least an extra $3 at retail; they probably desist from suggesting design changes that they would make if they thought in terms of, say, a $1.50 increase in retail price for each added dollar outlay by the manufacturer. (A ratio of 1.5 to 1 would actually permit the maintenance of existing margins for all.) As Table 7 indicates, small increases in price to retailers above the cost to them of the basic set will involve increases in suggested list price at a ratio of over four and five to one.

TABLE 7
RETAILER GAINS FROM UP-SELLING, BASED ON ONE MANUFACTURER'S 1960 PRICE LIST

Suggested Retail Price	Price to Retailer *	Addition to Retail Price	Addition to Price Paid by Retailer
$149.95	$117.00		
189.95	135.90	$40.00	$18.90
199.95	138.22	10.00	2.32
209.95	139.97	10.00	1.75

* Not including transportation charges.

This feature of television set pricing introduces price discrimination of a strange sort. Promotional models do not necessarily represent the best value" for the great majority of consumers—even though the manufacturer, distributor and retailer make little if anything by selling them. Ordinarily, they are offered only in unattractive cabinets; also, some attractive features of the "line" are omitted and some dubious economies usually have been effected in the circuitry itself. Also, as explained, they are produced in modest quantity, and output may be artificially restricted; consequently, few consumers can obtain the promotional set. Most consumers do not buy it but get the basic set plus some features for which they have been charged an unduly high price. The chief result of this price arrangement is to create a strong incentive for sellers to induce customers to buy additional features. In the process of pursuing the relatively great additions to gross margin that are obtainable by "stepping up" the consumer to a higher-priced model, great sales effort and expenditures may take place and inflate the costs of distribution. Existing pricing practices thus create very strong incentives to up-sell the customer and induce manufacturers and resellers to make strong and costly promotional efforts to do so.

ADVERTISING IN MANUFACTURERS' MARKETING PLANS

Of all the marketing activities television set manufacturers engage in, advertising is the most rigorously planned. It is a rare manufacturer in this industry who does not have an annual advertising plan. Some prepare enormous documents (one that is in my possession has 215 pages, most of which are single spaced). Others are far less pretentious, but nevertheless are much more detailed and thorough than plans for other parts of their marketing operation.

Despite the emphasis attached to the planning of advertising activities, advertising is far from the most important factor in a manufacturer's market success. That is the consensus of expert opinion in the industry, and there is no good reason to question it. This view explains the relatively modest sums devoted to advertising and the fact that these have often been diverted from "pure advertising" to other purposes. It also accounts for the fact that with few exceptions the top advertising executives in this industry are members of "middle management" rather than "top management," and for the frequency with which members of top management overrule the top advertising executive's decisions.

One advertising director described even the largest television set producers as "small-potato-advertisers." Relatively large manufacturers, such as Zenith, Motorola and Admiral spend about one and one-half million dollars on national advertising, a tiny sum compared with what is spent by producers of soap, dentifrices, coffee, cosmetics, liquors, etc. Their expenditures, as a proportion of sales, are in line with those of automobile manufacturers.

An almost unique feature of the advertising activity in this, as in most other industries, is that it is shared routinely with an outside organization by most large business firms. The advertising agency has become a fixture in the United States business system. While businesses are "do-it-yourselfers" in almost every other area, they routinely delegate a large part of the advertising function to a specialized outside agency. The main reason this situation exists is that the services of an agency cost the client nothing; the agency is reimbursed via the 15 percent agency commission on space and time purchases, which is paid by the media used to advertise, not by the client of the

Manufacturers' Distributive Activities

agency. However, the advertising agency's function varies from firm to firm in the television set industry and most companies have altered the division of advertising functions between the agency and themselves over the years.

To understand the advertising activities of television set manufacturers, one must know what they do within their own "shop" and what is done for them by the advertising agency. Also—and this will be discussed in a later chapter—it is necessary to know how manufacturers share the advertising functions with their distributors and dealers. At the outset, the main components of the advertising function will be described. Once this overall picture has been mapped out, we shall examine each component and see what the company does for itself and what the advertising agency does.

Manufacturers advertise on their own account; this usually is termed "national advertising" in this industry. They also share in the cost, encourage, and attempt to upgrade the advertising of their distributors and retailers. The second is usually termed "local" or cooperative ("co-op") advertising and accounts for about one-third of the total. (See Table 8) We shall discuss these two ingredients separately.

TABLE 8
COMPOSITION OF ADVERTISING OUTLAYS

	Percentage
Direct, manufacturer-sponsored advertising	60
Directed to consumers	48
Directed to trade	12
Cooperative advertising	30
Administrative costs	10
Total	100

National advertising includes advertising addressed "to the trade"—to retailers, distributors and servicemen—and advertising directed to ultimate consumers. Apart from differences in their advertising "targets," manufacturers' national advertising takes several different forms. It includes advertising in the conventional media—television, radio, newspapers and magazines—and point-of-purchase materials, sales catalogues, specification sheets, and the like. A substantial proportion of the total advertising outlays of television set manufacturers goes for the latter types of advertising.

Advertising expenditures data in this industry—as in most others—are, on the whole, very jealously guarded. So much is this the case that when one extremely cooperative member of the industry provided detailed advertising cost information, the author spent considerable time trying to "find the catch." It is difficult to explain the almost neurotic preoccupation of the individual manufacturers with the amount and uses of their competitors' advertising expenditures.

The best information available places expenditures on *national* advertising at between 2 and 3 percent of net sales, and their contributions to *co-op* advertising average approximately 1½ percent of net sales. Advertising outlays vary over time and among individual companies, but these variations apparently are not large.

The significance of advertising expenditure data is blurred by several circumstances. First, manufacturers include outlays for many items other than "pure advertising" in their advertising budgets. The most usual are purchases of printed materials like point-of-purchase posters, banners, catalogues, folders, etc.; public relations efforts; meetings and conventions for distributors and dealers; costs of sales promotions (including merchandise "inducements," bonuses, trips, and the like). The costs of certain price reductions are charged against the advertising department in at least one firm. Second, one important set producer, R.C.A., owns a major advertising medium, the N.B.C. network. It seems obvious that the amount and form of this firm's advertising efforts is affected thereby. (However, the major cost of a network program is for talent, not for the network facilities.) Third, much of the advertising for television sets is conducted in conjunction with advertising of other major appliances and even of unrelated products. (For example, G.E., Westinghouse, Admiral, R.C.A. and Philco produce several lines of major appliances; Zenith advertising often is accompanied by reference to its line of hearing aids.) Consequently, these data represent an arbitrary allocation of a joint cost. Moreover, advertising of a brand in conjunction with different products contributes to the sale of television sets.

Of its expenditure for national advertising, the average television set manufacturer spends approximately one-tenth for point-of-purchase material, including sales catalogues, specification sheets, etc. Variations among individual companies on this score are very large, and most manufacturers are determined to reduce these costs. (Ordinarily, distributors and retailers defray part of the cost of this promotional material.)

Media costs account for roughly 70 percent of the total; and the administrative costs involved are about 10 percent. The balance of 20 percent goes for artwork and "talent."

Responsibility for the preparation and control of all forms of national advertising material is vested in a director of advertising (known by a variety of different titles in each of the major television set firms). In turn, his responsibility for the company's advertising effort is shared differently from firm to firm with the advertising agency. He is responsible for the agency's performance, but since top management generally picks the agency, this responsibility is partial at most.

In almost all companies, advertising is a separate division of the marketing department. The director of advertising reports to the vice-president of marketing, although the former finds all members of top management involving themselves (some refer to it as "meddling") in his activities. As indicated earlier, most directors of advertising regard themselves, and properly, as members of upper-middle management and are largely confined to their specialty. They usually are not invited to participate in related top-level marketing and nonmarketing deliberations. (There are a few exceptions to this, of course.) The typical advertising department in a large television set manufacturing company has between 20 and 30 employees, including two or three secretaries. Most of them are concerned with the firm's national advertising effort, although at least one will be assigned the task of administering the co-op fund. Individual assignments vary, according to the duties delegated to the advertising agency.

Although it is dangerous to generalize about the manner in which set manufacturers share the total advertising function with their agencies, there are some broad propositions that do fit most cases. First, the advertising agency wants to participate in both the formulation of the client's basic marketing strategy and in every phase of advertising and marketing—if only to be kept appraised of what is done. Second, the client company wishes to participate in the selection of basic advertising themes as a minimum and reserves the right of review over the agency's selection of copy and customer appeals. Third, the set manufacturers determine, with weak influence from their advertising agencies, how much will be spent for advertising. Fourth, they delegate to their agencies almost complete responsibility for the execution of the advertising program: the preparation of copy, art work, selection of media and negotiations with them, and the many details involved in bringing together the various parts that make up a magazine, radio or television advertising program.

Agency practice in the preparation of basic advertising themes is far from uniform. Nevertheless, in the overwhelming majority of instances it is the agency's responsibility to prepare a program, widely called a "copy platform," that will embrace a substantial number of individual pieces of advertising copy. Such programs embody either a single theme or a few interrelated themes. The selection of themes represents one of the most crucial steps in the advertising function. In the television set industry, as in other industries which have a distinct model year, the copy platform is intended to dictate specific advertising actions for a long period—usually a full model year. The need or urge to prepare a new advertising theme stems from the newness of the merchandise. The manufacturer usually wants to inform customers of changes that were made and to convince them that they represent major improvements. Accordingly, the advertising theme is closely related to the changes in product. Its preparation starts with an exposure to the new line of the agency staff responsible for the account. Since advertising involves a long lead time, agency personnel will be shown the product long before it has been sent to market. They generally will be shown models made up for the purpose rather than sets taken from a regular production run.

When the agency has prepared a copy platform (in a manner described below), it is submitted to the client for approval. The copy platform together with the advertising budget represent directives to the agency that guide its activities until top management (or the agency) believes there is need to change the original advertising plan. Departures from plan are fairly frequent in the advertising sphere, for expenditures generally are adjusted to variations in sales. Changes result also from efforts to respond to rivals' advertising or to capitalize on some of the things that rivals say.

The whole vexing business of turning ideas (themes) into professional advertising copy, selecting the media and arranging for particular positions is left to the agency. Even in such matters, executives of the client company will sometimes involve themselves quite actively.

The following paragraphs describe in modest detail the national advertising operation of one large television set manufacturer and its agency. It does not differ markedly from the other companies that were studied, but a few minor features are unusual. The advertising effort of this company is the major responsibility of 33 people in the advertising section of the television set producing company. This group reports through the vice-president of advertising and sales promotion to the vice-president in charge of marketing. In the advertising agency 12 people work exclusively on this account. There are many additional creative people (copy writers, art workers, television show producers, etc.) who work on this as well as on other accounts.

Company personnel and agency personnel meet at least every week. The work in advertising planning is divided about evenly between the company and agency. The execution of these plans is divided approximately 70 percent agency and 30 percent company. Preparation of a yearly "copy platform" for the model year is a responsibility of the agency, but its creation and development take place in close contact with company advertising personnel.

Prior to any formal discussion of the current theme, the account representatives (agency personnel who act as liaison between the various creative people and the client), with the aid of information received from the company, prepare statistical data describing the firm's situation and sales objectives. They may detail such information as the number of set owners, market shares of the company, proposed future goals in sales, and demographic data on set owners. Also included may be company strengths and weaknesses. This information, which is revised twice a year, is promulgated throughout the agency by formal meetings, "bull sessions," inter-office memos and written reports. Dissemination of this information is continuous and acts as a pervasive background for the meetings concerned with the creation of the copy platform.

In preparing a specific advertising campaign, a group of approximately ten people (including account representatives, copy writers, art workers, etc.) travel from the agency to the company offices to be briefed on the new line. Agency group members are given kits demonstrating new engineering features as well as other samples to demonstrate new improvements and techniques. They mix freely with company personnel at meetings during which the agency staff is briefed by engineers on specific changes and by designers on cabinets, colors, designs, etc. They make notes and are encouraged to ask questions. The merchandise is discussed informally and frankly, highlighting the distinct advantages and the shortcomings. The agency is primarily interested in the consumer benefits incorporated into the line.

Occasionally a dramatic improvement is unveiled (such as remote control). This immediately presents itself as a benefit that can be "screamed from the housetops" and quickly emerges as the main feature of the future campaign. More frequently, however, no such single feature is outstandingly new. Further meetings and discussions are necessary to develop the main advertising theme.

One method used to develop a copy platform is to have each member of the creative group make tape recordings of his independent impressions when he returns to the agency. To avoid the danger of having one articulate, domineering person proselytize his own opinions and interpretations, and to achieve collective, creative thinking, each person individually records his impressions of the merchandise, its outstanding features, and his suggested approach to the advertising theme. These recordings are then played back to see if any uniform trend of thought exists. Frequently a common line of reasoning does emerge.

Copywriters who were present at the "briefings" are given a period of a week or so to mull over the information and suggest a copy platform. At the end of the week, four or five copywriters meet in the head copywriter's office and bring their ideas and suggestions in rough outline. Each copywriter is permitted to present his suggested approaches. These are discussed individually and criticized. Discussion

Manufacturers' Distributive Activities

continues until final agreement is reached on one "best" platform.

After the main theme has been selected, a copy platform is prepared, which sets up "the prime objective in which the campaign flows." Two or three members of the original group prepare this copy platform. It is three or four pages long. It does not present a specific advertisement but, as one account executive expressed it, "plants a thought about the manufacturer's reputation and the merchandise he has for sale this year."

Before the copy platform is submitted to the client it is presented to the account representative for his acceptance and to a "review board" made up of agency personnel not connected with this account in any manner. The review board is asked to give an objective criticism of the proposed campaign.

After the copy platform has passed the review board, its is presented to the client's advertising department to secure its agreement to the basic strategy selected. Following their approval of whatever mutually agreed upon refinements are deemed necessary, the platform is then cleared with the engineering and legal departments. It is then presented to the client's management for approval. The agency thereupon translates the copy platform into specific instructions and distributes them to each of the creative people assigned to the account for production of the actual advertising matter.

Occasionally, after a period of effort and preparation, it develops that the selected copy platform is confusing or is not evolving as anticipated. The campaign is then shifted to another theme. A change in theme during a campaign is mandatory if the readership ratings, which are subscribed to on a continuing basis, indicates the campaign is a failure. Other reasons for changing a copy platform are: discovery that a competitor has stronger claims on the same features being stressed, revelations of inadequacies in engineering performance, and voiced displeasure among the higher-ups in the company about the advertising.

Local advertising is mainly the responsibility of distributors, but the manufacturer must administer the co-op fund. This involves considerable routine paper work to keep a record of each distributor's co-op funds—both "earned" and spent. Also, the manufacturer frequently becomes involved in making special deals, with large retail accounts, for special use of co-op funds. The funds are sometimes diverted from use for conventional advertising to such things as payments to dealers, sales personnel, price reductions, special merchandise promotions and the like.

In recent years, some television set manufacturers have increased their efforts to make retail advertising more consistent with national advertising. One manufacturer, distressed by the fact that the tone of its national advertising was being canceled out by the shrill and blatent advertising claims of its retailers, constructed a long-range program, largely at its own expense, calculated to demonstrate that "quality" advertising pays off, even in the short run. This company believes its program has been quite successful, although not spectacular.

In the interest of brevity, other observations about how television set manufacturers manage the advertising function will be presented in the form of a list of statements, following the pattern employed in the preceding discussion of pricing.

1. Directors of advertising in this industry admit and bemoan the fact that "advertising is not a science." Almost every top executive, accordingly, and even some stockholders become self-appointed advertising experts.

2. Executives who direct advertising for the manufacturers appear to be among the most capable, intelligent, carefully organized and well-trained in their respective firms. This fact possibly reflects the influence of the advertising agency, which may serve as a competitive as well as a supporting force to the client's own advertising executives.

3. Advertising managers devote a great deal of attention to studying what their competitors spend, the media they use and their advertising copy appeals. (Their preoccupation with rivals' advertising behavior may even exceed their interest in rivals' physical product offerings.) To formulate proposed advertising programs, some executives will study their own and their chief competitors' programs over the preceding three or four years to see what the various companies have been doing and to obtain clues to "what works."

4. There is widespread admiration in the industry for Zenith's advertising efforts. The basis for this admiration is highly instructive,

Manufacturers' Distributive Activities

for the qualities of Zenith's advertising superficially do not seem very exceptional. Basically, Zenith is praised most for its consistency of theme. It has not diluted or departed from its claim to place quality and performance above everything else. More important, it has not sacrificed its basic theme to meet pressing, short-run goals which would have been better served if Zenith had departed from the theme. (Actually Zenith has very rarely found itself under great pressures to sacrifice its long-term goals in order to attain short-term objectives.)

5. The gulf between national and local advertising is great. There are important differences in the themes employed. At retail, "price is the big news." National advertising is more concerned with product quality and image building. There are also important differences in rates charged by media (primarily by newspapers), with very great price advantages enjoyed by retailers over distributors and manufacturers.

6. The frequent changes of advertising agency in this industry, as in others, seem to be almost matters of being in style. The reasons for change of agency do not seem to be great enough in most cases to offset the losses of continuity. References are sometimes made by advertising executives to the "great American game of changing advertising agencies."

7. The factors leading to a change of agency sometimes have nothing to do with agency performance. In referring to a recent change of agency by his company, one executive responsible for advertising said, "I was not personally involved in the dropping of our agency. I do know that there were personal associations between the top folks in this company and the top folks in our new agency."

8. There generally is a wide gulf between the agency's and the client's view of its relative contribution to the firm's advertising effort. In one case, the agency described itself as doing 70 percent of the planning, whereas the head of advertising for the company described the agency as doing less than half of the planning. The disparity of perceptions was even greater with respect to "execution of plan." The agency felt it was doing 98 percent, while the client felt it was doing only 70 percent.

9. In the early 1950s, most manufacturers set aside a proportion of sales (generally between three and four percent) that represented

"key city funds." These were used in various ways to "buy market penetration" in specific cities or to counter competitors' efforts to do so. Often these funds were used for massive advertising campaigns. Today these funds have largely disappeared, though at least one manufacturer is said to have continued their use.

10. Sales people in general and advertising personnel in particular are almost addicted to use of the word "creativity." An analysis of what advertising executives in the television set industry do and of the way they perceive their jobs suggests that attention to detail rather than brilliant imagination is the main qualification for success.

11. Even advertising agency representatives who work on television set accounts deprecate the importance of creativity in a successful advertising program. (On the other hand, it is impossible to reduce the activities of persons who write copy and do the artwork for advertisements to a routine that can be followed successfully by an intelligent individual.)

12. The problem of achieving consistency of local and national advertising appears crucial, yet effective action toward this end by manufacturers will involve them in indirect controls over retailer behavior. Without such control, manufacturers stand to lose the possible benefits they gain from their expenditures on national advertising.

13. The procurement of advertising materials and the purchase of communications media represent highly complex and vital business activities. It appears that the one price system does not particularly characterize these businesses. Also, qualitative considerations—e.g., "position" relative to other advertisers, and editorial matter—represent vital factors in appraising the true cost and value of media.

14. The mission of advertising has changed substantially over the brief life of this major industry. From original emphasis upon informing customers about the nature of television programs and reception, to stress on the enjoyment and educational benefits of television programs in general, advertising themes have shifted to direct competition. Manufacturers now try mainly to convince consumers that their brand offers better value than competing brands.

15. It appears that consumer interest in advertising by television set producers is far less now than it was shortly after the product was

Manufacturers' Distributive Activities

introduced following the war. The results of audience studies between 1949 and 1959 show a very dramatic fall-off in reader interest. These findings suggest a general tendency for advertising costs to rise as a product matures and loses its "news" aspect. (It appears that reader interest in advertising of color sets is much greater than in that of black and white.)

16. Executives are becoming troubled by the ups and downs in advertising outlays. In the first place, they are not convinced that advertising expenditures should fluctuate directly with sales. In the second, they recognize how difficult it is to plan and execute advertising budgets that do vary with sales. A few firms take the position that advertising outlays should be based upon estimated "standard sales." These reflect sales trends but are not affected by cyclical fluctuations. It seems that practice departs from this principle, but the principle has been adopted only quite recently and may come to prevail in time.

TABLE 9

VARIATIONS IN OUTLAYS FOR NATIONAL ADVERTISING MEDIA

(*Range of Outlays for the Period 1955 to 1959, as Percentage of Each Company's Total National Media Outlays*)

	Magazines	Newspapers	Radio and Television
R.C.A.	22 to 34	12 to 31	35 to 65
General Electric	14 to 45	17 to 37	18 to 59
Philco	25 to 70	16 to 41	8 to 59
Admiral	17 to 72	11 to 57	0 to 70
Motorola	28 to 81	19 to 72	0 to 10
Zenith	9 to 44	4 to 59	0 to 87

SOURCE: Published data derived ultimately from the individual media.

17. Almost every television set manufacturer has established a special accounting and financial unit within its advertising department. Such a special control unit is required to administer the co-op advertising fund; it is needed also to provide the flexibility required in advertising as funds are quickly diverted from one use to another. In addition, the sums administered by the advertising department are very large, and the products purchased are specialized and often intangible. Particularly stringent controls are therefore required.

18. In this industry, and perhaps others, advertisers tend to switch basic media—as, from magazines to television and from television to newspapers or billboards. (See Table 9) Although the reasons for such basic switches are not clearly expressed, it appears that advertisers hope to reach audiences not touched by the other media and to do it in suffcient depth to make an effective impression.

Selection of Product Designs and Level of Product Quality

A layman is likely to conclude, following Gertrude Stein, that a television set is a television set is a television set. Such is far from the case, however. A firm must pick a limited number from among the very large number of possible designs that would be considered acceptable. Especially in the early years of the industry, design decisions strongly affected a manufacturer's success. Even today, they affect more than trivially both the size of the market attained by individual manufacturers and their unit production costs.

Only recently has the selection of product design become regarded as a separate marketing activity. It is part of the "product planning" function and is a central responsibility of the chief marketing executive. Most of the people participating in this activity even now are not usually considered "real marketing men," however, and have ordinarily received no training in marketing or distribution. Part of the activity and expense involved in product planning are associated directly or indirectly with research and development—perhaps the most rapidly growing of business expenditures. No reliable data are available describing the amount and nature of television set manufacturers' research and development activities. It is nevertheless common knowledge that a few firms do considerable research, including some "pure" research, while most of them do almost none at all.

An important source of technological improvements in the industry is the research on government military projects that is carried on by set manufacturers at government expense. Manufacturers engaged in electronic research for the government must, however, provide a channel through which developments with commercial applications (among the nonconfidential discoveries) are made known to their television set designers.

One might ask many questions about the selection by manufacturers of particular versions of sets to offer for sale: Who makes such decisions? How frequently are changes in product design made, and how great is the cost of change? What have been the critical product feature choices made over the history of the industry, and how well have they turned out—both from the standpoint of producer profitability and consumer welfare? By what criteria and on what information are decisions made about product design? The answers to some of these questions possibly will never be known. These matters are discussed briefly, nevertheless, to highlight the issues, crystallize the points on which additional information should be gathered and to suggest tentative conclusions where it is possible to do so.

Most of the detailed decisions about chassis design and quality must ultimately lodge with engineers. These people possess the technical training necessary to design and produce a set, and they typically dominate spheres of production, research and design. They are also responsible for keeping top management informed about major technological developments as well as lesser "improvements." To do this, they may engage in research of varying degrees of "purity"; they are certainly expected to keep abreast of the technical literature; they typically maintain close liaison with their own firm's service personnel and with many of their distributors' and retailers' service departments; moreover, their duties keep them in constant contact with their production and purchasing divisions. These men, collectively, are expected to know all these is to know about television set technology. Their two main functions are to incorporate technical developments into the product that will reduce cost of manufacture and improve performance and reliability, and to design into their firm's sets the features that others believe will improve their attractiveness to customers.

The notable changes that have been made in sets either added features that were expected to be attractive to consumers or reduced production cost without impairing performance perceptibly. (Minor modifications are required, and fairly frequently, to adapt a chassis to changes in cabinet style and size and to take advantage of improvements in components.) In other words, the overwhelming majority of product design decisions in most firms seem to revolve about adding or eliminating specific "features"—elements of circuitry, etc.—rather than composing an entirely new set. However, drastic changes—e.g., printed circuits, remote control, wide-angle tubes, square tubes, portables and transisterized sets—obviously do take place.

Manufacturers consciously attempt to minimize retooling costs and to avoid the inevitable risks attendant upon major design changes. Unforeseen difficulties ordinarily arise when a set is redesigned, that cause interruptions in production; also some "bugs" often develop in at least the first sets produced that might give the firm's entire new line a bad reputation.[3] Retooling costs have been heavy in the television set industry—as much, as a proportion of sales revenue, as in the automobile and white goods industries, according to industry sources.

All major television manufacturers place responsibility for the selection of set design upon top marketing management. The vice-president in charge of sales for one of the largest set producers stated that he devoted one-third or more of his time to product design, along with styling, and attributed the success of his company to its preoccupation with these matters. Other companies locate responsibility for product design farther down the line and use a product development section plus a product development committee. For example, General Electric has a "Product Planning Section" on the same organizational level as the sales planning, advertising and promotion, marketing administration, service, and market research sections. This section, in 1960, consisted of the individual in charge of product planning and two men and one secretary. The person in charge is essentially a liaison officer between engineering, manufacturing and marketing. The two men in the section were engineers "with a commercial viewpoint." One of them was concerned primarily with the product features to include in the line and the prices to charge; he recommended the array of sets that were to compose the full line. The other engineer worked mainly on the physical product itself,

[3] In at least two cases involving very large producers the firms carried out a drastic reengineering program to raise the quality of their product and ended up with a line of sets so full of "bugs" that their already tarnished reputation was further damaged.

dealing with such matters as antennae, width control over picture, circuitry, etc.

In addition to engineering, manufacturing and marketing, General Electric has created a separate industrial design division to assist in product planning. The industrial design operation is separate from the others concerned with television set design in General Electric, for it has divisional status and its work deals with hi-fi and radio as well as television. The marketing research section also contributes to product planning. It does not function primarily as a tester of tentative design conclusions; its mission is to "be out in front of product development" and suggest the direction in which the product development people should be thinking.

At Motorola, which did not have an organization chart before 1958 and even in 1960 did not have job descriptions for members of its staff,[4] product planning occupies a more prominent position in the firm's organization than at General Electric. The company's consumer division, which is concerned with television plus automobile radios sold to the consumer through middlemen, contains two departments: the first deals with marketing and the other with engineering. Under the vice-president and director of marketing are four activities headed by a product planning manager, a manager of distribution, a merchandising manager and a group responsible for field services. In this arrangement, product planning ranks well above market research, which is only one of several responsibilities of the manager of distribution. The function of the product planning manager is to "get various departments together in a committee and direct and coordinate their activities."

The General Electric and Motorola organizational arrangements for product planning are essentially similar and are prototypes of what one finds at R.C.A., Philco (Ford), Sylvania and Westinghouse. The executive responsible for the function is lodged within the marketing "division"; he holds sufficiently high status to command the cooperation of persons in the manufacturing and engineering divisions.

[4] This situation reflected the resistance of Paul Galvin, then president of the company, to such things. Mr. Galvin died early in November, 1959.

Other major producers, among them Zenith and Admiral, place chief responsibility for product planning on the engineering division. They hope to obtain the contributions of other divisions by means of a "product committee." This appears to be a successful communication device, but it gives a different "division of power" and probably different decisions than would result from the sort of arrangements used by G.E., Motorola, *et al.*

In the smallest producers, the president and executive vice-presidents are actively involved in product planning. Often, as at Emerson, the president is the source of the major innovations; in other companies he will often dominate the decision involving a significant change.

Management often is offered a choice between improved design (consisting of better set performance, greater durability, ease of servicing and better style) involving high costs of production and less excellent design at a lower production cost. Not only must it strike a balance between quality and cost, it must also strike a balance between cost to produce and cost to sell. The addition of some special feature may increase production costs substantially and at the same time make the set so attractive in the retailer's and consumer's mind that the company could actually reduce its sales outlays.[5]

Improvements in basic quality reduce production costs. Improvements in quality of components and in workmanship save a producer large sums when they lower the rejection rate of sets on the production line. One executive estimated the value of recent improvements in the quality of receiving tubes to be roughly an extra month's output per year.

The attainment of the optimum balance between cost and quality is extremely difficult and requires a great deal of information. This information concerns the types of design changes that should be considered, the probable effect of these changes on production costs and sales costs, and the volume of sales that would be achieved with

[5] Of course, management could try to take advantage of special quality features to increase its share of the market, so that it might even increase its sales outlays. Even then, the increased sales attained through the combined effects of better product and larger advertising expenditures might reduce the company's *unit* promotional and sales expense.

and without each design change. The time and cost required to obtain such information would discourage most manufacturers from collecting it, even if it were highly reliable. Actually, even the best research techniques now known are subject to considerable error. The industry "scuttlebutt" includes tales of research that "could not have been wronger." As a result, they must balance cost against quality and select specific features to include in their models by methods other than research.

The executives and engineers concerned with set design are aware of many changes that might be made in the set. Some of their ideas come from knowledge of what their competitors have already done or have announced they will do. Others have been proposed and initiated by persons within the firm; some may start as suggestions from members of their family or acquaintances. However, these changes generally are minor and could be decided either way without serious repercussions by those responsible for set design. Usually, product design discussions revolve around such minor features. Occasionally, however, a truly major change is considered, one that would involve heavy retooling costs and the risk of being turned down by retailers and consumers even while offering an opportunity to win strong public favor.

These high-risk decisions involving product design are handled in several ways. Most set producers will include substantial redesign in only a few models of their sets. These will be produced with relatively little retooling—being made mainly by hand processes where the redesign would otherwise require extensive change in tools—and at substantially higher cost than would be incurred if the process were mechanized. The new sets will be put on the market and possibly featured in the companies' advertising, for advertisers are hungry for a special story to tell. Depending upon retailer and consumer response to the new sets, the firms will incorporate the new features in the other models or the new models will be dropped, or a few models with the new feature will be retained.

Another method of handling new product design is the "research method," in which the product is subjected to intensive market research to anticipate public reaction before it is put into production on a large scale. Although the executives are inclined to suggest that their firms do considerable new product market research, relatively little has actually been done to date.

Failure to employ market research as the basis for product design decisions is startling when one recognizes the enormous costs that could result from error. One might find several plausible explanations for this situation. First, those responsible for design (engineers and designers) hold the view that "a good designer knows what the public will buy" without making strenuous efforts to learn public tastes. Also, as a group, design specialists have done almost nothing to develop research techniques that would provide them with really reliable information.

Second, the television set industry has very quickly become "mature" in an economic sense. It probably has been afflicted with overcapacity since 1951. The product is sold through very many outlets in any community of even modest size. More than one brand is sold by most retailers. For these reasons and others, the competitive efforts of television set manufacturers have been oriented around price for many years. The result of this situation has been to put in key positions of authority executives who are skilled in selling on highly competitive markets and to relegate product design to subordinate status. Designers recognize that suggestions for "taking some of the guts out of the set to cut costs" will be warmly received; consequently, their proposals have been mainly of this type—which requires no special research.

A third possible explanation for the very limited marketing research done in the industry to test new product design is the conviction among manufacturing executives that "the industry moves too fast to take the time to research things out." Combined with this conviction is the unwillingness of any firm to tip its hand to its rivals. Rather than risk having an idea stolen, the firm prefers to go directly to market and incur the risk that involves.

A fourth explanation, and almost a necessary one, is that those who decide what methods should be used to make decisions have little confidence in the value of market research—and possibly for good reason. There have been several widely publicized examples in the industry where research (poor in quality, to be sure) produced wrong

Manufacturers' Distributive Activities

answers. One outstanding failure was the very low estimate of the potential market for a 14-inch portable set (especially at the time when the word "portable" was an extreme euphemism denoting "movable"—which a portable set is often not). General Electric executives rejected the conclusions reached by marketing research and demonstrated that a very large market existed. R.C.A. has had numerous experiences, it is said, in which consumers expressed preferences for particular kinds of designs and features but did not buy them when they were put on the market.

The experience of one large manufacturer is illustrative of the frequency and nature of product change most firms in the industry have experienced. It reported the following experience between 1948 and the beginning of 1960. During that period of approximately 11 years, it produced 222 different models of chassis. (Chassis should not be confused with individual cabinet models; a change is made in chassis designation only when circuitry, rather than surface appearance, is changed. Ordinarily, each chassis model will be used in many different cabinet models.) In other words, this company produced an average of almost 20 different chassis each year; many more chassis changes were made in the early years of the business than are made currently.

It has been this company's custom to bring out two new "lines" each year. That is to say, they have model change-overs twice a year. In addition, this company, like most others, produces a "drop-in" model or two. (A drop-in model is one that is added to the line during the slack period of the year—typically in December—in order to stimulate sales. It ordinarily will include some new feature absent from the current line—a feature that probably will be added to all models at the beginning of the next model year if consumers seem to like it.) In producing its new line, a completely new chassis or two generally is added by this company. There have, however, been instances when only minor changes were made in its offerings and no chassis changes were made at all.

In addition to the kinds of design changes involved in new chassis and new models, many other types of changes, called "running changes" have been made. Approximately several hundred such running changes are made each year on television sets alone. Each one of these running changes may cover many individual production changes; consequently the number of actual variations introduced each year is numbered in the thousands.

The purpose of all changes, whether they are of a fundamental sort or simply running changes is to achieve one of the following objectives: lower manufacturing cost; better performance; increased reliability; the incorporation of more advanced styling or greater ease of servicing. In addition, there are some very special reasons for changes, such as to overcome a bottleneck in factory test procedures or to permit the purchasing department a wider choice of component suppliers.

One finds general agreement among engineers that product change is too frequent in this industry. Some complain that they are "subject to excessive pressure to change design just to give marketing people something to talk about." Others complain of top management's "insistence on getting a product with some minor new feature into production before it is tested out." One executive in charge of engineering for a large producer explained the circumstances that brought him to the company in the following words: "This company had a serious product problem. Management insisted on adding new features before they were shaken out. Pressure for speed is by far the most important cause of product deficiencies in the whole industry. The companies in this industry all jump too quickly to be the first with a new feature. There is a general reluctance to test a product out for reliability."

Despite the numerous and frequent changes already described, there have been very few innovations worth mentioning during the last decade. Several engineers with different companies agreed that "very few companies have made any innovations worth mentioning." In their view, most companies just assemble components. They do not make, and could not justify the lack of, significant efforts in research and development. Another said that television sets were soon going to be like radios and added, "If you took ten-year-old radios and put them out on the shelf in prominent places, they would sell. The industry is going around in a circle; ten-year-old merchandise is good —as good as current stuff."

A few companies make special efforts to limit the changes in their chassis. In that way, they strive to avoid risks entailed when changes occur in production processes and in engineering design. In addition, they simplify the problems of and win the appreciation of television servicemen, who find it difficult to keep abreast of product modifications.

Another factor—unusual, to be sure—that may inhibit change is fear of a competitor's unfounded advertising charges. One executive explained why his company did not use a new viewing tube which uses no shield or cap. He said, "Even though the tube is very safe, your competitors would shoot you down if you used it. The first company to use this tube will be murdered because the consumer can be made to fear implosion." (Implosion is similar to explosion, in that it would mean flying glass with the danger of personal injury.)

Determination of Model "Line" and "Mix"

Much has been said already about the usual conflict between producing to meet the special needs and desires of consumers and to achieve minimum costs of production. This is essentially the same as saying that manufacturers must balance sales costs, which are heavy when few versions of the product are offered, against production costs, which are large when many versions are offered. The outcome of attempts to balance these costs takes concrete form in the firm's model line.

No television set manufacturer, however small, produces only a single model. Some produce a very large number, especially when account is taken of different styles of cabinet and wood finishes and colors. There has been a general tendency for the number of models to rise, though firms will "cut back their models" from time to time.

The length of a manufacturer's line reflects a balance of the following considerations, according to executives charged with responsibility for product planning in this industry. As indicated in the earlier discussion of consumers as a participant in the industry, increases in breadth of selection will enhance a manufacturer's ability to attract customers. Most set manufacturers try to appeal to a broad spectrum of consumers and are forced to offer a fairly broad set of alternatives to them to gain wide patronage and avoid inordinate sales costs.

Product planners have other reasons for adding models to their company's line than to serve customers better. One reason is to take advantage of "step-up selling," by which customers can be led, more or less gradually, from a low-priced model to one that is much higher in price. This is done by adding product features or cabinetry that "justifies" a price difference. Second, by broadening its assortment, the manufacturer can arrange for a certain retailer to receive an "exclusive" on particular models in his area and can therefore escape direct price competition on those models. The larger the number of models in the line, the more retailers can be favored in this manner in every area.

Great ingenuity on the part of the industry permits it to create a broad range of offerings with only a modest increase in production costs. Sets that have widely different sizes of viewing tubes use essentially the same chassis; many very different cabinet styles are combined with identical chassis. Although increase of breadth of a line undoubtedly does involve significant production costs, the manufacturers do not seem to know the amount. Those who were questioned about the cost of broadening their assortment agreed that it was "relatively small and probably much smaller than you think."

Paradoxically, some small television set manufacturers offer longer lines of models than most of the largest firms in the industry. One firm reported that it was quite prepared to make a "run" of a particular model composed of between 500 and 600 sets. This number would represent a "pre-production run" for the large companies, which would not consider a model composed of so few units. Because it has mastered the production of short runs at low cost, this firm has one of the longest, if not the longest, line of models in the industry.

The costs of a long line of models are not borne by the manufacturer alone, by any means; possibly the heaviest cost of a broad model line falls on the distributor and retailer. Here again, reliable information is lacking on which to base a conclusion. Manufacturers and distributors have also developed methods of reducing the cost of offering their customers a broad assortment. One of the most common is to persuade the customer to take something else—something the seller has in stock. Indeed, it is a rare distributor that stocks every model made by the manufacturer. No retailer carries every model that the manufacturer makes.

A function performed by set manufacturers that is closely related to but separate from the composition of a model line is the determination of the desired model "mix." That is to say, they prescribe the proportions in which distributors should try to sell different models. One might well ask why television set manufacturers need a model "mix" as well as a model "line." Why not simply estimate how many of each model would be sold in the ordinary course of events?

The existence of a model mix goal as separate from a *forecast* of what consumers will buy, implies several things: first, the manufacturer (and possibly the distributor and dealer too) has an incentive to sell in proportions that may be very different from those in which consumers desire to buy. It has already been indicated that producers set price in a manner that gives them a different unit profit on their various models. Second, the manufacturer believes he can influence the proportions in which consumers buy (or distributors and dealers sell) individual models. Third, the manufacturer believes that "it pays," taking account of the costs and risks involved, to try to influence consumers' model selections. When presented with these assumptions stated explicitly, executives in television manufacturing firms agreed that all were valid. They apparently have operated on these assumptions since almost the very first days of television set sale, and they have inherited them from other phases of the major appliance business.

As the industry has matured, the ability of manufacturers to dictate the mix has waned. Also, their efforts to do so have declined, though they have not been abandoned. More and more it seems that television manufacturers are "glad to sell anything they can."

Manufacturer concern with model mix sometimes is reflected in the compensation arrangements for regional salesmen. One company's written job description for its regional salesmen lists as one of their responsibilities that "they shall insure that the distributors' sales mix and volume of products offers maximum profitability to both the distributor and X (name of corporation)." The very first point out of ten discussing the basis for evaluation of regional salesmen states that evaluation of performance shall be based on "quota attainment in a product line for the district in the proper model mix."

It is not easy to learn precisely how executives in this industry determine the model mix they set as a target. The main principles applied, are, first, that the distributor and dealer should be discouraged from selling mainly the low-profit models. Even though it may be hard to do, they should be induced to make strenuous efforts to sell the most profitable models in the line. Manufacturers apparently believe that varying the margins to distributors and retailers either is not an effective or is not the *most* effective method of achieving this result. The second principle applied in selecting a target model mix is that it should represent a combination of models that provides a fair return for everyone along the line.[6] Manufacturers carefully compute their estimated profit for the model year, taking account of the variations in profit by model. They also watch carefully to see whether their model mix is departing from the target enough to endanger the firm's financial goals. If it is, they may shift prices or intensify efforts to push the high margin items.

Production Scheduling and Forecasting

The central pillar of the annual marketing program is an estimate of sales for the forthcoming year. Some television set manufacturers prepare their forecasts in great detail and set forth estimates for every individual model to be included in the line. Usually, however, the sales forecast is less detailed, stopping with estimated sales of table, console and portable receivers. In addition to such estimates, the marketing division is responsible for estimating the output requirements by individual models at short intervals—ordinarily every month. This forecast is used as the basis of production scheduling and the placement of orders from suppliers as well as for the preparation of short-period financial plans for the enterprise. The critical importance of the forecast of production requirements by model and by month becomes clear when one considers what happens if actual sales are significantly more or less than were estimated.

If more is produced than was estimated, the manufacturer faces a need to store inventories, for which space might be lacking. (Many television manufacturers have relatively little warehouse space close

---

[6] One can see in this an analogy to the planning procedures employed in the U.S.S.R. Controls in the form of physical quantities are used to supplement the cost price controls.

to the place of assembly.) Moreover, inventories tie up the firm's funds and might compel it to seek credit accommodation at a money cost or at some loss in credit standing. Perhaps most important, the firm ordinarily would feel compelled to cut production while inventories were being depleted. Output curtailment is a drastic step that most managements try to avoid in order to maintain labor morale, good management relations and to minimize the substantial costs of labor turnover. Also, periods of curtailed output ordinarily are characterized by high unit production costs. Not the least of the penalties for overestimating sales is the downward pressure on price that builds up when supplies are over-abundant.

If much less were sold than had been estimated, the firm would suffer mainly by losing customers and by creating distributor and retailer resentment. Especially in the television set market, few customers will wait long to obtain a specific brand or model, if another nationally advertised brand can be obtained in the desired style and size. Retailers are likely to minimize the expected length of time the consumer will be required to wait. Some retailers will not even mention that a delay will be necessary until they have closed the sale; others will not do so until after they were to have delivered the set. And, of course, some customers are willing to wait for the model and make of their choice. Consequently, the number of sales lost due to underestimating sales will generally be considerably smaller than the size of the error. Nevertheless, some sales are lost and resentments created, and these sometimes are costly.

For the foregoing reasons, television set manufacturers make strenuous efforts to predict sales accurately, especially for the length of time between the making of a decision about set output and the time the output is produced. In the television set industry, that period is approximately three to four months.

How are decisions made about how many to produce of each model of set? Although the precise methods differ widely from company to company, they are based upon the same basic principles. Different individuals given the job of setting production requirements for any set manufacturer probably would arrive at different conclusions, but the differences would be fairly small. In other words, it has been possible to reduce the estimation of output requirements almost to a mathematical formula. However, the importance of the task is so great that executives of very high rank participate actively in the process in this industry. Many a vice-president of marketing has on numerous occasions juggled numbers on an enormous columnar sheet. Increasingly, however, computers are being considered as replacements for personal estimates, and at least one major company in 1963 was accustomed to using a computer for deciding how many units of each model to produce.

The determination of output requirements rests upon the following factors: established seasonal patterns of retail sales, adjustment for changes in demand for sets in those regions where the company draws most of its business, trends in the sales of individual models (For example, have consumers been buying larger proportion of consoles or portables, and at what pace has this trend been progressing?), and adjustment for the size of existing inventories, by individual model. If one is willing to assume that recent changes will continue to occur in the same direction at the recent rate, it is possible to project output needs almost by simple mechanical procedures. Most manufacturers have resisted the use of purely mathematical formulas for making such vital decisions. They introduce judgmental considerations in reaching their conclusions. However, as explained, a drift to the use of computers has been under way for some time.

Most valuable in the preparation of production requirements is up-to-the-minute information about *current* sales and inventories at all levels of the industry, by individual model. Consumer sales of most appliances are far from regular and consistent. Consequently, failure to know sales accurately for the preceding week or two could represent the difference between making plans on the assumption that there is little merchandise in inventory or on the assumption that stocks are heavy. All manufacturers have, over recent years, increased the currency of their information about distributors' sales.

Strangely, the one problem that some marketing managements face in this connection, is to get the manufacturing division to produce the models that are wanted. In several well-documented instances, manufacturing divisions have pushed the production of selected models far beyond what the marketing department asked for, while holding back the production of more salable models. The result of this behavior was to create a glut of certain models that required an extremely costly "dump" of the surplus.

Manufacturing executives have preferences that find a way of expressing themselves in behavior. Some models are much easier to produce than others; most manufacturing executives like to produce these. Other models are unfamiliar and troublesome, and almost every manufacturing executive would be delighted if their output were eliminated or curtailed. Internal cost and price arrangements may work at cross-purposes with the marketing division's estimates of output requirements. Sometimes they permit the manufacturing division to show a considerable profit by concentrating on models that are easily manufactured; often they can show a higher profit by producing such models than by producing those which the sales department is most anxious to obtain. As a result, conflicts may arise between what the manufacturing department wants to make and what the sales department finds easiest to sell. Ordinarily, the top executive of the firm reconciles such conflicts, but sometimes the conflict does not come out into the open for some time. Possibly the manufacturing people are not even conscious of their tendency to over-produce the trouble-free models until inventories are bulging. Also, many top executives are too concerned with other matters to involve themselves in such disputes.

In one instance, a manufacturer accumulated between 35,000 and 40,000 sets of a few models in its own inventories; in addition, the distributors held large numbers of such sets. This surplus arose despite the marketing department's requests that these models not be produced and others be turned out in larger quantities. When the surplus became intolerably large, an intensive promotion program was devised (costing the company about $35 per set) to unload it. The program was quite successful, but when it was concluded, the manufacturing division continued to act in the same old way. Consequently, another promotion program was devised, more costly than the first. Finally, the top executive of this company put a very strong executive in charge of the television division, and the manufacturing division was instructed to produce what the marketing division ordered.

There is considerable evidence to suggest that the famous Westinghouse "dump" in the late fall of 1953 was at least partly due to a similar reluctance of the manufacturing department to produce what the sales division ordered. However, as is generally the case, other errors contributed to Westinghouse's difficulties at the time.

One finds universal agreement in the industry that sales forecasting is critically important to a producer's success. Most executives admit that their firms have not been able to forecast sales by model with substantial accuracy. Even though total monthly sales often are close to estimated sales, monthly forecasts of individual model sales frequently are in error by as much as 50 to 75 percent.

Manufacturers of television sets have devoted substantial resources and great talent to this forecasting problem, and they report progress. It nevertheless remains one of their most vexing problems. Indeed, the difficulty of adjusting output to sales goes far toward explaining the essential nature of this industry. One executive concludes that the television set business will never be profitable because, in his opinion, there is no intelligent way to control production and inventories. Certainly very few companies have yet found a way.

Chapter IV

MANUFACTURERS' ACTIVITIES RELATED TO DISTRIBUTORS

In tracing the early history of the television industry it was indicated that the largest manufacturers of the present day had inherited distributors from their radio or major appliance businesses. Very few companies that did not have an already established distributor (or retailer) organization when they started remain in business today (1963); not a single one of these is a major company in the television industry. This fact alone suggests that distributors are crucial to a manufacturer's success. Clearly, their functions and relations with manufacturers must be understood if one is to account for the present nature and development of that industry.

There are other reasons for believing that the television set distributor is a key link in the industry. First, one finds very great variations in the sales success of the same manufacturer from one metropolitan market to another. (See Table 10) The only factor to which *large* variations in sales success from market to market can be attributed is distributor performance, past or present. Second, set manufacturers attach great emphasis to getting and holding "good" distributors, and a large proportion of their thinking and some of the most talented executives are devoted to this problem. Third, the truly outstanding distributor will sometimes teach the manufacturer a thing or two about how to market his line. Consequently, a good distributor can represent the equivalent of a first-rate marketing executive added to the manufacturer's staff.

Analysis and description of television set distribution is vastly complicated by the fact that it is always combined with the distribution of other products. Consequently, all of the difficulties associated with "joint costs" and "joint demand" are here, and with a vengeance.

For example, how should administrative and occupancy cost be allocated to individual product lines, by what formula should the transportation costs for different appliances shipped from the factory be divided among them? There is not even a clear line of business to analyze and describe. Television set distribution embraces inherently dissimilar enterprises because the product "mixes" that are found in the industry cover a wide spectrum. Apart from these profound diffi-

TABLE 10

MARKET SHARES OF A LARGE TELEVISION SET MANUFACTURER
(*in Percentage*)

City	First Year	Second Year
A	7.4	6.6
B	1.6	2.9
C	3.4	2.3
D	5.1	8.0
E	4.7	5.7
F	10.0	10.6
G	11.3	13.1
H	6.3	6.7
I	8.9	9.1
J	5.4	6.2
K	6.4	6.1
L	3.4	3.8
M	5.4	3.8
N	4.0	5.8
O	3.3	2.3
P	10.6	10.7

NOTE: These data were obtained in confidence and are therefore disguised to conceal the identity of the company and the actual years involved.

culties there exist big differences in mode of distributor operation—not least of which is the difference between the factory branch and independent distribution—which limit the scope of any generalizations that might be drawn. Despite these complexities, a description of the nature and performance of television set distributors will be attempted in the following pages. To do this it is necessary to examine the trade that distributes major appliances. Since this chapter is focussed on those activities in which manufacturers are engaged relative to distributors, it will be unnecessary to describe every single

Manufacturers and Distributors

facet of the trade here. Most of the difficulties listed will return to plague us in Chapter VI, however.

Television set manufacturers are free to sell to whomever they choose. They could, if they wished, sell directly to the ultimate consumer, by mail-order or otherwise. They could sell to everyone—whether a wholesaler, retailer or ultimate consumer—on equal terms. Or, they might establish more than one system in order to appeal to different classes of customer.

Most manufacturers offer their merchandise to already established institutions for resale. These have costs that are ascertainable, known customer relations, habitual methods of operation, etc. Some are far better suited to the manufacturer's needs than others; some are far more interested in the manufacturer's products than are others. Mutual benefit ordinarily determines the channels through which products flow to market. Occasionally, manufacturers can create or cause to be created new institutions to handle their merchandise. This rarely happens, and did not occur in the television set industry.

Not all television set manufacturers employ the same system of distribution. Also, many employ more than one distribution system—in particular the special arrangements through which they handle the business of very large retailers. In addition, sales of television sets to institutional customers—hotels, restaurants, motels, hospitals, etc.—usually are handled by a special distribution system.

In the main, sets are sold through a three-step distribution system: they move from manufacturer to distributor to retailer to customer. This system will be termed the "normal" distribution system and all others will be considered "deviants." The deviant system of today may be the normal system of tomorrow, of course.

Management of Independent Distributors

Inasmuch as distributors are the biggest customers of manufacturers, distributors naturally occupy much of their attention. Manufacturers recognize the contribution that distributors make to their success and they talk about it a good bit. As with the weather, few do much about it—though increasingly manufacturers are saying that more can and should be done.

To understand manufacturers' activities relating to distributors, an earlier distinction must be revived. Reference is made to the difference between "physical distribution" and "persuasion." Distributors' great contribution to manufacturers' profitability has relatively little to do with physical distribution. A distributor's skill in transporting, handling and storing merchandise may explain the difference between his making a sizable profit or a loss, but will affect the manufacturer very little. The main contribution that distributors make to manufacturers, the skill for which they are prized, is that of persuasion—the creation of sales.

A substantial proportion (approximately 60 percent) of the average distributor's costs are incurred for physical distribution; most of these are almost beyond his control, as in the case of transportation and occupancy cost, or can be changed relatively little, as with general and administrative costs. (A detailed analysis of independent distributors' activities and their costs is presented in Chapter VI. It establishes the general conclusion that physical distribution accounts for a large part of the major appliance distributor's costs but only for a very small part of his time, effort, profits and growth.)

Although it may offend some students of marketing to see the conventional functions of the middleman treated so cavalierly, little will be said here about the physical distribution of television sets. These involve relatively small and unalterable costs; manufacturers do little more than "bill" their distributors for transportation (occasionally dropping transportation charges as one form of price-cut) and ship goods by the carrier that the distributor specifies. Television set manufacturers mainly regard distributors as a stage through which they must transmit their own sales efforts to retailers and ultimately to final customers, and as a source of information about the market. Although it is the distributor's skills as a persuader that the manufacturer desires most, he also is concerned with the distributor's capital resources, character and industriousness. As several executives put it, "When you appoint a distributor, you are hiring a man with money who is willing to take risks."

SELECTION OF INDEPENDENT DISTRIBUTORS

During the early post-war years, most large national manufacturers simply sold through the firms that were already distributing their

Manufacturers and Distributors

radios and/or other appliances. Distributor selection soon became a pressing problem, however. As discussed earlier, there is considerable turnover among independent distributors of major appliances. Manufacturers beset by basic sales difficulties generally suffer from staggering distributor turnover. For example, during a recent three-year period characterized by sales decline and internal "head-rolling," one major television set producer changed at least 50 percent of its distributors; a 20 percent turnover of independent distributors in a three-year period is about average.

High distributor turnover results from numerous causes. Manufacturer dissatisfaction with distributor performance is the major cause, though distributor disenchantment with the manufacturer or his product runs a close second. Also, death, sickness, or retirement from the business by the distributor generally compels the manufacturer to seek a replacement; in most cases, the manufacturer is primarily, if not exclusively, interested in the "principal" of the distributorship, rather than his organization. In addition, when a territory grows and cannot be served adequately by the existing distributor, the manufacturer usually will add another distributor.

An extremely vexing issue to top marketing executives in this industry is whether they should get a new distributor or try to improve present ones. Early in the industry's life, the tendency was to replace weak distributors very promptly. There followed a period when most manufacturers concluded that the new "devils" generally were worse than the old one and decided to work with the distributors they had, rather than take on new ones. Now again one hears things that suggest that poor distributors should be replaced rather than reformed. One top marketing executive for a major set producer said, in 1962, "If you have a weak distributor today, he'll be weak tomorrow. You cannot change the fundamental quality of a distributor. You have got to get different distributors to replace your weak ones. This is one of the lessons I have learned."

That executive's company has clearly been guided by that conviction. It changed 21 distributors within a period of 18 months. It would have changed even more, except that it takes time to work with new distributors and the costs of changing distributors are substantial —and perhaps generally underestimated.

The costs of changing a distributor take the following forms:

1. Costs resulting from taking back merchandise in sealed cartons and from the repurchase of "current" repair parts. (Most manufacturers do not want to permit any goods to reach the market as distress merchandise.)

2. The distributor may be over-spent in his co-op advertising. Some manufacturers will reimburse the distributor for his over-spending.

3. Special support is given to the new distributor, ordinarily in the form of promotional funds.

4. The factory ordinarily repurchases obsolete parts held by the distributor.

5. The new distributor does not understand the business for about six to nine months after he takes over. The manufacturer will not do much business during this period.

6. The old distributor will do almost nothing for the factory for at least a month before the change.

7. Top management from the factory must spend a lot of time training the new distributor.

Despite the large costs involved in changing distributors, television set producers have made many changes, apparently because of their disappointing experience with efforts to up-grade distributor performance. However, their efforts have not been great—not the kind that would appear to be justified by the great costs involved in making distributor changes.

If a manufacturer has lost a distributor or desires to add another to cover a growing territory, he has several alternatives. As already explained, he might establish a factory-owned branch. Sometimes he may extend the territory of an already established adjacent distributor. For the most part, he makes a replacement.

Lost distributors can be replaced basically in the following way: a firm that is a distributor for one brand may be persuaded to drop that line in favor of another brand; a firm that distributes another line may be induced to add television sets to its existing offerings; a person in an altogether different line of business may be induced to establish a major appliance distributorship from scratch (this person ordinarily already resides in the community); or the manufacturer may select an individual from within its own organization and assist him to become an independent distributor. Manufacturers presumably select the most promising person or organization from among these alternatives.

A television set manufacturer whose distributor is performing badly usually will try to persuade a successful distributor for a rival brand to give up that brand and take on his own. The most common method of replacing a distributor is to get someone already in the business. With this thought, at least one manufacturer requires its salesmen to make systematic efforts to become acquainted with and learn the thinking of rival distributors, so that if they should become dissatisfied with their present manufacturer's line they might switch to this manufacturer's products. As a routine matter, they call on rival distributors periodically and have informal chats. They drop by and introduce themselves and "offer to be of service." From time to time, they call again and inquire whether "anything is new." The distributors on whom they call generally welcome the opportunity to discuss the state of the appliance business and probably hope to learn something from the salesman about the current sales and problems of other brands. In this way, the field salesmen are likely to uncover distributors who are dissatisfied with their present line. Also, they are expected to chat with local bankers, members of the business press, etc., to get suggestions for prospective distributorship material—just in the event that it should become necessary to find a replacement. Ordinarily they will follow up on these suggestions and try to get to know the persons well enough to determine their capabilities.

This manufacturer apparently is unusual in requiring its field salesmen to operate in the manner described. Most of the others apparently become concerned with locating prospective new distributors only when they are needed, or when the home office becomes dissatisfied with the performance of the existing distributor and want to know whether a superior alternative is available.

Most television set manufacturers handle distributor selection as follows: the home office notifies the regional salesman that he should come forward with suggested replacements for the present distributor. He uses whatever resources he can, including some or all of those mentioned, to turn up some "good names." Also, inquiries are made of persons in the home office on the off-chance that someone there knows of some good prospects. Not infrequently, the chief marketing executive will go out into the area himself and will talk to bankers, executives of advertising agencies, the press, key retailers, etc. in an effort to find prospective distributors. One manufacturer sends out a team to investigate the market when it is considering a distributor change. Disguised interviews are conducted with retailers to see whether the present distributor has been building up loyalty; at the same time, dealers are asked who they believe to be the best distributors in the area. In the opinion of top executives responsible for distribution, in a small city these measures are very likely to uncover good distributor material if any exists—but they serve less well for finding good prospective independent distributors in large centers.

Thus, it appears that even the most systematic methods of finding prospective new distributors are very unsystematic. They essentially call for "just asking around." To characterize these methods in this way is not to criticize them: there does not appear to be a better way.

The uncovering of alternatives is only the first stage in the selection of distributors. The isolation of the best among the available alternatives is an extremely difficult task because the characteristics of a good distributor are not readily identifiable. The qualities desired in a television set distributor apparently are not uniform from market to market and from one stage in the history of the industry to another stage.

Ability to adapt to changes in the market has meant the difference between success and failure for many distributors. One manufacturer persuaded one of his distributors who also handled a wide variety of hardware lines to hire an experienced appliance man. This man established procedures for the radio and television end of the business that were completely different from the distributor's usual "style" of operating, which was primarily adapted to the hardware business. This change was very successful. On the other hand, one hears of many distributors who "started from nothing" and built up very substantial businesses in a period of expansion by entertaining dealers lavishly and effectively and who continued to rely on these methods when the industry became far more competitive. They were overtaken by competitors who, aware that times had changed, concentrated more on sales promotions and intelligent retailer contacts in their business efforts.

Many executives were questioned about the characteristics that manufacturers desire in their distributors, and they agreed that the features that were highly desirable in a distributor in one market might hamper success in others. They stated a preference for a smart, slick, shrewd, "operator-type" distributor in large metropolitan markets characterized by constant price-cutting and for a conservative, reliable, "nonoperator type" in stable markets. Then, too, if a distributor has alienated important dealers because of a particular fault, the factory will seek a replacement who, though he may have other shortcomings, will be free from that one fault.

Individual companies also place unequal weights on the many qualities desired in a distributor. These include good contacts and relations with appliance dealers, department stores, etc.; industriousness, intelligence in business matters; long business experience; youth; good health; and ample capital resources. Those manufacturers who are themselves short of funds are likely to put a premium on a distributor-prospect who will not require much financial assistance from them; those that are cash-rich will place far greater emphasis on business acumen and sales experience.

Despite its great importance to their success, television set manufacturers have not developed any new and specialized procedures for the selection of distributors. Distributor selection is handled mainly on a "crisis basis" and by methods that must be considered casual and personal—if not whimsical. Manufacturers of television sets devote far less attention to methods of distributor selection, for example, than to methods of selecting salesmen.

Their methods partly reflect the available supply of reasonably promising prospects in most communities. This number apparently is very small, especially in small and medium markets. Indeed, manufacturers generally retain distributors that they regard as mediocre in the conviction that any replacement would be even worse. This is true especially for those manufacturers whose brands do not enjoy strong consumer acceptance. It is possible that any and all distributor prospects are very conspicuous and few in number. Perhaps no special procedures are required to hunt them down and to select among them. Most marketing executives in the industry believe such is the case. Although they may be correct, since they have not experimented with different techniques for uncovering good distributor material, one cannot be sure.

DISTRIBUTOR SERVICING

In the ordinary course of business, there are several ways in which manufacturers are called upon to perform services for their distributors. Foremost, they must accept distributors' orders, arrange delivery and "bill" them. This function poses no special problems, but there is diversity of practice among manufacturers nevertheless. Some manufacturers have their distributors place orders directly with the factory, without using the local salesman for this purpose; others have their regional salesmen solicit and handle distributors' orders. The second arrangement is found in those companies which regard their regional salesmen in the old tradition and think of them mainly as salesmen. One of the leading manufacturers uses its regional salesmen to apply pressure on distributors to aggressively promote and sell; they are not involved in order taking, which is largely done by mail. Another company has men in the field "just telling the product story." They call on both distributors and dealers, attend sales meetings, and call on key accounts.

Inasmuch as distributors handle only one brand of set, it is not clear why distributors should "have to be sold." If they can make sales to retailers, they will order merchandise from the manufacturer. Since they have strong financial incentives to get retailers to buy from them, distributors should not require any urging from the manufacturer's salesmen. It would therefore appear that salesmen for the factory can best obtain orders from the distributors in his "charge" if he can help them—and their dealers—to make sales. The acceptance of orders is a routine clerical job that obscures the salesman's true function. (As will be explained later, television set manufacturers are not always clear and are not agreed about the regional salesman's function.)

Manufacturers' sales of major appliances to their distributors are rarely on a C.O.D. basis. (The exception is the distributor who is an extremely poor credit risk and whose franchise is about to be terminated.) To some extent, then, distributors are partly financed by manufacturers through credit accommodation.

Manufacturers can extend credit in the following ways: (1) sales

Manufacturers and Distributors

of goods to distributors with long deferred payment arrangements; (2) sales to distributors on a "field warehousing" arrangement (whereby the manufacturer continues to own the merchandise, which is earmarked on the distributor's premises; it is paid for as removed from a simulated warehouse established within the distributor's warehouse); (3) "floor-planning" for distributors—which is like field warehousing except that the goods are not isolated on the distributor's premises; (4) discounting of the accounts receivable acquired by distributors as the result of their sales to dealers; (5) discounting of dealers' receivables, thus providing them with funds so they can discharge their obligations to distributors; and (6) floor-planning arrangements for retailers who carry the manufacturer's line. (The manufacturer or distributor pays the interest charges for the retailer.) The most important forms of financial assistance that the manufacturers extend to their distributors are the first and sixth, and the first is greater by far.

The credit accommodation phase of television set manufacturers' distributive activities is complex and moderately technical. For the purposes of understanding the distribution of television sets, it is not necessary to treat this subject in depth. Several general conclusions regarding the amount and form of appliance manufacturers' credit accommodation for distributors in the television set industry are set forth in the form of a list:

1. Credit accommodation is on the increase; every manufacturer questioned on this point stated that he is tying up a larger proportion of his resources in financing his distributors' activities.

2. The amount of financial assistance that distributors obtain from individual manufacturers varies moderately, but the great disparity in manufacturer practice has narrowed greatly. At one time, General Electric provided far more financial aid than the others (relying on the G.E. Acceptance Corporation to carry out the actual arrangements).

3. Losses to manufacturers resulting from extension of credit have sometimes been extremely large; the largest occur when a distributor loses a large sum due to bankruptcy of a large retail account.

4. More and more institutions extend loans to distributors of major appliances. (These are commonly known as Commercial Finance

Companies, an outgrowth of the old "Factor"; they extend loans only against tangible security, such as accounts receivable, plant equipment and inventories.) However, most of these sources are relatively expensive and are used by distributors only rarely and then just to supplement the assistance received from the manufacturers.

5. Manufacturers generally charge very little for whatever credit they extend to distributors. Credit is used mainly to strengthen ties between the manufacturer and distributor, especially if the distributor is considered a "good merchandiser."

6. It is almost impossible to estimate the average manufacturer's costs resulting from the extension of credit to distributors. Although the actual outlays probably are not large, the risks are sizable and the amount of the manufacturer's resources that must be tied up in credit assistance often is large, and sometimes cannot be spared easily.

Manufacturers are the only reliable source of information about their offerings, guarantees, etc. They therefore try to inform distributors and their salesmen about changes in their "line." Since their purpose in providing such information is to make their distributor organizations more effective vendors, they have gradually expanded their activities to include the train of distributor salesmen. At the present time, all large television set manufacturers have "programs" whose purpose is to train distributors' salesmen, though several say, with emotion, that the "main job really belongs to the distributor himself."

Manufacturer efforts to train distributor salesmen take several forms: provision of training at the factory in the technical features of the product, formal classroom training of lecture-type sessions which deal mainly with sales methods, and on-site training whereby the manufacturer's regional salesmen visit dealer customers together with distributor salesmen and discuss sales techniques. In the major appliance business, activities of this type are expanding, even though they are still half-hearted and haphazard in many cases. Manufacturers apparently have ambivalent feelings about sales training; some do not see why they should do the distributor's job for him and still let him keep his "margin."

Manufacturers perform a variety of services for their distributors; of course, some companies do much more than others. For example, at least two firms provide, free at distributor request, the services of a specialist who will review the distributor's paper work and internal organization. Most provide suggested advertising copy, and some supply "mats" for newspaper advertisements. A few of late are assisting distributors with methods of inventory control and record keeping. All provide some point-of-sale brochures, display fixtures, etc. However, their policy regarding whether and how much to charge for these things varies considerably.

A few television set manufacturers are prepared to make great efforts to improve the performance of their distributors—to advance their own interests. They believe that they possess far more skill, personnel resources, experience, etc. than the average distributor and can do the distributor's job better than he. Consequently, they are moving in the direction of acting as management and marketing consultants; they even participate directly in some activities ordinarily considered the private preserve of the distributor. To the extent that the distributor recognizes that they can do the job better than he, their assistance is welcomed—and even requested.

Some TV set manufacturers are anxious to discover additional ways in which they might help their distributors and thus help themselves. Their viewpoint represents a conception of the manufacturer's role that is relatively new. As usual, practice lags far behind conception so that more manufacturers talk about aiding and training distributors than do it. Almost all believe that they are offering more assistance to distributors than distributors report that they are receiving.

MOTIVATION AND CONTROL OF DISTRIBUTOR PERFORMANCE

When a distributor accepts a manufacturer's franchise, he recognizes—and ordinarily he is also told—that he must "deliver." If he does not sell an acceptable amount of the manufacturer's merchandise, someone else will be sought to replace him, and he knows it. Distributors are extremely anxious about the cancellation clause included in their franchises. Those that hold franchises for actively demanded brands possess a valuable asset; manufacturers of such brands use this threat, generally implied rather than overt, to obtain maximum sales volume. If they have a very good distributor, they hope to make him even better; they are worried about distributors becoming complacent and turning into "fat cats." In discussions with poor distributors, manufacturers of strong brands rarely hesitate to show their dissatisfaction; generally the distributor whose performance is mediocre knows that his franchise is in jeopardy without being told.

Some franchises are not very valuable in that the distributor could obtain another one of equal value without much trouble. Manufacturers of relatively weak brands carry no stick and must speak in a soft voice.

The value of even a given manufacturer's distributor franchise varies enormously from city to city, depending particularly upon the intensity of competition in each city. For example, one distributor possessed a valuable brand's franchise for Los Angeles as well as San Francisco. He was quite content to give up the Los Angeles franchise when that became necessary and has no desire to get it back. On the other hand, he considers the San Francisco franchise valuable and is pleased with its level of profit. The Los Angeles market is very unstable and extraordinarily competitive; San Francisco is less afflicted by wheeling and dealing.

The motivation and control of distributors is not unlike the system employed to motivate and control individual salesmen in many industries. At the bottom of the motivation system is a measure of "what the salesman should be able to sell." This sum is generally expressed as a "quota" for both distributors and salesmen. Inasmuch as the maintenance or loss of a valuable franchise generally turns upon a particular "quota," there is great concern about the system that is used to set quotas for distributors. The successful distributors usually want to know why their quotas require them to get a larger share of their potential markets than most other distributors are expected to get of theirs. The unsuccessful distributors generally offer reasons for why their quotas should be set even lower than they are—simply to obtain greater insurance against loss of the franchise. To clarify the motivation and control of independent distributors, we need to consider the establishment of quotas and quota review and revision.

Although the mechanics by which individual manufacturers arrive at their sales quotas for distributors (they set quotas for both their independent distributors and their factory branches) are not identical, they all take account primarily of two factors. The first is the distributor's past market penetration—that is, the share of total television set sales in the distributor's territory that he accounted for in the most recent past. (The few large manufacturers that do not belong to the industry trade association, and therefore cannot measure market penetration, compute the distributor's share of their own total sales; although this measure is somewhat less valid as an indicator of relative sales success, it comes to much the same thing.) The second is the estimated market potential—that is, the share of the market that the distributor "should be able to acquire"; in turn, this generally means the average share the manufacturer has attained in all of his markets combined. A third consideration with some manufacturers is the "amount of sales promotion money they have poured into the market"; the markets receiving the greatest amount of sales support are required to produce a relatively larger sales result.

The basic principle that is translated into specific quotas is that "one cannot expect a distributor to change overnight." Another key principle that affects quotas is that those below the average for the manufacturer's entire distributor organization should be expected to move up toward the average with varying degrees of promptness. Both the distributor and the manufacturer accept the position that every distributor should be able to match the performance of the average distributor or "something is wrong with him." Discussions between manufacturers and distributors about failures to meet quota are dominated by this unspoken standard.

The function of setting distributor quotas usually is vested in the manager of market research—a post that does not ordinarily carry very high status or remuneration in most television set manufacturers' organizations. Typically, he will prepare rankings of distributors at regular intervals or only lists of distributors whose performance is inadequate. (One reported that he gave up preparing lists of poor distributors because the same names were always on the list. His company was unable to replace its poor distributors with better ones, apparently.) Also, the manufacturer's regional salesman is responsible for calling attention both to the distributor and to the manufacturer of poor performance and possible remedies. When an individual distributor's performance has been persistently bad and the manufacturer is contemplating a change, discussions usually are shifted from the market research department and the regional salesman up the line and end up in the lap of the vice-president in charge of distribution or even to the vice-president in charge of marketing.

Sometimes quotas are established and then almost ignored. Some manufacturers imply that such was the case not many years ago. As competitive pressures intensified in the industry, however, the administration of the distributor organization became more strict, and distributor quotas ceased to lie fallow. Programs for improving distributor performance were initiated in many manufacturing organizations, all revolving around the sales quota as a standard. These programs started with the premise that the "hopeless" distributors had to be weeded out, the poor ones had to be given to understand that they must improve or they would be dropped and those that were only fair had to be put under pressure and given counsel so that they would improve. Most manufacturers undertook such a program only when sales and profits began to shrink. When their sales were rising (even though their market share was not), they apparently were quite casual about the enforcement of distributor quotas.

Despite acceptance of the basic premise that the distributor organization should be improved, the programs developed to bring this result about generally consisted of little more than "good intentions." The market research manager was given the task of sending a list of the persistently poor performers to a designated executive. That executive was to "discuss the matter with the distributor" and get him to perform better. The link between the conversation with the distributor and his better performance was not spelled out. It apparently was believed that the manufacturer's representative would sense whether the distributor would and could improve his showing. The improvement, if any would occur, would result from implying or openly threatening that his franchise would be canceled unless market shares were increased.

The "jaw-bone" approach to improved distributor performance is not lacking in effectiveness. Like others, distributors become lax and can be coerced, intimidated, cajoled and enticed into stronger efforts. On the other hand, many distributors perform poorly for reasons unrelated to effort and incentive; they just are less skillful "businessmen" than their competitors. It is for this second and very large group that some television set manufacturers have taken measures to upgrade distributors. They may have been induced to amplify their programs for improving distributors' performance by the frequent experience of talking to extremely cooperative, well-intentioned and industrious distributors who were losing ground in their market. Once in a while, they faced the embarrassment of having a distributor say, "Well, why don't you show me what to do to meet quota? I want increased volume as much as you do."

Most manufacturers' relations with distributors have gone through the foregoing stages and have reached a point at which the average large television set manufacturer has decided to offer the distributor some help. At least one large manufacturer denies that he "owes it to them" but admits that it is wise to give them help, "though they should be able to run their own business without any help from the manufacturer. That is what they are being paid to do."

Very few television set distributors receive much help from their manufacturers; most could obtain greater help if they requested it. Manufacturers differ greatly in the amount of help they extend to their distributors who are making a mediocre showing and in the form that this help takes. Only as recently as 1957 and 1958 a few manufacturers first came to regard this as a wise course of action. It seems that in 1963, many still pay lip service to the idea and devote very limited resources to putting it into effect. In response to a questionnaire asking about formal programs conducted by manufacturers to improve distributor performance, only one of the five respondent companies reported ever holding such a program. Possibly a long time must elapse before a large organization can get around to doing something about what has now been recognized as a need. Alternatively, although they recognize the need to help, they may feel unable to do anything about it.

One other use of distributor quotas should be noted. At least one manufacturer at one time tied his production schedules and his shipments to individual distributors closely to the quotas set for them. This system gave rise to great hostility during periods of low sales, during which distributors found themselves loaded up with many more sets than they could sell. This manufacturer, holder of one of the most valuable franchises in the industry, was able to continue this system far longer than most other manufacturers could have. However, he was forced to abandon it some years back and currently uses distributor quotas in the same way that other manufacturers do.

Earlier it was noted that the interests of manufacturers are harmonious on many scores and yet conflict on others. The extent to which either party can achieve his goals depends partly upon his bargaining power and the skill with which he exercises it. Inevitably, both parties must compromise on some matters. Unfortunately, when respect is not mutual, compromise is often painful—albeit necessary.

One common form of conflict between manufacturer and distributor is disagreement about the kinds of credit risks that the distributor should assume. Some distributors adopt an extremely conservative policy and forego sales volume that the factory urgently wants. Manufacturers are almost powerless to do anything in such situations, even when they are certain that lucrative business is being turned away by the distributor. On the other hand, the distributor views such a situation as evidence that the manufacturer does not care about what happens to him.

Manufacturers often complain about their distributors' pricing policies. They favor what they euphemistically describe as "dynamic pricing." This was defined by one executive to mean that "the distributor will accept the shortest possible gross profit that he can live with in order to get maximum volume." It is doubtful that distributors would characterize such prices by the same name.

Although conflict of interest between distributor and manufacturer is a genuine problem, it cannot be considered a grave one. There are occasions, as a few executives in manufacturing companies admit in confidence, when the manufacturer must use its power to push a distributor around. They seem to be extremely rare, and there appears to be a basic feeling of warmth between most distributors and the factory personnel with whom they come in contact.

CREATION AND MANAGEMENT OF A PERSONAL SALES FORCE

In order to create and manage an independent distributor organization the manufacturer uses a personal sales force as a "control arm." This field sales force is composed primarily of Regional Sales

Manufacturers and Distributors

Managers (R.S.M.)—persons who, as representatives of the manufacturers, call upon distributors. (A variety of titles is used by television set manufacturers for these men.) They also call upon dealers from time to time; on those occasions they are usually accompanied by a representative of the local distributor. The R.S.M. usually does not have supervisory responsibilities but, in a number of companies, will himself report to an area supervisor.

The larger manufacturers have between 15 to 20 R.S.M.s in the field, who report to three or four area supervisors (in those companies that have them). Each R.S.M. has a number of distributors assigned to him, on whom he calls regularly and at length. One manufacturer expects his R.S.M.s to stay at least three days on each visit to a distributor: these are anything but hit and run calls. One company is an exception to this general description. This manufacturer, one of the largest, has 60 R.S.M.s. These operate in teams of three, calling on the same distributor together. (The manufacturer groups his product lines into consumer electronics, laundry goods and white goods; since only one team is concerned with television, then the number, 20, is around the industry average.)

A questionnaire survey of television set manufacturers to ascertain the role of the R.S.M. disclosed that most of the larger companies do not regard the R.S.M. primarily as a salesman. Far greater emphasis is laid on his ability to analyze the distributor's operations and to help him (and often his dealers, as well) with merchandising, sales and promotions plans. Some companies expect the R.S.M.'s to advise their distributor about internal management problems. A marketing vice-president for one large set manufacturer stated that if the R.S.M. performs these functions correctly, "it's unnecessary to pressure a distributor into an order. . . . He has to buy."

In addition to selling and providing managerial services to distributors, many companies place additional duties and responsibilities on their R.S.M.s. These can include:

1. Conducting sales training meetings for distributors and often dealers. Here the stress is laid on the ability of the R.S.M. to sell the manufacturer's program, and to convince distributors and dealers that the brand will make profits for them.

2. Reporting to head office on sales, on the intensity of competition

in the market, on the state of the market and on the efficiency of the distributors in the R.S.M.'s territory. (This last point is discussed separately in the next paragraph.) In effect, he is a relay station in the two-way communications constantly going on in the normal course of business. In one direction, he passes product and other information from the manufacturer to distributors and dealers; in return, he collects information about the effects of the manufacturer's various policies on the distribution system and the market. This feedback is vitally important "intelligence" that helps the manufacturer to plan ahead. In addition to his passive "relay" function, the R.S.M. also acts as a market "sensor." Through his close contact with the market, he is able to ascertain which models are selling successfully and which are "dogs"; he can find out what the competition is doing in his territory and devise ways to beat it. (One manufacturer, and perhaps many, requires the R.S.M. to follow closely the amount and form of competitors' advertising and to meet with representatives of the local press to learn whatever they can about competitors' expenditures.) Finally, at least one large manufacturer uses R.S.M.s in the planning and execution of their periodic market surveys.

3. Acting as a "trouble shooter," in the sense that he identifies weak distributors for headquarters. In some cases, he will be asked to take corrective action himself; in others, a special team is sent out from the factory.

Most manufacturers regard their R.S.M.s as key men in their organizations. (In all of the interviews I conducted, as well as in the responses to the special survey conducted to gather material for this section, only one executive from a manufacturing company expressed the opinion that the R.S.M. was not a key man.) For instance, several mentioned replacing a weak regional manager in one territory with a strong one. In some cases, sales in the territory just "took off"; occasionally the effects of a change were startling.

Starting salaries for R.S.M.s are about $10,000 per year and more; the average is around $15,000. Top men earn more than $20,000 a year in many companies. Some companies also add bonuses to regular compensation.

In view of the considerable responsibilities and substantial salaries that the position entails, manufacturers seek men of high caliber. In response to the question, "What special characteristics do you seek in your R.S.M.s," many companies laid primary stress on the person's familiarity with distributor operations, organization and management. Intimate knowledge of or ability to adapt to the particular conditions of a territory were also considered important. One company stated that it required its men to have an "ability to wheel and deal."

The main sources from which set manufacturers draw their R.S.M.s are distributor salesmen or managers, representatives of competing manufacturers, retail sales managers. Less common sources are the factory's own sales organization and advertising department.

Conditions and compensation would appear to be adequate, for the position is one with very low turnover. Many men stay in the position for ten years or more, and one executive "could not recall anyone ever quitting." Promotion within the company for R.S.M.s is mostly to sales management, and this can be in the factory, with a factory branch, or to a supervisory post in the regional sales organization. Two of the surveyed companies stated that there was nothing to stop a man moving right up to the top, providing he had the necessary drive, qualities, etc.

Opinion was fairly evenly divided as to whether there were enough "good men to go around." There was no correlation between a company's finding an adequate supply of men and its salary rates. The ones that paid least had as much success, or lack of it, as the ones who paid most—possibly because the variations in compensation among the few firms participating in the survey were not great. To keep the right men, all have to pay a competitive salary. The marketing executive of one large manufacturer who complained about an inadequate supply of good men said that there was no shortage of good salesmen—the management qualities required in an R.S.M. were the scarce resource.

Creation and Management of Factory-Owned Distributorships

The foregoing pages described the activities of television set manufacturers in connection with managing independent distributors. One manufacturer always establishes factory branches to replace independents when they prove unsatisfactory or give up his line on their own initiative. Most manufacturers have shifted back and forth in their policy toward factory branches. The independent distributor remains by far the dominant type at present (1963).

A sharp distinction was drawn earlier between independent distributorships and factory branches. Actually, these forms of business organization shade imperceptibly into one another. No firm that distributes exclusively for a single manufacturer is "independent" in the full sense of that term. It is heavily dependent upon the manufacturer whose products it distributes, even though a nominal financial independence exists. Some distributors say that their independence consists solely of the freedom to lose their own investment rather than the manufacturer's. Even financial independence is not a firm rule. Many manufacturers extend help to ostensibly independent distributors, especially in large metropolitan markets. For example, one "independent distributor" put up $50,000 toward establishing a distributorship in New York, and the factory "foots the rest of the bills." Someone who should know states that another manufacturer "cancels out all of its distributor's red figures" in a large Eastern city.

By establishing a factory branch, a manufacturer reaches forward toward the consumer and performs more economic activities. He extends his scope through ownership and thereby gains greater control as well as an opportunity for greater profit. In the process, however, he is forced to invest more of his own resources; by using independent distributors, he would use the financial resources of others.

Manufacturers describe their factory branch managers as being essentially independent profit centers. Some say that they have about as much difficulty in getting them to go along with a factory program as they do with independent distributors. If the factory branch manager is compelled to show large sales volume and profits, his behavior is likely to resemble that of an independent distributor, and conflicts between the factory and the branches will occasionally arise. Accordingly, factory branches are not totally dependent upon the factory in an operating sense. Thus, on grounds of the sources of investment and conflict of objective with the factory, the distinction between an independent distributor and a factory branch is smaller than one might suppose—though a vital difference does exist. If the factory wishes to increase its sales in a particular market or dump distress

Manufacturers and Distributors

merchandise, it has far greater freedom of maneuver if the distributor is a factory branch than if it were an independent. Indeed, the factory branch is more a competitive tool than a method of making profit on investment.

Many manufacturers report serious financial trouble with their factory branches, though a few claim that they operate at a profit. It is quite usual for television set producers to lose money consistently on their branch operations. This situation becomes extremely serious, as is the case with some companies, when they sell almost half of their volume through factory branches. However, faced with the choice of staying out of those markets or accepting only tiny volumes even at a profit, these companies prefer to establish a factory branch. They believe that these branches actually contribute to corporate profits by enabling the factory to run at a higher rate and thereby to achieve important manufacturing economies.

Even though a factory branch is completely beholden to the manufacturer and is required to do his bidding, it is no simple matter to insure that it performs its functions properly or efficiently. The factory must pick the personnel and location, provide financing, establish business methods and policies, etc., that will cause the distributorship to do what it was originally set up to accomplish. Because large distances frequently are involved, the problem of maintaining close liaison and identity of objective is not always simple. The greatest difficulty in managing factory distributors, however, stems from the fact that the distribution of major appliances is extremely competitive and complex. Few television set manufacturers make the mistake of assuming that they can easily hire and supervise the necessary talent to run a successful branch operation. On the contrary, they tend to agree that "a good independent is far better than a good branch any day of the week."

Almost every manufacturer establishes a quota for each of its branches and evaluates the branch's performance against quota. Also, it makes each branch manager "accountable" for the profitability of the branch, and his compensation is based—either formally and explicitly or as a matter of course—on its sales relative to quota and the profitability of its operations. It is not clear which of these factors is given greater weight in determining manager compensation. One would expect it to be the first, because the manufacturer generally establishes a factory branch to "get volume" and keep his plant operating near capacity to keep his unit production costs down. Also, it is not clear how the factory (or the branch manager) take into account instances where volume is obtained at a substantial loss.

The foregoing description applies to the activities of the "typical" television set manufacturer. Although it explains how most of the sets sold annually in this country reach the retailer for ultimate sale, it does not describe direct sales to large retail accounts. It also does not cover the distribution systems of such firms as Sears-Roebuck, Magnavox, Muntz and Packard-Bell.

If one considers all products in the United States that usually are sold through distributors it would appear that most manufacturers in those fields sell part of their output directly to large retailers. Direct sale of television sets to large retailers is relatively recent, dating from the time that the industry became afflicted with overproduction, and is still not permitted by some manufacturers. (It is difficult to get reliable information about direct sales; those companies which admittedly sell direct to many retail accounts accuse all others of doing the same.) Such sales, hereafter termed "direct sales," have increased rapidly with the growth in number, size and bargaining power of large appliance chains and discount houses. The large retailer of television sets possesses strong market power and apparently is growing. He is wooed by all manufacturers and distributors, for he offers an opportunity to move or "unload" large amounts of merchandise with just a single transaction. In addition, he usually is regarded as an effective advertiser, whose promotional efforts help to sell the brand in other retail stores. As a result, the fiercest competition in the industry is concentrated in the relatively small market sector involving "direct sales."

Many manufacturers designate very large retailers "associate distributors" (A.D.s). These firms pay only slightly more than distributors, providing a small over-ride for the distributor who serves that territory, and are required to order in substantial quantities. Retailers who are willing to meet these requirements have little difficulty in becoming A.D.s for manufacturers who have such accounts. As one marketing executive put it, "My company will make any strong retailer in a market into an associate distributor to get him and also will give him a big fat co-op advertising allowance."

Besides independent distributors, factory branches and associate distributors, television set manufacturers sell to other types of accounts: builders, key accounts, national appliance chains, regional chains, buying chains for department stores, buying co-ops for small independent retailers, national department store chains and PX stores. Some manufacturers are very alert to the differences among these types of customers for their products. Occasionally they devise special pricing and co-op advertising arrangements for each type and occasionally even make special changes in the product for particular types of customer. Of course, they are strictly limited in making such distinctions by the Robinson-Patman Act, which prohibits many types of price discrimination.

Why are the large chains, department stores and discount houses not served by some television set manufacturers through regular channels, just like other retail customers? In answering this question, it is important to separate "real economies" of serving retailers directly—circumstances that reduce the amount of labor, facilities, time, investment, etc., required to perform the necessary distribution function—from "bargaining power economies"—which reflect savings due to the buyer's ability to command advantageous terms because of his market power.

The distributor clearly could be of some service to the manufacturer in dealing with large retailers. He could provide local on-the-scene personal sales effort; he could give prompt delivery on merchandise that was not in the retailer's inventory; he could even deliver directly to the retailer's customers and thus provide low costs as well as speed; he could bill for merchandise and collect bills; he could keep in constant touch with the large retailers to learn their plans and needs; he might also lend assistance to large retailers in planning promotions and advertising programs. Thus, the distributor could help the manufacturer to win the business of large retail accounts and to serve them, and could perform some services that the manufacturer would find costly to provide.

One can turn the question around and ask what the distributor might do that would be of value to the large retailer. An answer would include at least the following items: he provides easy communications with the factory at low cost; he provides assistance in the servicing of sets that have been damaged in transit, that do not perform upon installation, or that fail during the warranty period; he offers flexibility in delivery arrangements, as already indicated; mainly, he makes it unnecessary for the retailer to carry large inventories. This list suggests that the distributor's services should be valued by the large retailer as well as by the manufacturer.

The use of distributors by television set manufacturers in selling to large retailers depends on how much these services are worth and how much the distributor must be paid to provide them. The manufacturer could perform them for himself and would do so if he would either reduce his costs or gain in sales effectiveness. Several noncontroversial observations about sales to large retail accounts will sharpen the issues involved:

1. By selling to large retail accounts through regular distributors, manufacturers usually achieve significant benefits and economies that are worth paying something to obtain.

2. The manufacturers could sell and service large retail accounts themselves for less than the usual gross margins obtained by distributors.

3. Large retail accounts are enormously concerned with price, and their business can be won only if margins are shaved all along the line.

4. Most manufacturers want to be free, if they want, to employ their own sales personnel in trying to gain key account business. They must be able to by-pass or supplement the efforts of the distributor when large sales volumes are involved.

Although the distributor has something to offer to both the manufacturer and large retailer, they will not pay his usual charges for those services. What are the distributor's costs to serve large retailers? Can he find a place for himself in handling large retail accounts and make a profit for himself in the process? For the present, at least, the answer seems to be affirmative. Most television set manufacturers either do not sell direct to any retailers or they use distributor personnel and facilities in serving them directly.

Manufacturers and Distributors

The large retail account is relatively inexpensive to cultivate and service. He is generally very accessible, for he is located in large cities, where the distributor himself is situated or where his salesmen call regularly; he usually is known to be a small credit risk; and he employs efficient methods of ordering and materials handling that make the cost of servicing him low. Economies of large unit sales added to the foregoing make the per-unit or per-dollar-of-sales cost of handling his business lower than that on a small retail account. In other words, the distributor apparently could afford to reduce his margins substantially on sales to large retail accounts.

The distributor would seem to possess great advantages over the manufacturer in handling large retail accounts. He already is on the scene and operates with a trained sales force in the territory; he possesses local information and contacts that should strengthen his ability to sell to the large retailer; he already does hold inventories to serve his smaller customers. Whatever the distributor's costs of servicing the large retailer, they would appear to be lower than those the manufacturer must bear to do the same thing. If the manufacturer could get the distributor to lower his margin demands to what it costs him to serve the larger retailer (plus a modest profit), he would save by selling to the large retailer through the distributor as compared with selling direct.

The foregoing line of argument suggests that there is a place for the distributor in selling to large retail accounts. The "real economies" of the situation are in favor of employing the distributor—*where he already exists* to serve small retail accounts. That is the situation prevailing at the present time.

How Manufacturers Handle Sales to Large Retailers

If one examines the methods by which television set manufacturers handle large retail accounts, he finds that the distributor performs important functions. His role varies from manufacturer to manufacturer and furthermore is changing. It seems to reflect bargaining power relationships and the individual distributor's negotiating skills quite as much as the "real economies" discussed in the foregoing paragraphs.

Some manufacturers ship merchandise directly from the factory to the large retailer, while others have the distributor handle the shipment of the merchandise. Billing, collection, extension of credit, service, etc., are divided between the manufacturer and distributor differently by individual manufacturers. Almost all television set producers, however, do participate in personal sales efforts to win the patronage of large retailers; however, most are careful to call on the large retailer only if accompanied by a senior member of the distributing company.

At least one firm has developed two separate systems for handling large retail accounts. The first mainly handles large accounts that are located wholly or mainly within a single distributor's territory; the second handles "national chain accounts." Especially when the large retailer operates in many territories, it may be necessary for the factory to involve itself in sales arrangements. Otherwise, the danger of "transshipment"—that goods purchased in one distributor's territory will be shipped into another distributor's territory and sold in competition with the local distributor's retailers—will arise and create serious problems for the manufacturer. (Usually purchases will be made in territories where prices are lowest and sent to the others.)

The industry will have to face the fact that as more sales are made "direct" to large retailers, the size of territories required to support a distributor will increase. Some attrition among distributors and realignment of territories would doubtless result.

THE SEARS-ROEBUCK SYSTEM OF DISTRIBUTION

Until about 1959, Sears sold television sets made for it by other firms. At present, it produces its sets through an independent manufacturing division, Warwick, which operates modern manufacturing facilities in the Midwest, and Pacific Mercury on the Pacific Coast. The shift from "private-label suppliers" to a company-owned manufacturing facility apparently did not bring significant changes in distribution arrangements; it may have resulted in improved relative set quality and lower costs, however.

The Sears-Roebuck system of distribution is distinguished by two features: first, only one brand is carried by the retail store; second, the salesmen in Sears's retail stores are very well trained and of far higher quality than the average retail salesman generally is. These two factors combined to give Sears a share of the market exceeded in 1963 only by from four to seven other firms.

Sears's sets are offered to the public in approximately 750 stores operated by this huge retail concern—and in its omnipresent catalogue. In the view of its executives, the Sears store is the "finest store in town" in 80 percent of the communities in which its stores are located. These stores generate a large and growing volume of traffic which insures the Silvertone brand wide exposure. Heavy store traffic, skilled merchandising techniques and high-quality salesmanship, plus the absence of competing brands on the sales site, appear to explain Sears's success with television sets.

THE MAGNAVOX SYSTEM OF DISTRIBUTION

Admiration, if not envy, of the Magnavox distribution arrangements is almost universal in the industry. It therefore would be interesting to understand the attractive features of that system and learn why others have not emulated it.

Magnavox distributes directly through retailers on a very restricted basis, without intermediaries. Its salesmen call on retailers directly and service them, much as do distributors' salesmen for other retailers, and the company sells to relatively few and carefully selected retailers. Certainly this system is not remarkable in its novelty; it is, however, remarkable in its effectiveness, because it fits the particular circumstances that prevail in the television set industry. More specifically, distribution directly through retailers permits Magnavox to limit sales of its sets to retailers that will do a creditable sales job for the brand. By limiting the number of retailers to which it will sell, Magnavox enlists the cooperation of retailers who want to avoid the very intensive price competition prevalent in this industry.

Magnavox sells through approximately 2,000 retailers at present. (This is a tiny number compared with those of other manufacturers.) In almost every community the department store or music shop or appliance dealer that leads all others in prestige will be one of the few stores that handle the Magnavox line. This fact explains why others cannot emulate the Magnavox system: the very best retailers are already part of the Magnavox system and it would be extremely difficult (nothing is impossible) for any other firm to lure them away. The circumstance that makes retailers handling the Magnavox line so loyal is the relatively high margin their retailers actually obtain.

It is not clear whether the costs sustained by Magnavox to get its merchandise through to retailers are reduced by virtue of dispensing with distributors. In their absence, Magnavox is compelled to maintain a costly sales force that sells to retailers. In addition, it operates 12 warehouses which, in many ways, resemble factory branches. Distributors perform that function for manufacturers who sell to retailers through intermediaries. The strength of the Magnavox system seems to derive chiefly from exclusivity, which affords profit protection to dealers. Although most Magnavox retailers also carry other lines, their salesmen invariably concentrate upon selling the Magnavox line—under the spur of higher margins.

Just before this manuscript was readied for publication, Magnavox announced what might represent a major change in its marketing strategy. In November 1962, the company "franchised" 16 selected Singer Manufacturing Company retail outlets (10 in metropolitan New York and 6 in Philadelphia) to carry its television and other home entertainment products on a test basis. Singer operates 1,700 retail stores, less than one-fifth of which possess the necessary floor space to handle Magnavox's products. Nevertheless, this test might well be offering Magnavox television sets in metropolitan areas and may be a severe test to the proved Magnavox system of marketing.

THE PACKARD-BELL SYSTEM OF DISTRIBUTION

Two factors chiefly account for the uniqueness of Packard-Bell's distribution system. These are: first, that distributors are essentially "one man shows," and second, that the distributor handles only television sets—no "white goods" or other appliances are carried, as is usually the case. Ordinarily, Packard-Bell distributors are salesmen who have had some success in the appliance business. If they are prepared to put up some capital to show their "genuine interest," Packard-Bell will "put these guys on ice," helping to sponsor financial programs, and assisting them in other ways to secure additional bank finance.

Because of the small size of operation—one man plus secretary and bookkeeper—(an extra helper is the exception rather than the rule) overhead costs have been kept very low. However, an individual distributor's sales rarely exceed a million dollars. The typical distributor carries about a month's sales in inventory, and he services between 40 and 50 dealers, with whom he maintains a close personal relationship.

This policy and the company's paternalistic outlook has led to a very loyal set of distributors who remain with the company for many years. The problem is not one of turnover but more nearly, as one executive put it, to keep them "from getting fat, dumb, and lazy."

Packard-Bell's system has worked well for its essentially Western regional operations, especially in the larger cities. Despite its Western concentration the company has some Eastern accounts that buy direct from the factory. Whether such a system will work effectively and efficiently for national distribution remains to be seen.

THE MUNTZ SYSTEM OF DISTRIBUTION

Perhaps the most unusual distribution system is that used by Muntz. Like Magnavox, Muntz deals direct with the retailer, but it solicits dealers primarily by mail and phone; there is virtually no personal contact with the factory except in a few key cities.

Muntz has a policy that calls for the sale of its sets in every city with a population of 2,000 or over. Its search for retailers in such communities is quite systematic. The process begins with a letter from the factory to the local Chamber of Commerce requesting a list of furniture and appliance dealers in the locality. If this fails, a local phone directory is obtained and names taken from it. Next, the names are checked for credit rating, and the best rated firm (usually) is sent a letter plus promotional material explaining that the company is interested in establishing representation in the town and that it has been chosen as the best for the job.

Some days later, the dealer is phoned by one of a staff of five girls especially trained for this task. She in effect repeats the theme of the letter and answers any questions asked of her. If the dealer accepts the offer to become a representative (about 10 percent do), the girl who phoned becomes his contact with the manufacturer.

The phone remains the primary medium of communication between the factory and the dealer after the necessary dealership arrangements have been made: orders can be phoned to Muntz collect, and goods are shipped, often on the same day. In addition to its regular production, Muntz has a large "private label" business, which is also on a direct-to-the-retailer basis.

Muntz experimented with a variety of distribution arrangements. It started originally with a direct-to-the-consumer method of distribution. It initiated a policy in 1953 of having its regional branches do the final assembly work on sets. These branches were essentially warehouse operations and were to receive chassis, tubes, cabinets, etc. directly from suppliers and assemble them. This system worked very poorly, for Muntz was not able to maintain production efficiency.

After its bankruptcy, Muntz decided to use dealers and cut out its branches. It took some people from within the company and set them up as exclusive dealers in key areas. This policy also failed, partly because one key dealer was not sufficient to give Muntz substantial volume in most areas. Immediately prior to turning to their present distribution system, Muntz used factory representatives who carried related lines. They abandoned this system because the factory representatives concentrated on those items that were in demand at the time and did not give year around sales support to television. Muntz thereupon decided to sell to established dealers and developed the unique method already described for soliciting dealers.

MANUFACTURERS' COMMUNICATIONS WITH DISTRIBUTORS

Communications are part of every management function—even as are decision-making, organization, assignment of job responsibilities, etc. Communication is peculiarly a marketing function, for selling depends heavily upon the transmission of information between seller and buyer and to resellers along the way. In addition, selling is largely a process of persuasion, which depends upon communication between the seller and the prospective customer.

Advertising is one device by which television set manufacturers communicate with ultimate consumers, resellers and servicemen. Although not described explicitly as a communications mechanism, the personal sales force retained by set manufacturers permits two-way flow of information between them and those upon whom sales-

Manufacturers and Distributors

men call. This section discusses one other communications mechanism between manufacturer and distributor that is widespread in industry generally, and is central to the communications system erected by television set manufacturers.[1] Reference is made to the "annual meeting" or "annual convention," which consists of a series of carefully arranged face-to-face meetings between manufacturers' personnel and distributor principals and sales personnel.

Manufacturers' communications with distributors cover a variety of subjects. The most important information transmitted by annual meetings concerns product. This subject will therefore be discussed first and in some detail. Thereupon, we shall sketch other matters that are communicated at such meetings.

A manufacturer of television sets who sells nationally, as most do, finds it difficult to communicate product information to the many firms within its own distribution system. The number of people involved is very considerable, especially if one includes distributor salesmen and sales managers. Also, the large amount and technical nature of the information that the manufacturer wishes to communicate cannot be transmitted effectively by paid advertisements or by personal correspondence. It is true that a substantial body of printed material flows between the manufacturer and his distributors, and much of this does deal with product specifications. Moreover, the average television set producer employs about 12–15 field salesmen who call on distributors at fairly regular intervals and frequently discuss product information with them. Despite these communication efforts and channels, the manufacturers were compelled to create a specialized communication device to transmit information about new lines of models that they introduce to the trade in May and June. This device, once created, came to be employed for other purposes as well.

Every year manufacturers hold meetings with their distributor principals and their key personnnel. At these meetings, new models are displayed—often with the skill and lavishness reserved for Broad-

---

[1] Another communications device between manufacturers and distributors of growing importance will not be discussed here—the distributor advisory panel. Some manufacturers have established or are contemplating the creation of a distributor advisory panel. These panels serve various purposes, but mainly give the manufacturer his distributors' reactions to contemplated policy changes, information on marketing and style trends, etc.

way musicals. Usually the new line is described and discussed by factory executives and then placed on display, where distributor personnel can examine it in detail and at leisure.

The annual meetings are also used for other purposes than product information by the manufacturer, who understandably tries to get as much benefit as he can from having his distributors together at one place. The cost of these annual meetings sometimes approaches $1 million for a large manufacturer. In particular, they are used to discuss advertising and sales promotion campaigns; sales training meetings often are held at such meetings; and, most important, manufacturers engage in fairly intensive sales efforts at such times.

Manufacturers try to create a festive—almost a carnival—atmosphere at these annual meetings. Distributors live in luxury at the manufacturer's expense. They often develop an exuberant and optimistic mood that is not wholly realistic. Some distributors complain that they "weaken under this lavish treatment and over-order on the new line of merchandise." Manufacturers seek to induce distributors to place large orders for new merchandise at annual meetings. They ordinarily offer special inducements, most often in the form of easy credit terms, together with free merchandise with purchases of large packages of sets. Partly through the actual sales process, but also by means of personal discussion with distributors, manufacturers try to learn their ditributors' reactions to the new product features and styling of the new line.

The annual meetings provide factory executives with an opportunity to tighten the personal bond between themselves and their distributors and to build morale by making them feel like members of a friendly and a powerful organization. They offer the manufacturer an opportunity to provide distributor personnel with pleasant out-of-town trips. Lavish entertainment is generally provided, and the distributors often are given a small gift which usually is selected to please their wives. By these measures, the manufacturer hopes to tighten the personal ties that hold their distributors.

The manufacurer may develop films which show the selling features of its merchandise and which might be used to teach sales techniques. These are not only shown at the annual meeting, but will be made available to distributors to be used by them in their own presentation of the new line to dealers.

Annual meetings pass through cycles. Manufacturers feel obligated to keep up with the others in lavishness and luxury. For quite a few years now, many firms have held their meetings in Miami Beach and Las Vegas—generally alternating between those two cities. Lately, there seems to be a movement away from those cities, as distributors complain that they have been there so often that it is no longer much fun.

Exclusive Distribution

In substance, if not in legal form, distributors in the television set industry enjoy exclusive franchises. Territories are allocated to individual distributors (including factory branches), and it is clear to all concerned that the boundaries are not to be violated—though because of antitrust considerations the written franchises do not explicitly delimit the territories or enjoin against sales beyond their borders. Basically the same results are achieved by making the franchise cancellable by the manufacturer after six months notice, without cause. Similarly, it is mutually understood that the distributor will not carry any other brand of television set. Indeed, it is assumed that any contemplated significant change in the kinds of items he carries will be discussed with the television set manufacturer.

Why does the industry employ exclusive distributors? What consequences result from these arrangements?

As frequently noted, television sets are distributed in the same way that radio sets and other major appliances were sold previously. That pushes the question back one step and to a different time: why did manufacturers employ exclusive distributors in major appliance distribution? Why did manufacturers favor such an arrangement? What were the gains and losses to distributors? Rather than answer these historical questions, we will examine appliance manufacturers' and distributors' current viewpoints toward exclusive distribution.

We start with the assumption that major appliance manufacturers have decided to sell to retailers through distributors of some sort, rather than sell directly. Given that decision, the following choices would be open to them:

1. Sell to any and all distributors who want to resell the merchandise—as long as they pay their bills. They could allow these distribu-

tors to sell as many brands as they wish to whomever they wish, wherever they wish and at any price they please.

2. Sell to a limited number of distributors (possibly twice or three times the present number) and permit each of them to sell as they wish.

3. Sell to a large number of distributors, but attempt to prescribe the terms (essentially price) at which they resell the merchandise.

4. Sell to roughly the present number of distributors but do not delimit territories, and allow them to do whatever they wish with regard to price.

5. Employ an exclusive distributorship system.

It would be extremely cumbersome to compare all of these alternatives; however, their mere listing suggests several observations. Most important, manufacturers of appliances want more from their distributors than that they resell their merchandise. They want them to develop a retail distribution system, based upon a stable and close relationship with individual retailers and composed of retailers of above-average quality. Also, the manufacturer is anxious that the retailers who carry his brand should earn a reasonable return upon his merchandise so that they will continue to handle it and give it at least as much sales support as they give the other brands they carry. To achieve these ends requires efforts to mitigate price competition and to give help and advice to many retailers. Also, manufacturers seek a maximum of promotional support, of the "right" type and merchandising practices that enhance the "image" of the brand.

In addition, the manufacturer wants to be assured of the distributor's loyalty to the brand, to insure that he will be willing to invest effort and monies in establishing a following among dealers and consumers. The manufacturer does not want to compete constantly with others for his distributor's time and loyalty. If he occupied such a weak and insecure position, he would incur high costs to gain and retain distributor support.

With these goals, manufacturers are emphatically not indifferent to what happens to their merchandise once it leaves their hands. They want resellers that act much as they would act themselves if they were to engage directly in distribution—i.e., as a factory branch. The many services that manufacturers wish the distributor to perform require him to make a substantial investment and to incur considerable risk. The distributor must be offered returns that would justify large investment and risk or he will not enter or remain in the business. What can the manufacturer offer to induce talented businessmen to enter the major appliance business?

One might think that manufacturers could lure persons into distribution by selling them sets at a low price, but he would be mistaken. A low price that is matched by competitors is no insurance of profit. Unless the manufacturer can, in some way, protect the price of his merchandise against erosion under intensive competition, distribution will be unprofitable for these engaged in that trade even though they pay the manufacturer a low price. Without a "protected" profit margin, the distributor will have no interest and little ability to develop retailers.

A major appliance distributor presumably seeks the business opportunity that promises him the biggest return on investment taking account of his risks and alternative uses of his funds and talents. To be one of several distributors attempting to sell a given brand of television set in any given territory carries the following risks: that other distributors may, when hungry for a particular piece of business, cut the price so that he is forced to do likewise; that a rival distributor of the same brand may attempt to win away one of his best retail accounts by some form of concession; that other distributors may give the brand a "black eye" by their selling methods and poor service.

A prospective distributor would consider these risks in combination with the heavy financial investment required to engage in appliance distribution. As explained, the retailer generally requires credit accommodation; to meet the local retailer needs, the distributor must hold sizable inventory; due to the bulkiness of major appliances, substantial warehouse facilities are necessary; in addition, a personal sales force is needed to service and win new retailers. It would be extremely difficult to justify the heavy investment required to be a distributor if one were exposed to competition from other distributors of the same brand. The profit experience of distributors—even under an exclusive system of distribution—establishes this conclusion. Rates of return, as explained, are quite low at present and have been for some time.

The distributor wants some offset for his heavy investment and for the large risks faced in appliance distribution. The manufacturer can give him only a few things that would make participation in this industry worthwhile; we already observed that a low price would not help him much if other manufacturers were obliged to match it. First, he can give the distributor merchandise that is in strong demand—largely due to the manufacturer's own efforts. Second, he can protect the distributor as far as possible from competition—and particularly from competition from the factory itself (in the form of direct sales to retailers) and from the competition of other distributors for the factory. Only geographical exclusiveness will free distributors from the most direct and painful form of price competition.

Distributors want also to develop an asset in the form of a going business value. They want to create a business with stability and security that has "regular customers" and that could be resold or passed along to members of their families. The distributor is willing to invest in the creation of a "retail organization" on behalf of the manufacturer if he can share in the fruits of his investment. On the other hand, he will not invest his funds and efforts to create a following for the manufacturer's brand if his efforts redound equally to the benefit of other distributors who are selling in the same territory. These distributor goals require territorial exclusiveness also.

In addition, most distributors apparently want to identify with the factory—even as the factory feels the need for the loyalty of distributors. The manufacturer and the distributor of major appliances have many economic interests in common. It therefore serves the manufacturer's interest to protect the distributor as much as possible and establish close and personal ties with him.

It must be stressed that the manufacturer could not, even if he wanted to, "spoil" his distributors by shielding them from competition. The presence of distributors whose livelihood depends upon selling competing brands subjects even exclusive distributors to considerable competitive pressure. In that way, all manufacturers are protected against distributors' demanding unreasonably large margins of profit for their services. If competition from rival brands were to slacken so much that distributors could command very high margins and thereby curtail sales of appliances, manufacturers might be obliged to reconsider their policy of exclusive distribution. At present, exclusive distributorships represent a tolerable balance of opportunities and risks for distributors and an acceptable quality of sales support for the manufacturers. The balance may be precarious, however. As manufacturers increase their "direct" sales to large dealers, the opportunities available to distributors shrink and may turn a barely tolerable profit into something that is quite intolerable for many of them.

Since this study is mainly concerned with the "why" and "how" of marketing activities rather than with results, the consequences of a system of exclusive distribution *in this particular context* will be discussed very sketchily. Any discussion of consequences implies some alternative with which present arrangements are compared. A few pages back, four alternatives to exclusive distribution were listed. One can make such a comparison only if he can forecast how alternative systems of distribution would function, their costs, the service they would render to consumers, the intensity of competition they would generate and the form that competition would take. Persons associated with this industry disagree as to how these alternative distribution sysems would work out. Not many people in the industry are very concerned with this problem because the interests of both manufacturers and distributors seem to require the present system. A few general points might help to set down the little that can be said on this subject with some confidence.

1. Intensive competition is quite consistent with exclusive distribution; under a system of nonexclusive distribution, competition would be even greater, all other circumstances assumed identical.

2. Costs of managing and serving distributors probably vary pretty much in proportion to the number of distributors, rather than to their sales.

3. Distributor turnover probably would be far greater with a nonexclusive system, increasing costs to manufacturers to replace them.

4. Quality of service—caliber of marketing functions performed—probably varies directly with the stability and security of distributors.

5. Direct sales to retailers who possess strong bargaining power put exclusive distributors under very direct and powerful competitive pressure.

Chapter V

OTHER MARKETING ACTIVITIES OF MANUFACTURERS

The preceding two chapters, although very long, did not describe all of the distribution activities in which television set manufacturers engage. This chapter will complete the picture of their distribution activities and should establish that manufacturers of consumers' products have become involved in many marketing activities that are above and beyond the traditional and obvious ones. Moreover, it appears that a manufacturer's success depends partly upon how effectively they perform these nontraditional marketing functions. (What is said here applies also to manufacturers of producers' goods, but to a lesser degree.)

Some of the activities described in this chapter have not yet won acceptance among manufacturers in the television set industry. Only the largest and most "scientific-management-oriented" firms in the industry undertake *all* of the functions discussed here, though some are now routine. Many top executives in this industry have been reluctant to undertake some of them and hope to avoid doing so. (Most foreign manufacturers seem even not to realize that they might make these kinds of marketing efforts.)

Perhaps the major conclusion that comes from this and the preceding chapters is the paradoxical one that "A manufacturer is mainly a marketer." That is, a manufacturing firm's success depends largely upon its marketing skills. More and more of a manufacturer's outlays go for marketing, and its top management increasingly is preoccupied with sales and marketing problems. As they have devoted more attention to marketing problems, ingenious executives have discovered means of gaining an advantage over rivals and new ways of rendering

Other Activities of Manufacturers

a service to their customers. In this way, the range of marketing activities in which manufacturers engage has tended to expand.

Most of the activities described here may be considered secondary. Consequently, they will be sketched briefly, rather than described in depth. They are of interest chiefly because they may suggest incipient trends.

Marketing Activities: Manufacturer to Distributor to Retailer

The preceding chapter has already discussed manufacturers' direct sales to large retailers. This section describes their activities which involve retailers to whom they sell indirectly through distributors.

When a manufacturer takes actions that are directed toward the retailer, he involves himself in another's—the distributor's—normal sphere of control. This involvement may be welcomed; in time it may be considered "natural." However, it does require diplomacy on the part of the manufacturer and acquiescence if not explicit permission from the distributor, since, in principle, he is responsible for retailer relations. In addition, the distributor largely creates the climate in which these activities take place. If he supports them and wins the cooperation of retailers, these measures are carried out actively and usually achieve considerable success; if the distributor is lethargic, the manufacturer's efforts get nowhere.

HOW MANUFACTURERS TRY TO IMPROVE THE PERFORMANCE
OF RETAIL SALESMEN

Most television set manufacturers hold their regional salesmen responsible for conducting sales meetings with dealer salesmen. The purpose of these meetings is to instruct retail salesmen in sales methods as well as to convey product information. Manufacturers' salesmen usually carry out this responsibility by giving talks at retailers' regular sales meetings. On such occasions, the regional salesman is usually only one of several persons who speak. A manufacturer's salesman will sometimes request an opportunity to address a particular retailer's salesmen and may conduct the entire meeting himself. Part of a regional salesman's training includes instruction on conducting such meetings.

Small retailers who have only one or two salesmen—a very common situation—generally must train their own salesmen; regional salesmen ordinarily do not hold formal sales meetings with such small groups. Nevertheless, on their occasional visits to retailers, they will generally speak to salesmen and try to give them specific sales "pointers" and "sell them on the line."

The amount of help the manufacturer is able to give dealers in this way depends very much on the dealers themselves. If they feel no need for the assistance and regard it as an intrusion and an implied criticism, the regional salesmen will be able to accomplish very little—and even that with great difficulty. Conversely, when dealers welcome the help that manufacturers offer, often they derive a variety of benefits.

Most of the manufacturers distribute booklets that are designed primarily to instruct retail salesmen. Ordinarily they carry titles like "Guides to Step-Up Sales" or "Step-Up Features in the 1963 Line." Although these booklets might appear to be mainly descriptions of the manufacturer's merchandise, they serve the equally important purpose of suggesting sales arguments that retail salesmen can use in an effort to persuade consumers to purchase more costly sets than they had originally planned to buy.

HOW MANUFACTURERS TRANSMIT PRODUCT INFORMATION TO RETAILERS AND THEIR SALESMEN

Although closely linked, sales training and the transmission of product information are essentially different. Manufacturers employ three major devices to transmit product information to retailers and their salesmen. The first consists of clinics, the second is "open houses" and the third is factory visits. Ordinarily, dealers and their salesmen are invited to clinics, which usually feature the showing of a motion picture and the demonstration of specific product features. When elaborate presentations are made, both distributors and dealers' salesmen are invited to attend; often dealers will be invited from a considerable distance. These clinics, which are ordinarily held on a distributor's premises, are moderately costly and manufacturers expose them to as many people as feasible.

Manufacturers also transmit product information to dealers and their salesmen in conjunction with the introduction of each new line of products. As already indicated, they occasionally invite selected dealers to attend the elaborate annual sales meetings at which they introduce the new line to their distributors. In addition, they participate in the introduction of the new line to dealers by the distributor—though this function nominally is the distributor's responsibility.

The chief device that has evolved for displaying the new product line to dealers and their salesmen is the "open house." This function takes place shortly after the manufacturer's annual sales meeting and is an annual sales meeting on a far smaller and less lavish scale—and held for dealers rather than for distributors. The average distributor will conduct several open houses in rapid succession in order to cover his entire territory, occasionally holding them in different cities for his dealers' convenience. In addition to the display of merchandise and the placing of orders, there is sometimes entertainment and social activity at open houses. Manufacturers contribute to them by having their top executives attend them and sometimes actually present the new merchandise. The actual cost of open houses is borne by distributors, however. It is not an exaggeration to say that during the period of distributors' open houses—lasting about three weeks for the average manufacturer—almost no top executives are to be found in the home offices of the major television set producing companies.

Increasingly, open houses are of the "flow through" rather than the "sit down" variety. The latter is like a regular meeting at which dealers are seated and the new line is presented to them, together with formal talks on a variety of subjects. The "flow through" type of open house is one in which appointments are made with dealers at staggered times; each dealer is shown the new line, which is artfully displayed, by a salesman who will also take his order. Some distributors characteristically take their dealers out to dinner and to a show in conjunction with their open houses, but entertainment seems to be a declining aspect of distributor open houses.

A third device that some manufacturers employ to transmit product information to dealers and dealer salesmen is the "invited factory tour." These consist of a several-day visit to the factory for an examination of production processes, demonstrations, lectures and intimate discussions by invited dealers and their senior salesmen. Usually these days are cram-packed, starting very early in the morning and ending late with some local entertainment.

MANUFACTURERS' ADVERTISING DIRECTED TO DEALERS

A small portion of most television set manufacturers' advertising budgets is devoted to "trade advertising." It accounts for between 10 and 15 percent for most of the large firms in the industry. These expenditures mainly pay for printed advertising in a handful of periodicals. Although accurate figures are not available to the author, it appears that three publications account for almost 90 percent of all trade advertising of television sets. One is a daily newspaper and probably accounts for about half of all trade advertising outlays (*Home Furnishings Daily*). Another is a weekly publication (*Electrical Merchandising Weekly*), while a third is a monthly magazine (*Mart*). Relative to many other trades, major appliance manufacturers (television set producers in particular), are compartively heavy users of trade advertising.

Most trade advertising by television set manufacturers is characterized by two themes: the first, that the line yields an attractive profit to the dealer; and second, that the quality of the particular brand is superior to others. Manufacturers apparently believe that retailers are deeply concerned with the quality of the lines that they carry. Consequently much of the trade advertising would also be quite suitable for use in consumer media.

MANUFACTURERS' EXTENSION OF CREDIT TO DEALERS

Some appliance manufacturers extend credit accommodation on three levels: to their distributors (as discussed elsewhere), to dealers and to consumers. These activities ordinarily are concentrated in one division or subsidiary company, which operates much as any other commercial finance firm—except that it is motivated by the desire to increase appliance sales as well as the desire to earn income through finance charges.

The financial needs of dealers, as with distributors, arise from two sources: the need to "finance" merchandise held in inventory and the need to "carry" customers until they pay for their purchases.

Other Activities of Manufacturers

Commercial finance companies that have no connection with a manufacturer also lend money for both of these purposes so that the television set manufacturer is not creating a new form of accommodation for his dealers (and distributors). However, he typically arranges his financial operations so that they are particularly suited to the needs of dealers who sell his brand—and to the consumers to whom they sell. Specifically, he extends to them larger amounts of credit, for longer periods and with less onerous penalties and pressure in the event of delinquency, than independent commercial finance companies offer them.

Several aspects of manufacturers' financing activities are generally overlooked. First, when a television set manufacturer extends loans to dealers, he usually does so for all of their needs—not simply to finance inventories or sales of his own brand of set. He also lends against other brands and other appliances. Second, these appliance-company-owned finance companies have been quite profitable and are not simply devices for supporting television set sales. Third, manufacturers meet one of the largest financial needs of a distributor or dealer by lending to its customers. Manufacturers extend financial help to dealers mainly by "buying their commercial paper." That is, they purchase the installment contracts signed by customers, thereby lending money to the ultimate consumer [1] so that he can pay the dealer immediately; as a result the dealer is enabled to pay his debts to the distributor, who can then pay the manufacturer. Of course, a loan to an ultimate consumer does not *automatically* result in a roughly equal payment to a distributor and manufacturer. Moreover, when a loan to a consumer results in such a payment it may be made to another manufacturer than the company making the loan.

Not all television set manufacturers have "captive" finance companies. One sold its finance division in 1962 but stipulated that its dealers and distributors were to be served just as they had been up to that time. There is considerable disagreement about the extent to which the possession of a captive finance company helps the manufacturer to makes sales *currently*. It is generally agreed, however, that

[1] From a strict legal standpoint, the finance company is lending money to the retailer, for the title to the appliance does not transfer to the consumer until he has discharged his debt in full.

it *was* a substantial help some years back—before 1954. Since that time, competition among independent finance companies for commercial paper has been quite keen, so that fairly ample credit facilities have become available to almost all dealers. Nevertheless, two slight advantages are still enjoyed by dealers who obtain credit from captive rather than independent finance companies: more liberal loans for holding inventory of that manufacturer's sets—usually arranged with the finance company by the manufacturer's sales department—and less stringent requirements to be met by retail customers. These advantages are small, though real enough. A manufacturer who withdrew from television set manufacturing in 1960 gave the lack of a separate finance division as one of the most important handicaps he had to overcome and a major reason for his decision to leave the business.

Several manufacturers are now experimenting with another method of assisting retailers to meet their financial needs. In a few test cities they have established a local warehouse from which they deliver directly to the ultimate consumer's premises after the dealer has consumated a sale. Since the warehouse and the inventory are the manufacturer's, this arrangement obviates the need for the distributor and the retailer to hold anything but "floor" stocks; it thereby greatly reduces the drain on distributors' and retailers' capital resources. It does not, however, substitute for loans to set buyers through the purchase of dealers' receivables. Those conducting these experiments have finance companies that do provide credit to consumers, which, as explained, can trickle down and thereby provide funds at all levels of the industry.

WINDOW DISPLAY SERVICE FOR DEALERS

Most television set manufacturers believe that good window display contributes to sales. Appliance dealers as a group lack both the time and talent—even when they possess the inclination—to change their window displays frequently and to make them very attractive. It is not an easy job, for window space in most appliance stores is inaccessible and appliances are bulky and heavy.

Several manufacturers provide virtually free window display service to dealers carrying their brand. They have full-time employees specially equipped with the trucks, equipment and supplies required to make window displays. These are assigned to designated areas and call on dealers by appointment to discuss their taste preferences and learn what merchandise they wish to display most prominently. Without being obtrusive, they usually win a more prominent position for their company's products than they would hold otherwise, and they help to determine which of their firm's lines will be featured in the dealer's window.

The extent to which individual manufacturers help dealers arrange their window displays varies greatly. As a rough general rule, the smaller manufacturers do more of it than the large—possibly viewing it as an inexpensive substitute for mass-media advertising, which they can afford only in modest quantities.

Some manufacturers seek to upgrade their dealers' window displays by less direct and costly means. One device employed for this purpose is the window display contest. The hope for a prize induces some retailers to make special efforts on their own to achieve attractive displays—to both their own and the manufacturer's benefit.

Manufacturers' Activities Relating to Consumers

As already explained, television set manufacturers devote approximately one-third of their advertising outlays to national advertising directed to the public, and the balance goes to cooperative advertising. "Co-op" represents the manufacturers' contributions to the advertising costs of their distributors and dealers. Distributors and dealers advertise almost exclusively in local media; these media are directed to persons in a single metropolitan area, although they reach a small proportion of persons outside the local area.

Manufacturers advertise to the ultimate consumer both to help the dealer to make sales and to exert some pressure upon him. Specifically, the manufacturer strives to create a strong preference among consumers for his brand so that they will press dealers to carry it rather than—or in addition to—rival brands. Most dealers believe that a "prestige brand" enhances the image of a retail store. They moreover fear that customers would gain an adverse impression if they did not carry some of the "best" brands. The fact of the matter, however, is that a majority of dealers do not carry either Zenith or R.C.A. the two most widely purchased and highly regarded brands. Apparently no manufacturer has been able to create such a strong position for his brand that dealers cannot afford to be without it.

An important connection between the manufacturer and the ultimate consumer is via product guarantees. Most consumers look to the manufacturer to enforce—though not necessarily to execute—guarantees of materials and workmanship. Very few consumers recognize that the regional distributor actually gives effect to the warranty. The great majority assume that the manufacturer "stands behind" the product. Many will take comfort from whatever confidence they have in their dealer, but even these assume that the manufacturer will give effect to the guarantee.

It is the manufacturer who formulates the terms of the guarantee and communicates them, however imperfectly, to the consumer, even though the distributor executes it. In recent years, television set manufacturers have aroused the resentment of their distributors, independent servicemen and dealers by extending the length of the warranty period. Since the sums involved in the servicing end of sets are very large, such changes usually cause conflict. An extension of the warranty period increases the distributor's costs and obligations to provide service while reducing the opportunity for dealers and servicemen to repair sets at a profit. Part of the emotion generated over this issue undoubtedly results from the fact that the manufacturers can unilaterally take a step that affects the fortunes of its dealers and distributors and of independent servicemen.

Manufacturers' Activities Affecting Independent Servicemen

As explained, distributors execute the manufacturer's "warranty," and are paid a specific sum per set to do so—or are allowed to claim up to a certain amount from a special fund. (A warranty is a guarantee of product performance and quality of material and workmanship for a designated period following purchase.) To carry out the warranty, distributors must maintain service departments and a stock of repair parts. Manufacturers who sell direct to retailers—mainly

Other Activities of Manufacturers

Magnavox and Muntz—require their dealers to execute the warranty.

Most television set repair service occurs outside the warranty period and is performed by a variety of servicing enterprises. Firms that engage in television repair service vary the extent to which they are linked to and subject to the influence of the manufacturer. A ranking of service organizations according to the closeness of their link with a manufacturer is presented below:

1. Factory-owned and operated service companies. R.C.A. is the best-known example and is the only large firm that operates its own service company over the entire market it serves.
2. Factory-owned branches' service departments.
3. The service departments of independent distributors.
4. "Authorized" independent service repair men.
5. Service departments of dealers who are tightly linked to a particular brand—or who sell only a single brand.
6. Independent servicemen who also sell several brands of television sets.
7. Independent servicemen who do not sell sets.

The manufacturer is concerned with all of these types of servicemen, but their activities vary with respect to the different types. Their communication links are much stronger and their community of interest is far greater with those at the top of the list than with those near the bottom. Also, their control and potential influence varies considerably from class to class. Partly because they must deal with different types of servicemen and because the service function is inherently complex, manufacturers have experienced great difficulties with this function. Owing mainly to those difficulties, most of them conduct sizable departments which are responsible for relations with servicemen.

The cost to a consumer in time and money to repair an appliance affects its manufacturer. If a television set is expensive to repair or performs poorly because of incompetent repair, the manufacturer's product often is held to blame. Especially during the early years of set production—say, up to 1955 or so—television set owners and prospective customers were extremely conscious of service costs, and the frequency and expense of set breakdown were common subjects of parlor conversation. At that time, many television set owners purchased insurance contracts which guaranteed them full service. The cost of such contracts declined as sets became more reliable; the R.C.A. service company charged $100 in most communities for a service contract in 1950 and reduced their charges to $69.95 in 1955, and they are now $39.50 in most communities. Today, relatively few owners of black and white sets have service contracts, but a majority of color set owners do.

For many years a substantial proportion of independent servicemen had little knowledge of how to repair defective sets. Generally they were radio repair men who were self-educated in television set repair. Until they gave themselves a good education, many of their customers suffered from high charges and poor workmanship. Also, opportunities to defraud the owners of defective sets were too great and lucrative for some servicemen to resist. Consequently, heavy charges for repair—especially after the set was removed from the owner's premises—were far more common than were justified. Manufacturers feared that they would suffer more from these abuses than the consumers upon whom they were perpetrated.

The eventful history of television manufacturers' relations with independent servicemen need not be related here. Our interest is in the activities of manufacturers that relate to independent servicemen.

At present, manufacturers give a great deal of attention to the independent servicemen for several reasons. Perhaps the most important is that Zenith's rise to first position in the industry is partly explainable by its having won the independent serviceman's support. It did so partly by designing its sets so that they provided especially easy access for servicemen. Later the company's refusal to adopt printed circuits at a time when many servicemen had not learned how to service them won Zenith their appreciation and strong support. Also, as already mentioned, servicemen often are asked for advice by persons contemplating a purchase, and their advice is believed to carry weight. In addition, an increasing number of servicemen also sell sets. (Similarly, many retailers now indoctrinate their servicemen to sell sets while out making service calls.) But manufacturers are mainly concerned with the independent serviceman to insure that those who own their sets will receive speedy and competent repair service at reasonable cost.

Other Activities of Manufacturers

All television set manufacturers are apparently reconciled to the fact that their ultimate customers will mainly call on independent servicemen when their sets require repair. Their efforts to insure good service for their customers from independent servicemen lead them to:

1. Take measures to insure that their distributors hold adequate supplies of repair parts.

2. Provide opportunities for independent servicemen, as well as others, to get information about or actual training in the repair of their own sets—which are, to a degree, unique and pose special problems. All manufacturers of television sets issue special service manuals for servicemen, giving wiring diagrams and schematics that are intended to help them with repairs. Most companies sell these materials at a nominal charge, just covering their costs.

3. Designate certain independent servicemen as "authorized" by the factory. Some manufacturers require an examination to establish competence, others require servicemen to take a course of instruction at the factory to earn the title of "authorized serviceman" for their sets. On the other hand, a few manufacturers allow just about any serviceman to call himself "authorized" if he buys a sign from them which he displays, or if he carries at least a minimum inventory of repair parts for their sets.

4. Insure relative uniformity and moderation of service charges, by requiring authorized servicemen to post a schedule of charges—or simply by issuing a book which gives suggested charges for the most common repairs.

Independent servicemen apparently are mistrustful of the manufacturers. Possibly they fear that the "factory" is trying to participate in the huge repair business, esteemed at over one-half billion dollars per year. In the past, several manufacturers felt obliged to offer direct service essentially as a defensive measure. A residue of mistrust remains. Consequently, manufacturers treat servicemen almost as an independent arm of the government; they curry their favor and avoid any action that might displease them.

A very substantial decline in service business has occurred due to vastly improved reliability of receiving tubes. (Tube failure represented by far the major source of set failure in past years.) Dealers with television repair departments are finding them a source of loss more often than profit. (Of course, the department may yield indirect benefits, if its service personnel is able to boost its sales.) Some have taken to repairing small traffic appliances in order to build up their revenues. Others prefer to give up their own service department and rely on the distributor's department; they find this difficult to manage, however, when the distributor is located in a distant community.

As the service business becomes less profitable, television set manufacturers must insure an adequate supply of servicemen. Even more pressing, they must avoid measures that will turn independent servicemen, already sensitive due to the decline in their business, against them. Hence the high level of interest and concern of the manufacturers with the independent servicemen.

Although something of a digression, it is perhaps appropriate to ask why the independent serviceman is so much more prominent in the television set industry than in, say, refrigerator, stove or dishwasher repair. Several hypotheses suggest themselves: First, the high service charges during the early years of television (as suggested by the cost of service insurance contracts) were highly attractive especially to men engaged in radio repair and men recently discharged from the armed forces who had worked with or around electronic equipment. Second, the parts required for television set repair are "general purpose" to a large extent, that is, they can be used for many different brands of sets, in contrast to replacement parts for washers, dryers, refrigerators, stoves, etc. Third, the distributors and dealers in the appliance business in the late 1940s and early 1950s lacked the trained manpower to handle all of the repair business available and were disinclined to build up large service departments that might divert their energies and funds from profitable sales operations. Fourth, television set service is a relatively easy trade to enter and does not require large financial resources. Also, special schools were established soon after the Second World War to train men in television set repair, and veterans were able to have their training costs defrayed under the G.I. Bill of Rights. These factors, and perhaps others, combine to make television repair essentially a trade composed of independent servicemen.

Public Relations Activities of Manufacturers

Most television set manufacturers are very large corporations, with many employees and stockholders. Their brand names are better known by far in the average home than the names of cabinet members and members of the Supreme Court. They are as vulnerable to gossip and adverse criticism as a motion picture star—and about as careful not to arouse public disfavor. To handle their potentially delicate relations with the public all television set manufacturers have public relations departments, which are largely engaged in marketing communications.

It is possible to distinguish quite a few different publics with which the average television set manufacturer is concerned. They include: their employees (labor), stockholders and the financial community generally, the local communities in which they produce sets, local and state officials, voters generally, and the federal government—especially regulatory agencies. This activity was not studied in depth, although enough information was collected to indicate its key features. These will be set forth briefly.

The enormous variation in the extent to which the individual manufacturers are engaged in public relations activities is striking and complicates a description of those activities. One of the companies least concerned with public relations, strangely, is Zenith, the largest producer of sets during the last few years; ordinarily the largest firm in an industry assumes the major public relations burdens for its industry. By far the most preoccupied with public relations in the industry are R.C.A. and General Electric. While Zenith has about three persons plus one secretary engaged in public relations activities—and those mostly concerned with "pay television"—R.C.A. employs almost ten times as many, even if one counts only its divisions that are similar to divisions of Zenith.

Public relations embraces a motley conglomeration of activities. For such large firms as R.C.A. General Electric and Westinghouse, it includes "antitrust" as a central concern. In some companies, the public relations department spends a considerable proportion of its resources trying to create and embellish the popular image of its top executives, far beyond the call of its public relations value. Usually the public relations department is responsible for releasing information about the company to researchers and writers for trade magazines —as well as for preparing press releases for the daily press, which is perhaps its major job. Also the public relations departments of television set producers generally become involved in preparing and "clearing" public statements and speeches of its executives.

The manufacturers apparently do not regard the public relations function as part of their marketing activity. These companies have not followed the current trend of placing public relations under the director of marketing or marketing vice-president. In the largest companies, public relations is treated as a separate function which reports directly to the president of the company. It is considered here, in the discussion of marketing activities conducted by television set manufacturers affecting others than their direct customers, because much of public relations is indistinguishable from advertising in its objectives and is quite similar in method. By the various devices employed by public relations specialists, appliance manufacturers communicate with actual and potential customers, and others, in an effort to transmit information and impressions that are favorable to the company. Their main object is to improve the image of the corporation among potential customers and to increase its sales.

Chapter VI

THE ROLE OF THE DISTRIBUTOR

Much has already been said in preceding chapters about the television set distributor. Earlier references treated him mainly as a tool employed by manufacturers in designing a distribution system that serves their needs. This chapter examines the distributor as a businessman in his own right—one who uses manufacturers and retailers in his own interest.[1] In particular, we shall be concerned with the activities performed by the distributor, their costs, and the chief differences among individual major appliance distributors' approaches to their business.

Specifically, this chapter considers the following: (1) the experience of television set distributors since the inception of the industry; (2) the functions that major appliance distributors perform and how much they cost; (3) the chief differences in approach to the market taken by individual distributors; (4) the essential character—described in terms of competitiveness—of the major appliance distribution industry.

The reader should recall an earlier discussion which explained that the television set distributor is a major appliance distributor in the overwhelming majority of cases. Television set sales are usually the distributor's biggest single source of revenue, however.

[1] Other viewpoints from which the distributor might be examined are: from standpoint of dealer—what he does for the dealer or as perceived by the dealer; the economic functions performed by the distributor; what the distributor does for the consumer.

The Experience of Distributors
Since the Inception of the Industry

To explain why firms are in any business it is necessary to understand the conditions that existed at the time of their inception rather than prevailing circumstances. This statement applies with particular force to most distributors of major appliances. These men, on the whole, entered the business during the 1920s and 1930s when the chief product carried was radios and when a distributorship was essentially a one-man firm that required very modest capital investment. Attracted to this business were mainly men of limited financial resources and managerial skill, but with high ambitions and considerable sales talent; a large majority of those in business at the end of the 1930s possessed these qualities.

During the 1930s a few large manufacturers of major appliances possessed far greater bargaining power than did their distributors. It was far easier for them to obtain the services of effective distributors (for there were numerous applicants with good qualifications for distributor franchises) than for effective distributors to obtain a manufacturer's franchise of any value. The manufacturer was really "hiring a salesman with money" when he took on a distributor. Accordingly, distributors for these manufacturers were in constant fear of losing their franchises during this period. With the 30-day cancellation clause in the typical franchise agreement at that time, their economic security was far from "total." When a manufacturer's sales representative sat at the desk of a distributor and said, "The factory is concerned about the way things are going in this territory," the distributor usually became deeply and visibly concerned too.

Major appliance distribution remained essentially small business until the early post-war period, for the major appliances of the present day had not yet become commercially available. Television sets, the automatic washing machine and dryer, and stereophonic phonographs were all post-war developments. In addition to such major appliances as radios, refrigerators and stoves, most distributors sold the so-called traffic appliances (toasters, irons, mixers, grills, etc.) in order

The Role of the Distributor

to develop a sales volume sufficient to support a business. Few major appliance distributors were highly profitable prior to the Second World War, but, then, few businesses in the nation were.

The war, and especially the post-war years changed all that. Just how distributors carried on during the war, when most metal-using appliances were no longer produced, is not altogether clear. Nevertheless, most of them did survive and some managed to thrive. In the post-war period they fell upon truly golden days. Sales were assured for almost any appliance they offered for sale. Virtually no sales effort was required to dispose of all the merchandise they could obtain from manufacturers. (Supplies available to them were small and manufacturers were selling on an "allocation basis"; the supply available was divided among distributors according to some formula.) The distributor who barely eked out a living from a small enterprise during the 1930s became a very prosperous and sometimes a rich man during the late 1940s and early 1950s. Many did not possess exceptional talent for the major appliance business but were fortunate enough to be in the business when it would have required exceptional lack of talent in order to fail.

Well before the middle of the 1950s, the bloom was off the major appliance business. In most metropolitan areas, competition became severe and even highly efficient distributors found their financial returns quite modest. With each passing year, more and more distributors found it difficult to avoid losses—and in some years, most did sustain losses in their television departments. The fact that a manufacturer was "concerned" about a distributor's performance did not frighten him very much any more. The distributor himself became very concerned about the business, and many were tempted to give up their franchises. A few did so. Also, as the trade became increasingly competitive, manufacturers exerted greater efforts to strengthen their distributor organizations. They dropped their weakest distributors and sought to attract into their organizations the strongest distributors carrying competitive lines.

By the late 1950s many distributors of major appliances had become deeply disenchanted with the business. It was fairly usual to find that fathers who started a distributorship were discouraging their sons from entering or continuing in the major appliance distribution business. Even manufacturers of major appliances became troubled about the low returns that could be earned on capital in distribution near the end of the 1950s. Some took measures designed to increase the financial returns to distributors in order to insure that they would have an adequate supply of independent distributors to resell their merchandise.

At the time of this writing (Fall, 1963), it appears that most firms engaged in major appliance distribution are there because it was a good place for them to be a quarter century or more ago. A majority apparently do not consider it a "good" business to be in right now. However, they have invested fairly heavily in their present facilities, and these could not easily be adapted to other uses. Few of them know any other business to which they might transfer with a reasonable likelihood of success. Consequently, they stay on. Many major appliance distributors, however, have not reinvested much of their resources in their business. They have, rather, invested in other enterprises and in the stock market, which were far more profitable than their distribution enterprises. Because of the high returns obtainable on most investments during the middle-late 1950s and early 1960s, these men prospered, and many became financially independent. Indeed, some are now very wealthy. Not a few of these regard themselves as proven business successes. They are quite independent in spirit as well as in financial status and are not likely to jump at manufacturers' suggestions. They do not depend on their franchise for a livelihood, and the really good distributors among them are constantly courted by rival manufacturers. They must be handled very diplomatically by manufacturers' representatives, and they are—unless or until they are considered expendable.

This broad characterization of major appliances distribution since the 1920s admittedly does not take account of many factors. In particular, it ignores the very substantial differences among individual geographic regions and among the individual brands of appliances. Distributors handling the many brands that could not survive the period of intensive competition experienced famine long before the others. Also, the distributors for at least one major brand are prospering at present in absolute terms, as well as relative to the others. Despite these exceptions to the pattern described, the pattern does accurately summarize the present state of most major appliance distributors and what they have been through.

The Broad Economic Functions Performed by Distributors

The term "functions" has an honored place in treatises on marketing. Until quite recently, marketing has consisted largely of a discussion of the individual sub-functions that compose the marketing functions and a description of the institutions that perform them. In this sense, "function" denotes socially necessary and valuable services. More recently, the term "functions" has been applied to the chief activities of business enterprises. One therefore distinguished the functional areas of manufacturing, engineering, marketing, finance, personnel, etc. Also, within these broad areas, distinctions are made among the marketing functions of advertising, sales management, merchandising, point-of-sale, public relations, marketing research, etc.

To avoid confusion, we shall first discuss the broad economic functions performed by major appliance distributors and then discuss their concrete business activities. The term "activity" is employed because it is neutral, implying neither the desirability nor necessity of any activity; some of the activities described may be unnecessary, or even objectionable.

The reseller situated between the manufacturer and the retailer traditionally performs three central functions: (1) he "assembles"—that is, he constructs new assortments of merchandise by combining in one place the offerings of several manufacturers, thereby facilitating purchase by his customers; (2) he engages in "physical distribution"; and (3) he sells goods in smaller quantities than those in which he purchased them to meet the requirements of retailers. The television set distributor performs all of these functions; however, he performs a different form of assembly function than the one described.

As marketing specialists use the term, "assembly" means to bring together in one place the offerings of rival manufacturers in order to facilitate purchase by the customer.[2] As a result of assembly, he reduces his cost and inconvenience in seeking out the wares of many manufacturers. In addition, assembly involves the distributor in performing "purchasing agent functions." That is, he makes a critical review of available offerings and selects those that represent the best value for his customer (the retailer).

Distributors of televison sets and other major appliances almost never perform the assembly operations just described, for they handle only one brand of any one product. They will stock, for example, Motorola television sets, Norge refrigerators, Fedders air conditioners, etc., or only G.E. or Westinghouse or Philco appliances. Consequently, if they serve as a purchasing agent, they do so only in electing to distribute a particular brand of appliance. This view implies they had a choice of brands, which rarely is the case. As long as a distributor handles a single brand of an appliance, he exercises a selective function only to the extent that he may carry only part of the line of products and models offered by that manufacturer. Thus single-brand distributors do not perform the purchasing agent function.

On the other hand, distributors of television sets do perform another type of assembly function. They carry a variety of major appliances, which they offer their customers. By this type of assembly, they offer their customers essentially the same benefits as do traditional types of wholesalers: they make it easier to make purchases and reduce the time and money costs involved in retailers' purchasing. The usual appliance retailer handles many appliances including, in the usual case, refrigerators, stoves, washing machines, dryers, television sets, phonographs, radios and air conditioners. By carrying inventories of many different appliances in one location, the distributor clearly renders a useful service to the retailer as well as to the manufacturer. The joint sale of many appliances by a single business is to be explained by economies of operation quite as much as by customer convenience. The physical movement, storage, sale, service and financing of major appliances is much more economical

---

[2] Assembly also denotes the collection into large aggregations of the small outputs of individual producers—as in agriculture—for purposes of storage, grading and shipment in economical quantities.

when many items are stocked by a single firm than if sold separately. These products require similar facilities, sales materials, handling skills and servicing facilities. The cost of these operations can usually be spread over many items in a way that makes the cost of any one item lower than if it were handled alone.

Business Activities of Major Appliance Distributors

The activities of distributors are determined largely by the manufacturer. If he were to elect to perform some function now carried out by his distributors, he could do so. Both through direct contractual arrangements and as a result of forces in the market, the distributor would drop the function that the manufacturer had decided to perform for himself. The distributor in the television set industry—and in others—thus does what the manufacturer elects not to do. Stated differently, the manufacturer decides what functions the distributor is to perform. Much the same holds for the division of functions not performed by the manufacturer between the distributor and the dealer, with the distributor in the deciding position.

Partly through a process of trial and error, the division of functions among manufacturers, distributors and retailers comes to be worked out. The result varies over time and differs slightly from company to company in the industry. The division of the total distribution function among these three parties has not shifted much in the last few years. However, it is not wise to assume that this division is permanent—or even the best one possible.

The distributor might be viewed as an independent businessman who performs some services that manufacturers might otherwise have to perform. He does so in the expectation that his efforts will yield him a profit; the manufacturer permits him to perform these services because he believes that the distributor will perform them more effectively or at lower cost than the manufacturer could do himself, or because the manufacturer lacks sufficient funds to finance those activities while conducting his manufacturing operation on the desired scale.

Nothing has yet been said about the chief business activities of major appliance distributors. These consist mainly of "selling" and servicing appliances. The traditional view of distribution stresses the physical distribution and assembly functions, possibly because it assumes that businessmen simply offer goods to customers who come and buy without solicitation, after comparing the wares of competing sellers. Wholesaling as a separate line of business arose at a time when sales skills mattered far less than they do today; certainly, wholesaling originated before brand names achieved prominence and power. Whatever the reason, the main function performed today by distributors of major appliances for manufacturers—and their chief activity and largest expense—is selling. In the case of a television set distributor, this means that his job is to persuade retailers to carry his brand of sets and to help retailers to persuade ultimate customers to purchase that brand.

TABLE 11

COSTS OF MAJOR APPLIANCE DISTRIBUTORS, 1959
(*Expressed as a Proportion of Net Sales*)

	Composite Average	Range
Direct selling expense		
Total selling compensation	3.18	2.90–3.49
Expense	1.22	1.03–1.40
Advertising	.35	.18– .61
Total direct selling expense	4.75	4.26–5.19
Control and variable overhead		
Total warehouse cost	.78	.66– .96
Total shipping cost	.45	.38– .53
Total service cost	.42	.31– .51
Total general salaries	2.10	1.78–2.50
Miscellaneous overhead	1.09	
Total constant and variable overhead	4.84	4.68–5.06
Non-Control overhead	1.22	1.03–1.53
Provisions (bad debt)	.26	.11– .39
Total expenses	11.07	10.31–11.48

In other words, the main function that the television set distributor performs is not one of the traditional economic functions of assembly, physical distribution and disassembly—though he does these too. Principally, he is engaged in selling his brand of appliances

The Role of the Distributor

to retailers. In addition, he performs repair service and related activities involved in giving effect to the manufacturer's product warranties.

One method of describing the chief activities and functions of television set distributors is to analyze their costs. Tables 11 and 12 present the best cost data available to the author, and they differ fairly substantially. Most of the differences between these two tables are due to the fact that they measure somewhat different things: Table 11 presents a breakdown of major appliance distributors' costs on their total sales, which include far more than television sets; Table 12, on the other hand, is an estimate of the distributors' costs for television sets alone. Also, the tables refer to different years, but that fact would not account for much of the dissimilarity between them.

TABLE 12
ESTIMATED DISTRIBUTORS' COSTS ON TELEVISION SET SALES, 1962

	Percentage
Cost of merchandise (including in-freight)	85
Pre-tax profits	1.5
(There has been a downward drift in this figure, but distributors have managed to keep their nets fairly stable by cutting back certain optional costs when sales declined.)	
Direct advertising costs	1.5 to 2.0
Interest costs (reflects difficulty of getting distributors with adequate capital)	1.5
Reserve for price reductions	1.5
Sales cost (for salesmen)	5.0 (just a speck less)
General and administrative	4.0
	100.0

The financial information that major appliance distributors collect for control purposes are, understandably, very detailed. For other purposes than internal control such detailed information is more bewildering than illuminating. Table 11 was compiled from the operating records for the year 1959 of 40 major appliance distributors of various sizes and locations. These data are essentially comparable, having been based upon a common set of definitions. There has been some slight rounding of numbers for purposes of simplification.

Another estimate of distributors' costs, lumping together the experience of large, medium and small firms, is presented in Table 12, just as received from a high executive of a large television set manufacturing company. The grouping of expenses here is very convenient. Of particular interest are the comments that accompany several items and are enclosed in parentheses.

No detailed analysis will be made here of these costs or of the activities of distributors that they reflect. However, the chief lessons that they teach may be observed. First, sales costs are substantially higher than the costs of physical distribution, though the degree of the difference between them cannot be estimated with confidence. Second, sales cost is far greater than advertising cost. Third, a large proportion of a distributor's costs are relatively fixed.

The following discussion of the activities of distributors will divide them into physical distribution, internal marketing activities and external activities. Other classifications are possible, of course. This division was selected partly to insure that adequate attention is given to the physical distribution aspect of the business, which has been passed over lightly hitherto. It is also similar to the organization of the discussion of manufacturers' functions.

PHYSICAL DISTRIBUTION ACTIVITIES OF DISTRIBUTORS

Physical distribution designates the transportation, storage and "handling" (movement of merchandise essentially on a single site) of merchandise. In the television set industry, these activities are performed primarily by distributors; what they do not do, retailers do in the main. Manufacturers have held their activities in this sphere to a minimum.

The average television set travels a long distance from the end of the production line to the home of its ultimate owner, and it makes several stops along the way. Occasionally, it will move from the end of the factory assembly line into the manufacturer's warehouse on the factory site; generally it will move from the production line to the shipping platform. It is then loaded aboard truck or train for transportation to the premises of the distributor. (If shipped by train, it must be transshipped by truck from the freight yard to the distributor's warehouse.) Upon arrival, it must be unloaded and will usually be moved into the distributor's warehouse. It is likely to be moved around a bit within the warehouse before it is moved from the warehouse to the shipping platform for loading aboard truck for shipment to the retailer's store. Upon its arrival there, it again must be "handled" and placed somewhere until the retailer again moves it to the point at which it will be loaded aboard a truck and taken to the customer's residence. At this point, it must again be "handled" until it is settled at its initial point of operation.

All of this movement and handling involves sizable costs, most of which are borne by the distributor. He ordinarily pays for transportation from the factory and to the retailer. Although these costs vary considerably with the proximity of a distributor to the factory and the size of his territory, they apparently average out to be about 2 percent of the retail price of the set. Of course, some of the costs of transportation—paper work, insurance, materials handling, storage and direct transportation costs—are borne by the manufacturer and retailer. Physical distribution represents a major ingredient in the total cost of a television set, variously estimated to be between $20 and $25. No one pretends to be able to measure these costs precisely, but there is general agreement that the correct figure lies within this range.

Manufacturers do not transport sets in their own carriers to distributors located in other cities. (Some use their own trucks to transport sets to distributors located near their factory; one manufacturer actually holds all inventory for his local distributor. Deliveries to retailers served by that distributor are made directly from the factory.) The function of moving merchandise from the factory to the consumer is performed almost entirely by specialized agencies outside the industry—mainly the railroads and trucking firms. Television set manufacturers, distributors and retailers participate in the process by doing most of the paper work involved and by making the decisions as to when and how much to ship and by what carriers.

It is sometimes possible to effect substantial savings by shipping under the least costly circumstances. A manufacturer or distributor who is forced to send a few sets over long distances in a big hurry to accommodate an important retail account (who may be pressed for speedy delivery by a key customer) may spend twice or three times as much for transportation as he would if he had shipped those sets as part of a carload shipment. Transportation costs obviously vary according to the distances involved, the size of shipment, type of carrier used, and the rate arrangements (not at all standard in the case of trucking concerns) made between the sender and the carrier. To appreciate the magnitude of transportation costs, they should be compared with other expenses incurred in conjunction with the production and distribution of television sets. They are as great, for example, as the cost of a mahogany cabinet on a 23-inch console model set, and about half the cost of the chassis on the same model.

During several of the early years of the industry, all manufacturers shipped their entire output directly from the production line to distributors. They held no inventories of finished products whatsoever. This practice, a significant cost-saver for the manufacturer, was made possible by distributors' acquiescence to the arrangement. The distributor was required to store the merchandise or to reship it to dealers or to do a combination of these things.

When sets were in short supply, the distributor could immediately reship merchandise received from the manufacturer. At the time that manufacturers held no finished goods inventories, distributors also held relatively small stocks of sets. When the set shortage ended, however, distributors usually had to hold sets in inventory if manufacturers shipped merchandise that dealers did not order. Occasionally, distributors did send sets to dealers that they had not ordered, although that happened only under very special circumstances.

The manufacturer's policy of shipping goods to distributors just as soon as they were produced created numerous situations in which more goods were available for shipment than had been ordered. The manufacturer's determination to hold no inventories meant that distributors sometimes received more goods than they wanted. To hold a valuable franchise, distributors were forced to accept these arrangements for quite some time—particularly during the period when substantial profits were to be earned in television set distribution. As the industry matured and distribution profits declined, almost all

The Role of the Distributor   155

manufacturers were forced to retreat from the "no finished goods inventories policy." Accordingly, manufacturers' policy compelled distributors to perform a substantial storage function. In addition, the very nature of the services that distributors render requires them to be prepared to make speedy delivery in response to dealers' orders. Failure to do so would alienate dealers and might induce them to give their patronage to some other brand that offers better service. For these reasons, one finds that major appliance distributors own or rent very large warehouses, and their occupancy costs represent a substantial proportion of their total cost. One estimate places occupancy cost in the neighborhood of 1.77 percent of distributors' net sales—or about 15 percent of their total operating expenses. Of this amount, almost 60 percent goes for warehouse space. ("Occupancy cost" equals .76 percent, "warehouse cost" equals 1.01 percent.)

The costs of physical distribution are thus very substantial. If transportation, materials handling and storage are performed inefficiently, the distributor will dissipate large sums that could make the difference between a moderate profit and a sizable loss. Nevertheless, skill in physical distribution rarely accounts for the success or failure of a distributor. His fortunes depend mainly upon his talents and industriousness in selling. Moreover, his ability to obtain and hold a franchise bears virtually no relationship to his efficiency in physical distribution, but depends almost entirely upon his ability to "move merchandise."

INTERNAL MARKETING ACTIVITIES OF MAJOR APPLIANCE DISTRIBUTORS

Virtually all activities other than physical distribution and the creation and servicing of a dealer organization are internal, the most important being: forecasting of sales and purchase requirements, preparation of marketing programs, pricing and advertising—both on the distributor's own account and in connection with the co-op advertising program.

Forecasting sales and purchase requirements by individual model. Distributors forecast sales in much the same way that manufacturers do. Indeed, more and more television set manufacturers are helping distributors to prepare sales forecasts. Manufacturers are compelled, directly or indirectly, to forecast their distributors' sales in order to estimate their sales to distributors. Consequently, their assistance to distributors involves little additional effort on their part.

The forecast of sales by model is generally the starting point in the making of several key decisions by a major appliance distributor. First is a determination of the quantities of merchandise to order. The distributor rarely will order just the quantity that he expects to sell; he must consider such factors as the size of his current inventories, the availability of quantity discounts, special "deals" and price promotions, his supply of liquid funds and the various demands upon those resources, and the confidence he can attach to his sales forecast. These factors, among others, must be balanced in order to arrive at the number of sets of each model to order.

Second, the distributor's decision as to how much credit to extend to dealers and how much to seek from suppliers usually starts from the sales forecast. Sales do not automatically result in equal cash income; similarly, purchases do not necessarily result in a cash drain. Varying payment arrangements ordinarily will have been made with individual dealers and with the manufacturer. Some dealers pay for their purchases very promptly; others require open book credit from him. Conversely, at some times the manufacturer will extend liberal book credit (especially at the beginning of a model year) whereas at other times payment must be fairly prompt. These cash flow considerations necessarily influence the distributor's financial plans as well as his decisions about the amount of merchandise to order and the time at which to place his order.

Preparation of marketing programs. Distributors rarely prepare market programs that carry as far into the future as those of manufacturers, and these are rarely rigorous or for a long term. Even the largest independent distributors are essentially one-man businesses, at least if one considers only the television set department operated by the distributor. For example, the largest independent distributor of major appliances is Bruno of New York City. One man is at the head of this organization and operates it with relatively little assistance at the senior executive level. For practical purposes the television division is an independent enterprise under the active direction of this person. Possibly for this reason, written rigorous marketing plans are virtually unknown among major appliance distributors. They continue to conduct their operations largely "out of their hats," according to all accounts.

Pricing. Distributors of television sets are free to charge whatever they wish for their merchandise. Even factory branches are, on the whole, autonomous in the exercise of the pricing function. It appears that substantial variations sometimes exist in the prices charged by different distributors of the same manufacturer at the same time. In part these differences reflect fundamental price policy variations—some pursue a large volume at low margin while others seek "full margin and modest volume." Also, price differences result from errors in ordering. Distributors will generally try to push models of which they hold excessive inventories by some form of price inducement. It is not uncommon for one distributor to be relatively short of a model that another distributor holds in excessive amounts.

Pricing is regarded as a critically important and fairly rare skill among major appliance distributors. When executives in manufacturing firms refer to pricing skill, they speak of an ability to devise "promotions." Promotions offer an opportunity for great ingenuity and experimentation. In addition to the specific terms of a promotion, its timing—the season of the year and its duration—will often be crucial to its success. A description of television set promotions will be presented in a later section of this chapter.

Pricing is a responsibility that has grown in recent years, as manufacturers have increasingly dropped the practice of naming suggested retail prices on some or all of their models. However, pricing is not an activity that requires much planning on the distributor's part. With his own costs, by model, as a starting point and with the information he gains from talking to salesmen about customer relations—and with one eye on his inventory figures—he decides what sets to promote, when to do so, and how strongly. He must set price on the basis of very current market information rather than long-range plans.

Nowadays, a major appliance distributor is almost as concerned with the prices at which retailers resell his merchandise as with setting his own prices. He recognizes that the prices he can charge depend heavily upon what his retailers are able to obtain. More important, distributors recognize that their ability to gain dealers for their brand depends to a large extent upon the profitability of carrying the line, and this in turn depends primarily upon their obtaining prices that will more than cover their costs; in practice that means that there must not be extensive "discounting" and price cutting on their brand of sets. The distributor's concern with retail prices involves him in very subtle and complicated activities that are of great importance to himself and to the manufacturer whose line he carries.

All retailers of television sets in any area compete with one another. Competition is keenest among adjacent retailers who carry the same brands. If one retailer advertises a substantial price reduction for a particular model, other retailers in the area face great difficulty in getting "regular price." In this sense, the individual dealers served by any distributor are quite interdependent, and a small minority can strongly influence the welfare of everyone. Consequently, an appliance distributor usually tries to maintain an orderly and stable price structure among his dealers and to protect the vast majority from injury by a small predatory group.

Distributors of major appliances apparently have no intention of maintaining uniform retail prices for television sets and recognize that they probably could not do so even if they tried. Moreover, most distributors want dealers to exercise initiative and imagination in price making; they seek out and cultivate dealers who are expert in promotion. Nevertheless, they are sensitive to "trouble makers," "chiselers" and "opportunists." These, and other terms less likely to pass censorship, are used to describe dealers who may damage the reputation of a brand by some of the shady practices described in the following chapter.

Even if distributors did not want to prevent such activities, the dealers hurt by them would urge their distributor to take action. The connection between the major appliance distributor and his dealers is sufficiently close for them to give almost immediate expression to grievances. The distributor who is indifferent to the distress caused by shady pricing practices of his retailers earns no loyalty among his dealers and is not likely to hold his franchise long with the manufacturer.

The Role of the Distributor

Brief reference has already been made to the fact that increasing use is being made, by distributors, of minimum prices on television sets. The move toward minimum pricing has been very rapid in recent years. A survey by a trade publication of major markets in March of 1963 found it to be confined essentially to four major markets: New York, Los Angeles, Boston and Philadelphia. These have been among the most competitive markets in the nation up to now. In New York City, for example, 15 brands of major appliances and television were found to be fair-traded in whole or in part. These included almost all of the major brands of sets. In other major markets, including Chicago, Washington, Cleveland, St. Louis, Milwaukee and San Francisco, price maintenance has not grown to an appreciable extent.[3]

Minimum prices for any set usually are set below the list price, if the manufacturer names one. Determination of the point at which the minimum price is set is in the hands of the distributor. On rare occasions, a particular model will carry a minimum price equal to the list price all across the country—suggesting that the manufacturer can exert strong influence on retail price if he is determined to do so for a good reason.

"Minimum prices" have been employed by major appliance distributors for some time, dating back in some markets at least to 1955. However, the determined application of the policy backed up by strict enforcement is still the exception rather than the rule. The upsurge in use of minimum prices is dated by many persons in the industry at the beginning of 1960.

The experience of one distributor with a minimum price program should reveal the very great difficulties encountered and explain why such programs are not universal and are not likely to become so. Early in 1960 in a large metropolitan market, a newly appointed distributor who had strong factory support (financial and otherwise) decided to establish a strong minimum price program. He allowed himself three years to make it work. Day after day for two months, he met both at lunch and at dinner with groups of ten dealers and explained his minimum price program, its rationale, why he thought it would help them and that he was resolved to make it work. He

[3] *Home Furnishings Daily* for the week starting March 11, 1963.

initiated a rigorous system of "shopping," spending approximately $375 per week to get reliable information about the prices that individual dealers were charging. At first, dealers were given a warning when apprehended in violations of the minimum price restriction. After a while, all violators were cut off. As late as two and one-half years after the start of the program, this distributor learned that his second-largest dealer in a sizable city had sold below the minimum price level. Painful though it must have been, he cut off that dealer.

In the process of establishing this system, the distributor lost substantial market penetration in his sales area. After a while, however, he began to regain position as dealers happily discovered that they need not fear being undersold at ridiculously low prices on his line. By the middle of 1962, his market had become one of the best in the country for the manufacturer he represents.

This story is being repeated in many markets, though not all distributors are attempting to establish a minimum price program. The determined efforts to do so, accompanied by costly and painful enforcement programs, are a recent phenomenon. At the time this is written it is difficult to forecast the success distributors will achieve with minimum pricing and even to guess how much effort they will expend to make it work. It is even more difficult to forecast the actions of regulatory authorities and the interpretations of the courts with respect to minimum prices.

Advertising. As indicated earlier in Table 12, major appliance distributors average approximately 2 percent of their net sales for direct advertising. There are very great variations in this figure; in some cases, according to persistent rumor a distributor can sometimes show an actual profit on this phase of his operation. This possibility and others no less exotic will be discussed presently, when we consider co-op advertising.

The power of local advertising, mainly in newspapers, to move television sets is universally recognized by executives in all three levels of the industry. There is considerable dispute, however, about the ability of newspaper advertising to sell a particular model of a particular set, unless it is offered at extremely low price and the retailer actually wants to push it—a most unusual combination. Advertising at the local level aims chiefly to build retail traffic and give the retailer "a shot at the customer." Once he has the customer in his sights, the retailer will try to sell a set (possibly of a brand that was not advertised) that offers a better margin of profit than the advertised models.

Local advertising affects more than retail traffic. It is generally agreed that it affects the acceptability of a brand. Certain kinds of local advertising can build a manufacturer's reputation and image for quality, dependability and "value."

Some manufacturers have learned to their sorrow that local advertising is a double-edged sword. It can damage the image of high quality, luxury and prestige that a manufacturer tries to achieve by his national advertising and creates in its place an impression of the brand as "promotional," low in price and low in prestige.

Accordingly, manufacturers and distributors want heavy retail advertising support for their own brand, but they want it to be of a particular kind. It is to achieve these two goals, which often conflict, that the distributor may become heavily engaged in advertising activities. With very rare exception, the distributor does almost no advertising on his own account. Instead, he encourages retailers to advertise by offering to share the cost using both the co-op fund (held by the manufacturer) and the substantial sums he sets aside to be devoted strictly to advertising. By so doing he gains some control over the content of the retailer's advertising.

The foregoing paragraph summarizes the broad picture of the major appliance distributor's advertising functions. However, it omits many very interesting details—including the one that makes it possible for some unusual distributors to actually make money, rather than spend it, on advertising. The practices described below have become quite rare, and possibly extinct. Moreover, even when they were most flourishing, only a minority—and possibly a small one—engaged in these practices. The two chief practices that represent departures from the picture are misrepresentation of advertising expenditures and the use of co-op funds as a substitute for price reductions. To understand these practices, it is necessary to become more familiar with co-op advertising arrangements in the television set industry.

In basic principle, cooperative advertising is simple. When the manufacturer sells sets to a distributor, he sets aside a predetermined amount in an account for the distributor to use for co-op advertising. The amount set aside generally is a fixed percentage of sales. (There currently appears to be a shift to a sum fixed for each model of set.) These sums are clearly earmarked for the distributor and are paid to him if he meets the general requirements of the co-op program. Basically, these provide that the distributor must, out of his own funds, match the expenditures from the co-op fund. (In theory, at least, distributors set up specific funds that match the amount of money the manufacturers hold in their name.) The distributor is thus induced to encourage retailers to advertise and is given an incentive to get the retailers to pay as large a share of the total advertising cost as possible. Whatever cost is not borne by the retailer is divided equally between the distributor and the manufacturer's co-op fund.

One of the major abuses of co-op advertising in the past has been its discriminatory use; it was an important source of price reductions for those retailers it favored. It is well known that some large retailers "never spent a penny of their own to advertise a television set." On the other hand, small retailers generally were forced to pay about half the media cost plus most of the costs of creating the advertisement. Vigorous action by the Federal Trade Commission during the last few years has greatly reduced such discrimination. Certainly, there is far greater awareness and fear of F.T.C. action now (1963) than there was even in 1960. However, it is unlikely that complete equality of treatment is accorded to all retailers. Manufacturers take great pains to avoid complicity in co-op "violations." They have not, and probably cannot, and possibly would not if they could, compel distributors to bring them to a halt. Any distributor might lose considerable ground in his market, especially with his key retail accounts, if he did not give preferential treatment in the disbursement of co-op funds.

The second abuse is more interesting and intricate. Perhaps it can be explained most clearly by an illustration. The Ace Retail Company (an imaginary company), may run a local newspaper advertising campaign on television sets, for which it actually pays $10,000. Because Ace is a very large advertiser and an effective bargainer it commands a highly preferential rate from the newspaper; another retailer would be charged $20,000 for the same space. The newspaper bills the Ace Retail Company for $20,000, at the latter's request. (In truly extreme cases retailers have paid 8 cents a line and presented bills for 82 cents.) This $20,000 invoice will be presented to the Brown Wholesale Company, Ace's distributor, for "sharing" under the terms of the co-op program. As an accomplice to the arrangement, Brown will pay Ace, say, $8,000 (80 percent of Ace's actual cost) and will pass along to the manufacturer the bill that Ace received from the newspaper for $20,000. Brown may claim that it was necessary to pay Ace all but $3,000 toward the $20,000 advertisement in order to persuade Ace to run it. Brown might allege that other distributors were offering Ace an even larger contribution. Brown thus declares that his contribution was $17,000, toward which he is entitled to receive $8,500 from the co-op fund. This amount yields him a $500 net profit, for he paid Ace only $8,000 toward the advertisement.

The foregoing instance is extreme, but by no means the most extreme the author has heard. Such abuses involve collusion—and downright fraud—on the part of the media, the retailer and the distributor. They can occur only if the manufacturer is lax or unwilling to correct them. No one familiar with this industry denies that cases like that cited occurred frequently in the past. A few claim that such abuses, though less extreme and common, occur even today. Manufacturers are aware of the abuses and not infrequently know the chief offenders, but they are not always in a position to prevent them. There has been a tightening up of the administration of co-op funds in the last few years. Now some manufacturers and distributors allow a flat rate per line of local advertising, regardless of the actual rate paid.

Apart from administering the co-op fund, the average television set distributor operates a small advertising department designed to help retailers prepare ads. Occasionally, a retailer will request assistance from the distributor. If the distributor believes that a retailer is doing an ineffective job with his advertising, he'll tell him so and help him to improve. The task of discussing this with the retailer usually falls on the distributor's salesman, who calls on the retailer.

For the most part, the distributor tries to help by making up a series of advertising lay-outs which are available to retailers without charge. The lay-outs are made up mainly from mats, glossy photographs and specification sheets provided by the factory. They do very little special advertising work for individual retailers.

Distributor promotions. Promotions are directed to and initiated by different parties in the television set industry. By and large, the major appliance distributor is the main source of promotions. Retailers occasionally initiate them, but far less frequently than the distributor or manufacturer; often, too, the retailer promotion is run at the behest and with the strong behind-the-scenes support of the distributor, who in turn occasionally is using the manufacturer's ideas and funds. Distributor promotions are directed: (a) to retailer "principals" (and here a sharp distinction must be drawn between the big and the small dealers; (b) to retailer salesmen; (c) to the distributor's own salesmen; (d) to the families of these three groups; or, (e) to consumers.

All promotions are motivating devices designed to increase sales. However, the immediacy of that goal is far greater in some promotions than in others. For example, a distributor may organize a trip to a big city for his dealers, wine and dine and entertain them lavishly—all to build up good-will. In this case the number of items that the dealer must purchase (the qualifying quota) would be low. On the other hand, to move overstocked merchandise in a hurry, an elaborate trip may be offered, requiring dealers to order a large number of sets to qualify for this trip.

Aside from the common aim of sales promotions to increase sales, they can be divided into at least the following significant categories: package deals, premiums, free merchandise, trips, money, "gimmicks" (imaginative stunts, etc.). Each of these types will be discussed in turn with particular reference to distributor-initiated promotions.

Package deals: A package deal is an offer of a selected "package" of sets—two or more of a certain combination of particular models and types—at a lower than usual price. Package deals generally are offered for only a limited time. A common form is: For every 2 consoles and 1 portable that the dealer buys from a given list of models, by a certain date, he gets a reduction of $10 per set from the usual price; a variation of this is a lump sum reduction on the whole package of, say, $25. Package deals often create severe difficulties with reorders; especially if the reorder quantity is less than a standard package.

Premiums: Premiums are similar to package deals but take the following form: Buy this particular group of items for the regular price and you will become entitled to price reductions on *other* items. A most common premium for retailers is greatly reduced prices of television set stands, with the purchase of portable sets. Distributors sometimes offer greatly reduced prices on portable phonographs with the purchase of a certain model of portable television set. Another variation is to give United States Savings Bonds for the purchase of certain packages.

The use of premiums for consumers is not uncommon, although this is found more in "white goods" appliances than in electronics. Common examples would be reduced prices for stands, indoor antennae or radios if bought in conjunction with certain "special sets." More often than not, the premium to the consumer represents the direct passing on of a premium received by the dealer.

Free merchandise: In this instance merchandise is given away with certain sets or packages. "Give-aways" by the distributor to the dealer may be intended for the dealer to keep himself or resell, or to be passed along to the consumer. The former can and do include almost anything one can think of, from wrist watches to cases of liquor. Free merchandise intended to be passed on to consumers generally consists of small appliances or toys for the children. (Stuffed dogs were used by one distributor, whose brand motif has a listening dog.) One distributor commented that the trouble with merchandise gifts for the consumer that are arranged through the retailer was that if the merchandise was salable, it often ended up on the dealers' shelves to be sold, rather than offered to the consumer as a gift if he made a purchase. He quoted one such specific instance where the give-away was an electric blanket. Toys, he said, are less susceptible to such misdirection.

Free merchandise is a popular promotion for salesmen—those of the distributor and of the retailer. The distributor's salesmen often have a participation right in the merchandise deals to retailers. Thus, if a salesman sells ten packages which involve the giving of a basket of wine to the dealer, he is entitled to a basket himself. Another type of "free merchandise" promotion directed at retail salesmen is less common. Immediately after the salesman closes a sale on sets from a certain list, the salesman phones a special number where a girl draws a prize from a barrel for him. He is told immediately what prize he has won, and this is mailed to his home the moment his sale is verified.

Other forms of merchandise give-aways that are intended to foster competition among dealers and/or salesmen will be discussed below.

Trips: Trips for retailers have become so common in the last few years that one distributor was moved to say in all seriousness, "Today's appliance dealers are the best traveled class of businessmen in the United State." Almost all television set manufacturing companies organize trips for dealers through their distributors. Of course, trips are "given" for other durables besides television sets.

It is possible to distinguish four different types of trips offered to retailers. Each has a different objective, and to be successful, as one distributor put it, "You have to be clear about objectives and how to achieve them." We may distinguish, first, the "loading program" trip, designed to move large quantities of merchandise in a relatively short time following their introduction to the trade. As one would expect, minimum qualifying orders are high, although some allowance is made for the smaller retailers. These trips, usually lavish, will range from the Miami weekend to an overseas cruise. Second is the "goodwill trip." Often these are weekends of entertainment for dealers and their wives in a large city. It is used primarily by distributors in smaller cities. The offer of a "sophisticated good time" with few strings attached is designed to build up good personal relations in areas where this is essential for good business. An ex-distributor commented, "If you want goodwill it is wiser to give trips than to establish a straight quota for earning them. You cannot offend the big fellow so you have to take him along anyway, whether he fulfills his quota or not." This person found that he obtained as good results this way "without ramming the merchandise down their throats."

Third is the "reward and stimulate" trip, where qualifying dealers are flown off to a luxury resort or big city, and, mixing business and pleasure, are shown the new line. It appears that "they don't mind the commercials mixed in with the fun."

Finally, dealers may be flown to the plant to be given some product indoctrination. Although the emphasis is primarily on business, considerable "entertaining" takes place on these occasions.

The trips spoken of here are offered primarily to the retailer-owner. On some occasions, when a retailer is entitled to more than one trip, he may send one or more of his salesmen in his place.

The competitive strategic value of trips to manufacturers and distributors has declined as everyone has had to "get into the act." According to some, they have got themselves into a rat-race with no hope of getting out. Despite the fact that trips have become almost "promotional clichés," one could hazard the guess that they will continue to be used for some time: "People are still willing to travel."

Money: The use of money as a promotion is generally resorted to only when it is conceded that nothing else works. It is used primarily in two instances. One is to large retailers who are not interested in promotional gimmicks but only in price; the other is to retailer salesmen, who some distributors regard as being interested in little else. Money deals to retail salesmen would include "spiffs" and "P.M.s," which are discussed elsewhere. Money prizes have also been offered to distributor salesmen for opening up new electronics dealers, which often means persuading a franchised white goods and/or laundry retailer to take on television sets. From time to time, too, dealers are offered price reductions on "one day specials" of certain models.

Gimmicks, competitive promotions and traffic builders: This category subsumes all the different promotions not classified above. Man can be moved by motivations other than cash. Salesmen, it is said, must be kept amused, otherwise their efforts will flag. To keep up spirits, competitions among salesmen are held for fairly short periods. The more unusual and humorous these are, the more successful they appear to be. One common form is to establish a "point score" for each sale, these points contributing to some prize. One distributor added a new wrinkle to this traditional form of promotion. The points earned by the salesmen were used to "buy" articles of clothing for his salesmen. At the end of the competition the salesmen attended a special dinner, each dressed only in the clothes he had won. The distributor claimed great success for this promotion, both in terms of short-run output and in improved *esprit de corps* of the sales force.

The families of dealers and salesmen can be easily implicated in such competitions, so that the dealer or salesman is urged on by his family to greater exertions. Prizes in such competitions include family trips, mink stoles or even automobiles.

One imaginative distributor combined a number of elements into a grand annual "jamboree." He gave out "phony dollars" on a point-system basis to dealers who bought his merchandise. A festive jamboree was held in a huge, specially stocked warehouse, to which the dealers were invited along with their families. On that day the "phony dollars" became currency that could be used to buy the goods on display at marked prices. The distributor accumulated large reserves of merchandise to be offered during this event. In addition, he was able to sell large amounts of regular stock to dealers on jamboree days because their families goaded them into obtaining more "phony dollars" to purchase some chosen goods. To be sure, far more than television sets are involved in this promotion, illustrating again the difficulty of separating out jointly distributed goods.

An important class of promotions is conducted by the retailer for his customers, but the promotions are designed and often financed by the distributor. The distributor may reduce prices of some goods for this special promotion; even more often, he will design and help execute the particular stunt. These promotions often are built around a spectacular and imaginative traffic building idea, and will feature the sponsoring distributor's brand more than the others. Such traffic builders will range from free pieces of pizza, keys to open a treasure chest, and "back door sales," to entry forms for a world cruise—"no obligation to purchase, just come into the store to get your form." The variety of ideas is great, and new ideas are ever required to capture, even fleetingly, the attention of the over-promoted public.

One may well be moved to ask whether promotions differ from equivalent sums of money in their effects. In other words, why not give the money away in the first place? Distributors believe, and rightly, that these have very different effects. Money promotions, if widespread, lead to lower prices. These, in turn, lower margins, which generally dampens sales effort—precisely the opposite of what is intended. Moreover, merchandise promotions appear to have greater value to most recipients (whether retailer, salesman or final consumer) than they actually cost the giver. It is perhaps fitting that many of the people in an industry known for this kind of "doublethink" are taken in by it themselves.

In recent years, promotions have become increasingly common. For example, one distributor in a large city ran 20 promotions in eight months. And this number would have been far greater but for a two-month showing of the new line, which drained off most of the available promotional funds for the period.

EXTERNAL ACTIVITIES OF MAJOR APPLIANCE DISTRIBUTORS

The chief activities of major appliance distributors, as already noted, are directed toward selling. Their financial success depends mainly on how effectively they sell, for their value to the manufacturer depends upon the volume of sales they produce for him. Sales of television sets to retailers are made in two steps: first, a dealer is persuaded to "handle" a particular brand; second, he purchases larger or smaller quantities of that brand. Accordingly, we shall discuss what distributors do to create and service a dealer organization, the measures they take to increase set sales, and then consider their activities related to service.

The creation and servicing of a dealer organization. The volume of sales that a distributor gains for his brand depends primarily upon the number and quality of dealers in his area that he can persuade to carry it. Manufacturers and distributors have conflicting goals regarding the type of dealers to include in their dealer organization. In his desire for profits, rather than volume, the distributor usually does not want to serve very small, inaccessible and uncredit-worthy retailers. Such customers would build the manufacturer's sales volume, however, contributing to greater revenues and reduced unit costs of production. Consequently, many manufacturers would like their distributors to serve such retailers and try to persuade them to do so.

Retail representation is a most significant ingredient in the success of almost every consumer product. That is especially true when the product is complex and involves a large expenditure. In such situations, the retailer is somewhat analogous to a doctor: he can almost prescribe what the customer should take. Certain retailers are sought by all distributors. They sell large quantities of appliances, and the competition for their patronage is extremely keen. Even though such retailers ordinarily carry several brands, and often many brands, they almost never carry all of them. (A distributor with a spectacular promotion on one or two models usually will be able to get his sets on the floor of such a retailer, at least until he disposes of the promoted sets.) The distributors who are able to get a disproportionate share of the business of such dealers are regarded as the most efficient and will be treasured by the manufacturer whose brand they carry.

At the other extreme, an occasional distributor will create a weak and unbalanced dealer organization out of ignorance or negligence. He may, choosing the easy path, find himself saddled with dealers whose business is not wanted by other distributors, who are difficult to service, and who must be caught before they will pay their bills. Such derelict distributors are relatively rare, for the financial losses from an operation of this type would insure their speedy exit from the business.

Even distributors who are alert to the heavy costs of servicing small dealers and the dangers of selling to dealers with a poor credit rating sometimes will sell to them. That is likely to occur when their sales are below quota and they feel that their franchise is threatened.

A distributor can strengthen his dealer organization by: inducing those dealers to carry his brand who had not done so before—either by increasing the number of brands he handles or by dropping a rival brand; inducing retailers who theretofore never carried television sets to do so; and improving the effectiveness of dealers currently in his organization. It is essential to understand the means by which distributors seek to achieve these goals and the services they must render to dealers in order to retain them as customers. In particular, we shall discuss the measures that distributors take to induce dealers to carry their brand and the things they do to persuade retailers to "push" their brand.

Distributors rely mainly upon a personal sales force to build a dealer organization, although they also use other methods. Accordingly, they recruit salesmen, provide field and home office supervision, offer training and devise a system of motivation and control in order to create an effective selling group. Some distributors devote great effort and make sizable expenditures to develop their salesmen, bringing in outsiders as a regular part of their training program. These distributors generally say that they "want much more than sales" from their salesmen. They want their salesmen to be "consultants to dealers" as well as salesmen.

Distributors' salesmen call on dealers and, in the manner of personal salesmen, attempt to persuade them of the superiority of their brand and of the high quality of the service that the distributor renders. To a large extent, the effectiveness of the distributor depends upon the number and quality of his salesmen. This in turn depends heavily upon the number and closeness of their personal relationships with appliance retailers, as well as upon sales and management skills.

Reference has already been made to the highly personal nature of the relationships between distributors and retailers. Especially in small communities, business is strongly colored by personal acquaintanceships and family ties; they are rarely completely absent even in large cities. Accordingly, distributors will capitalize upon their personal contacts and try to increase and strengthen them.

Apart from such personal bases for winning the patronage of retailers, most of the measures that distributors employ to persuade retailers to carry their line are equivalent to direct payments. Indeed, on rare occasion, distributors have made outright gifts to retailers to induce them to carry their line. Generally the manufacturer does not even know when this has been done.

Almost every business is actually short of cash or its owners fear that it might soon become so. Consequently, distributors can try to induce retailers to carry their brand by offering easier credit terms—both in terms of amounts that may be bought on credit and the amount of time before they must make payment. In effect, the distributor makes a gift to the retailer of interest-free loans. The attractiveness of this gift, as the retailer perceives it, can be appreciated if one understands that many retailers pay an interest rate of between 20 and 25 percent on loans made from sources other than commercial banks—and sometimes suffer some personal embarrassment and damage to their credit standing in the process.

A distributor who is anxious to place his line in a particular retail store will sometimes pay for facilities that the store is about to acquire. He may, for example, pay to redecorate and provide lighting and display fixtures. He may contribute to the downpayment on a lease for a new location. Any capital expenditure made by a retailer may be underwritten in whole or in part by a distributor who is anxious to persuade the retailer to carry his line.

One common method of gaining customers, used in virtually all trades, is to do favors for them and attempt to put them under obligation. A distributor's salesman will typically welcome opportunities to entertain a potential valuable retail customer and to make him feel that he has received a favor and feel some obligation to the salesman. Retailers who accept big favors do so only because they are contemplating a switch to another brand; to accept a "big treat" otherwise is regarded as highly unethical by most businessmen. The amount of entertainment and its form varies from situation to situation. Theater tickets and lavish dinners are quite commonplace; heavy drinking sprees and the favors of call girls are far less common—though in these matters no one has bothered to keep score. Indeed, one sees no reliable figures on the size of distributors' salesmen's expense accounts—and particularly on their special entertainment costs.

It should not be overlooked that the relationship between a distributor and his retailers involves mutual trust. Specifically, dealers depend upon their distributors to charge the same price to all "equal" dealers—"equal" under the terms of the Robinson-Patman Act. They must be able to believe him when he says that certain models are not available. They sometimes suspect distributors of reporting "out of stocks" on certain models to get them to buy other models that they wish to unload. Distributors who have not won the trust of dealers suffer considerable turnover among dealers and find it difficult to replace those they lose. Word travels pretty fast about such matters.

How distributors attempt to persuade retailers to push their brand. (1) Special deals. Most retailers carry more than one brand of set. Consequently, the distributor's job has only begun after he has persuaded the retailer to carry his line. To insure that the retailer will produce sales requires that the retailer's sales force give special support to his brand; window displays, prominent floor position and advertising all are desired—and preferably in disproportionate amounts. Complete objectivity is no more common among retailers than others; they generally play favorites.

Distributors attempt to become the retailer's favorite by offering him special "deals." Two main possible elements in a deal are: a lower price to the retailer, which widens the spread between his cost and selling price so that sales of that brand give him a higher profit than he might obtain from other brands he carries; or, an opportunity for the retailer to lower price to the ultimate consumer and thus persuade him to buy this brand rather than other brands that the retailer carries. Some dealers use deals to combine both elements; most attempt to keep the wider margin all for themselves.

(2) Push money. A variety of names, including "push money," "spiffs" and P.M.s are used to describe one widespread practice. This practice consists of giving the retailer or his salesmen an extra bonus for selling a particular brand or model.

In certain trades, spiff money has become so commonplace that the salesman receives a spiff of equal size regardless of the brand he sells. Under such conditions the push money gives no brand a differential advantage but merely becomes part of salesmen's compensation.

In the major appliance business, spiffs are "now and then things." The spiff is "on" only during a certain period and is obtained on a single brand—and possibly only on certain selected sets in the line. Push money occasionally is offered to salesmen without the knowledge of the store owners, although that practice has been ruled illegal. Some television set manufacturers and distributors require signed authorization from the retailer for any spiff.

(3) The wide markup. If his brand loses market position, the distributor may offer his retailers a wider margin (i.e., charge lower prices) in the hope that the latter will attempt to switch consumers to his brand. This may be likened to deals, except that it may endure indefinitely.

A retailer's margin is best defined in terms of the price he pays and the price he *actually receives*. Ordinarily, however, it is based on a "list" price, a "regular" price, or the price that is "usually charged" for merchandise bearing that cost. But the list prices of some brands (these days, they are called "suggested lists") are deliberately "puffed" to abnormally high levels. Some manufacturers consciously "sell against list price"—that is, they knowingly set high prices so that the retailer can offer a large-seeming discount, even while earning his usual percentage markup over cost. Although these brands seemingly offer the retailer a large margin, in fact they end up by selling at the usual margin. The phony big discount from an inordinately high list price apparently works effectively with certain kinds of customers. This method of pricing is therefore found in areas where such customers do their shopping.

(4) Currying favor with retailer's salesmen. As explained, retail salesman can often switch a customer from the brand in which he had greatest initial interest to some other brand. In other words, they exert far greater influence upon customer brand selection than both national and local advertising combined; it is widely agreed that good salesmen can offset a very substantial price advantage for one brand by derogating its quality. Under these circumstances, distributors are most anxious to gain their support. Distributors are also extremely anxious to avoid and offset any favoritism that dealer's salesmen might feel for a competitive brand.

There are many ways to win the support of a salesman, but their effectiveness differs widely from person to person. Some salesmen apparently respond exclusively to short-range profit motives and will push the brand that gives them largest dollar commission during that week. These salesmen must be "bought," and the spiff is intended for this type. Many salesmen, even while they take spiffs, cannot be "bought"—they must be sold on the merchandise. These salesmen will not push a set with which past customers have had trouble or that is clearly overpriced or that alienates the customer for any other reason. Once assured that they would not be doing the customer any harm, however, they usually try to influence customers to buy the brand and model that gives them the highest commission or spiff or recognition from their employer.

Beyond their regard for money in the current pay envelope and for avoiding customer ill will, retail salesmen allegedly show favoritism for purely personal reasons. That is, they sometimes try to help out a particular salesman for whom they have a fondness or close personal friendship. They may develop a conviction that one brand is better than another and be motivated to sell what they regard as the best brand on the ground of merit alone. With these kinds of retail salesmen, it is imperative for the distributor to establish cordial relations. He must arrange either personally or through his own salesmen to develop close personal ties, perform favors, "educate" them to the special features and strength of the product and the manufacturer, and if possible create a feeling of obligation or affection that will cause them to favor his brand over others. To achieve these objectives, the distributor must allocate considerably more of his salesmen's time to sales activities than is required to simply take orders and to discuss changes in product, price and availability.

CONSUMER-ORIENTED ACTIVITIES OF MAJOR APPLIANCE DISTRIBUTORS

The discussion up to this point has covered only those distributor activities which directly affect retailers. These certainly are the most costly and the most significant (from their standpoint and from the standpoint of the manufacturer) activities in which they engage. Nevertheless, distributors of major appliances routinely go over the heads of their dealers in an effort to "pre-sell" to potential customers. It is appropriate to investigate why dealers are not left to do this on their own, and to describe the measures by which distributors try to create demand among ultimate consumers for their brand.

The distributor helps to create consumer demand mainly because he is dissatisfied with the way that most dealers perform this task. He regards the average dealer as incapable of and unwilling to use the available instruments for customer persuasion. He is concerned because the success of his own business depends upon their performance.

It is common to find that businessmen at one stage of an industry have a low regard for those to whom they sell and from whom they buy.[4] Under these circumstances, they usually help out their customers in one way or another. In certain lines of business, the help extended by businessmen to their customers consists of almost "running their customers' business." In the case of major appliance distribution, the help given rarely reaches such proportions. However, the methods are numerous and include direct newspaper advertising,

[4] Some distributors consider the sales promotion activities of the manufacturer to be quite ineffectual. They feel obliged to do some of the manufacturer's job themselves. One major appliance distributor, who was speaking primarily about television sets, asserted that this organization had taught the manufacturer a great deal and had helped him in many ways to do a better job of national advertising and merchandising.

the most common and most costly aid; actual selling effort on the retailers' premises; and preparation of advertising copy for newspaper or circulars. In addition to these, the distributor, as explained, creates consumer demand indirectly by helping to train dealer salesmen, to motivate them and to educate them on the merits of his line and the weakness of competitive lines.

Activities of distributors related to product service. Television set distributors are involved in the servicing of sets in several ways: first, they maintain inventories of repair parts required by dealers, independent servicemen and their own service departments. This activity is absolutely essential if the manufacturer is to maintain customer acceptance for his product and the support of servicemen. In addition, it generally produces revenue for the distributor beyond the cost of operating the service department.

Second, the major appliance distributor is largely responsible for carrying out the terms of the manufacturer's warranty agreement. In the usual case, he adds a specific sum, fixed by the manufacturer, to the price he charges the dealer to cover his warranty cost. Even if the receiver is basically defective and it would be uneconomical to repair it, the distributor will not return it to the factory for replacement. Distributors apparently spend much less to effectuate the warranty than the amount they charge to do so, because tube failures have declined sharply in recent years.

Third, the distributor is at least partly responsible for informing and training local independent servicemen in the best methods of repairing current models of its sets. This responsibility involves the dissemination of "schematics" and detailed instructions; occasionally, the distributor will conduct clinics for the purpose of training or retraining local servicemen. Ordinarily, the factory provides the printed material that must be distributed to local servicemen and will supply personnel to give servicemen instruction.

It appears that most manufacturers of television sets were slow to realize that servicemen exerted a powerful influence on consumer brand preferences, and even on the brands and models of sets that retailers urged customers to buy. Several manufacturers became directly engaged in servicing sets for a profit and aroused fierce antagonisms and strong countermeasures among independent servicemen. There is unanimous agreement that the servicemen were able to exert a pronounced effect on the sales of brands to which they were opposed. Other manufacturers set up systems of authorized or approved servicemen and aroused misunderstanding and resentment, with resultant opposition from independent servicemen and a decline in sales. Product service in the industry has an extremely involved history, and almost every firm's experience constitutes a fascinating illustration of misunderstanding, conflict and frustration.

At the present time, the servicing of television sets is handled mainly in the manner described below. This description is of one specific company but applies to most set producers in 1963.

Responsibility for service is clearly lodged with the distributor, even though the manufacturer and retailer do become involved in service also. Every distributor has an appliance service manager and an electronics specialist. In each of these departments, there are one or two "bench men" who repair sets on the distributor's premises; on the average, a distributor will have six service people. The appliance service manager and electronics specialist will be men of high quality who will have been trained by the parent corporation.

Each distributor's territory is divided into sections; in each section, the distributor selects a "servicing dealer." This person is the "authorized servicing dealer" in his area. He is brought into the distributor's shop and trained in the servicing of that company's sets. Also, these authorized dealers are required to attend meetings held throughout the year. Part of their training consists of a fairly intensive course extending over a three-week period at night.

The manner in which the distributor performs his servicing functions within the foregoing system can best be explained by a hypothetical illustration. Mrs. Jones bought a set from the Ace Appliance Company, and it stopped working two weeks after purchase. She called Ace, who in the overwhelming majority of cases would not be the authorized serviceman for that area. Ace then called the distributor. A girl on the switchboard who received this call from Ace immediately identified the area in which the consumer was located and the authorized serviceman for that area. She then called the authorized serviceman, who called on Mrs. Jones and repaired the set. He billed the distributor, basing his charges on a prearranged schedule. If the serviceman could not make the repair because the set was basically defective, he would report this to the distributor. The distributor would then send his own man to examine the set—generally accompanied by the authorized serviceman. If the set could not be repaired, it would be replaced by the distributor—who would *not* make any claim on the manufacturer for reimbursement.

Chapter VII

DISTRIBUTIVE ACTIVITIES
OF DEALERS

To gain a full picture of any transaction or relationship, it is necessary to understand both participants' viewpoints. Accordingly, this chapter will help to flesh out the picture of the distributor's activities as it describes the distributive activities of television set retailers.[1]

The retailer of television sets (almost universally called a "dealer" in this trade) is a seller. As such, he faces essentially the same problems and performs the same functions as the major appliance distributor. Consequently, most of the television set dealer's functions can be described very briefly. Particular emphasis will be attached in the following discussion to those respects in which dealers differ from distributors. Most of the following discussion is organized around the distinction between internal and external distribution. Other topics that do not fit comfortably within this structure are discussed mainly at the end of the chapter.

Structure of Television Set Retailing

According to the best figures available, there were over 72,000 retail outlets that sold new television sets in April 1962. This total

[1] In addition to the data collected by personal interviews with television set retailers, members of the trade press, a trade association representing appliance dealers, and officers of a large cooperative buying group, this chapter draws heavily upon several retail market studies conducted under my direction. One such market study was made in New Orleans, Louisiana, during 1960–61, another was made in Freeport, N.Y., mainly during 1962 and a third was made in Rockville Centre, N.Y., during 1961–62. Detailed results of the individual market studies will be published separately. Some of the findings will be presented here, with grateful acknowledgment to Sperry & Hutchinson, whose research grant made those studies possible, and to Mr. Sidney Bloom, whose dogged efforts and ingenuity made them so illuminating.

may understate somewhat the number of television outlets, for it is very difficult to get adequate representation of the tiny and exotic forms of retailing—and there is little interest in doing so.

There apparently have been two cycles in the number of retailers selling television sets. The number of outlets increased very rapidly after the war as manufacturers expanded their output of sets. The number increased further as television spread to new areas, after the ban on new television transmitters was removed in 1954. Sometime in the early 1950s, the number of television outlets started to decline, possibly reflecting the withdrawal of many small appliance dealers under the pressure of competition from discount houses. The sharp drop in the number of manufacturers of television sets may have contributed to this decline, also. (A national study places the beginning of the decline in 1955; a highly detailed study of Kalamazoo, Michigan, by *Mart* magazine showed the decline started there in 1951.) The decline in numbers of outlets apparently continued until about 1959.

The number of retail stores selling television sets increased again in about 1960. Between that year and 1962, the increase amounted to over 25 percent and is expected to carry forward for several years more. Some people in the industry believe that television sets are gradually turning into a "traffic appliance" (bought on impulse, rather than after long and careful deliberation) and are therefore finding their way into retail stores that did not carry them before. An examination of the kinds of outlets that have increased in numbers show them to be mainly either very small or very large stores; in the miscellaneous category, consisting to a large extent of television repair shops and credit jewelers; and located in metropolitan centers. Strangely, the North Central States did not share in the increase, which occurred in all other regions of the nation. (See Tables 13–16)

An enormous variety of retail stores have sold television sets since the end of the war. Beauty parlors, gas stations, drug stores, etc.—indeed, any retailer who could persuade the local distributor to give him some sets for sale—went into the retail television set business when the industry was in its infancy. These exotic types of dealers disappeared rather quickly. However, dealers still vary greatly in the companion lines of products they carry.

Table 13 indicates the product classification of retailers that sold sets in April 1960, 1961 and 1962. As that table indicates, the largest single group consists of household appliance and radio-television stores. The second largest category is termed "other" and is said to consist primarily of shops operated by television servicemen and credit jewelers. Furniture stores are very important outlets and are growing in importance.

TABLE 13
OUTLETS CLASSIFIED BY PRODUCT CATEGORY, 1960, 1961 AND 1962

Type of outlet	1960	1961	1962
Furniture stores	14,370	15,590	16,950
Household appliance stores	10,620	14,290	17,290
Radio and television stores	10,710	7,800	9,280
Department and other general merchandise stores	5,700	5,850	5,140
Other	15,720	21,440	23,400
Total	57,120	64,970	72,060

SOURCE: Audits and Surveys, Inc. These data apply to the month of April in each year.

Tables 14, 15 and 16 show the number of retail television outlets in the years 1960–62 classified by sales size, geographic region and size of community. An analysis of the changing number of retailers, so classified, yields clues to the forces behind the recent expansion in the number of retail outlets selling sets.

TABLE 14
OUTLETS CLASSIFIED BY ANNUAL SALES VOLUME, 1960, 1961 AND 1962

Breakdown by Annual Sales Volume (all products)	1960	1961	1962
Under $30,000	9,330	12,994	15,565
$30,000–100,000	22,200	20,790	26,950
$100,000 and over	25,590	31,186	29,545
Total	57,120	64,970	72,060

Data are unfortunately lacking that classify television outlets by merchandising approach. We therefore do not know with any accuracy the proportion of outlets of each type, size, region or size of community that are discount houses or that are located in suburban shopping centers.

TABLE 15
LOCATION OF OUTLETS ACCORDING TO REGION, 1960, 1961 AND 1962

Breakdown by U.S. Census Region	1960	1961	1962
Northeast	8,970	11,695	13,475
North Central	20,400	18,841	22,555
South	21,120	25,338	24,861
West	6,630	9,096	11,169
Total	57,120	64,970	72,060

TABLE 16
LOCATION OF OUTLETS CLASSIFIED BY CITY SIZE, 1960, 1961 AND 1962

Breakdown by Number of Outlets by City Size	1960	1961	1962
Metropolitan over one million	13,590	16,892	20,393
Metropolitan under one million	17,010	20,790	23,060
Nonmetropolitan, Urban	13,500	16,243	14,987
Nonmetropolitan, Rural	13,020	11,045	13,620
Total	57,120	64,970	72,060

It is now a cliché to state that retailing is passing through a revolution. The major changes taking place in retailing are so numerous that one does not know to which revolution reference is being made. Since the Second World War, the trades that carry television sets have undergone the following major changes: (1) application of self-selection and self-service; (2) a sharp decline in the number of small stores and a more-than-compensating rise in chains; (3) a growth in the discount house and of the discount-house chain, with a dramatic adaptation on the part of many department stores; (4) a move of large retail units to suburbs, especially into shopping centers; (5) the growth of retailer buying cooperatives; and (6) the decline of the one-price system, with the delegation of price-discretion (within limits) to some salesmen. Most of these changes have affected the amount and the type of service that appliance dealers provide for their customers, and the activities that customers perform for themselves.

The Consumer and the Nature of Retailing

The foregoing section described the various types of retailers engaged in the sale of television sets and listed the dramatic changes that are taking place in retailing. One major cause for the emergence of different types of retail firms and for the ferment in retailing is the growing recognition by businessmen that major differences exist among customers. (These differences probably are not new in themselves.) Customers seek different product features and want dissimilar kinds of service. In the retailing of such things as clothing, drugs, appliances and hardware, consumers were offered essentially the same blend of service at essentially the same price until relatively recently. The customer who placed overriding emphasis upon low price had no place to go. He would have been willing to forego such niceties as spacious and attractive premises, convenient locations, ample parking, numerous and attentive salesmen and speedy delivery service in order to effect a saving. But no retail institution met his desires. Other customers place chief emphasis upon pleasant surroundings when they purchase, attentive and informative salesmen, iron-clad guarantees, etc. Clearly, the same kinds of shops do not meet the needs and desires and whims of these dissimilar types of customers. Accordingly, new types of retailers—in particular the "mass" or "volume" retailer, now called the "discount house"—emerged. This type of retailer essentially applies to the sale of such things as appliances and clothing the same principles that had been applied for decades to the sale of food products in supermarkets.

We can hypothesize, then, that the distributive activities of appliance dealers represent adaptations to the desires and behavior of their customers. Similarly, distributors of major appliances pick their hours of operation, methods of display, salesmen, etc. on the basis of the number, location, and expressed or implied preferences and actions of retailers. To understand why and how appliance dealers do the things they do, one must study the ultimate consumer and determine how the retailer sees him.

Every appliance dealer does business with consumers that vary greatly—even though customers of a given type tend to be attracted to a particular type of retail outlet. At one extreme, there is a substantial and apparently growing class of consumers that retailers and their salesmen regard as "the enemy." These are aggressive and well-informed but dishonest (at least as buyers) customers who consider a major purchase a challenge to outsmart the retailer. They place an unreasonably high value on tiny monetary savings, because for them it is a matter of pride and principle to make purchases at the lowest possible price. These consumers are found mainly in large cities. They have no store loyalty or personal friendship with a retailer or salesman and buy wherever they can "get the best deal." The notion that the dealer is "entitled" to make a profit is foreign to their thinking; if they were able to buy an appliance below the dealer's actual cost, they would ordinarily boast of it rather than feel compassion for the dealer.

At the opposite extreme are consumers that salesman call "gentlemen." These customers feel and show genuine concern for the retailer's interests. They would not beat down a price even if they believed that they could. These consumers regard retailers as basically honest and trust their advice almost completely.

Another important type of consumer, as viewed by appliance dealers and their salesmen, is the "lamb." "Lambs" are very uninformed and unsophisticated buyers; moreover, they are gullible and malleable. Ordinarily they are anxious to own the item for which they are shopping and welcome any advice and sales arguments that facilitate their purchase.

As indicated, every salesman meets all types of customers, though "the enemy" gravitates to the discount houses and appliance chains; he comes out in greatest numbers when those stores are runnning special promotions. "Gentlemen" and "lambs" are found in all kinds of retail stores. The former tend mainly to patronize local shops and become acquainted, if not friendly with the retailer and some of his salesmen. "Lambs" are attracted to stores that claim to offer bargains.

Appliance salesmen who have had numerous contacts with "the enemy" tend to become wary. Until they have conducted a reconnaissance to form an estimate of "the enemy's" intentions and capabilities, they withhold their fire. Once they find an "enemy," most appliance salesmen expect and offer no quarter. All tactics are considered fair in what they regard as a no-holds-barred struggle—on both sides. Whatever qualms of conscience they might have felt if they used shady tactics with "gentlemen" never arise. They regard their behavior as more than justified—indeed, they consider it necessary for survival—by the nature of the enemy they face.

It is not clear whether all appliance salesmen's behavior is very different when they meet a "lamb" or a "gentleman." Doubtless there are substantial differences among salesmen in this regard, with many matching customer consideration, if it does not involve a *large* financial sacrifice. On the other hand, one finds some who seem to be motivated solely by short-term gain and try to get their customer's name on a contract by any device that might work, regardless of the customer's demeanor.

It is impossible to explain the low ethical standards one finds among metropolitan salesmen of appliances unless one recognizes the aggressiveness and unscrupulousness of many consumers. Consumer avarice certainly reinforces sellers' deceitfulness, though it does not excuse it. The aggressiveness and avarice of many consumers can be explained in large measure by the unenviable position they occupy when they come to the market place. They confront an enormous variety of similar items among which they must choose. The most important attributes of the product are far too technical for them to appraise. Many of them, moreover, have lost any personal ties with the retailer, for more and more of them buy from department stores or large chains which are impersonal and characterized by rapid turnover of personnel. Moreover, their purchase involves a sizable outlay, so that the penalties of a mistaken choice are substantial. Then, too, every consumer gets to meet the "sharp salesman" who deals loosely with the truth and, finding a trusting consumer, will take advantage of him outrageously. From this strange mixture of dependence, mistrust, insecurity, feelings of inadequacy, and strain because of the large expenditure, comes strange and varied consumer behavior. And that is precisely what one finds in the market for major appliances. Consumers vary at least as much as the stores in which they buy and the salesmen with whom they deal.

Customers have been divided into three broad types on the basis of their approach to the purchase situation and the way they relate to retailers. Within these broad classes of customers are many and very important differences to which skilled retailers are sensitive. Customers differ in income, in education and in the number and condition of their present sets. Some are interested in auxiliary equipment (like hi-fi or stereo), some are brand loyal, some are regular customers, etc. Many retailers try to identify the types of customers they attract and study how best to serve them, as well as other types. No retailer meets only one type. The adaptable retailer is able to retain the patronage of many classes of customers, even while concentrating his efforts on certain selected types.

Analysis of Dealers' Costs

Even more than major appliance distributors, dealers in television sets handle a very large number of diverse products. Also, they are far less rigidly compartmentalized than distributors, so that their cost records generally apply to a wide variety of items. As a result, any data that purport to describe costs incurred by dealers in conjunction with the sales of television sets necessarily represent a rough guess.

Compilations of appliance dealer costs are made periodically by the chief trade association composed of appliance dealers—namely, the National Appliance and Radio Dealers Association (NARDA). These cost figures apply to all items carried by the dealers rather than to television sets alone. They have only slight value as a measure of the expenses actually incurred by dealers to distribute sets, for such a measure would require elaborate time and motion studies that cover a wide variety of dissimilar retail establishments—and no such studies have been conducted. They are of chief interest in what they show or imply about the *composition* of an appliance dealer's costs and the *direction* in which the individual items have changed in recent years. The best available data on appliance dealers' costs are presented in Tables 17 and 18.

Of even greater interest, perhaps, than the foregoing data is an understanding of what appliance dealers believe their costs to be. As is explained later, few appliance dealers are "fact men." They do not keep exhaustive records; the records they do keep are treated with extraordinary neglect. A small group of dealers were interviewed to learn what their impressions were of the costs of selling sets. Mainly

TABLE 17
COSTS OF APPLIANCE AND RADIO DEALERS, 1947–59
(National Averages, in Percentage)

Line	Item	1959	1958	1957	1956	1955	1954	1953	1952	1951	1950	1949	1948	1947
1.	Net sales (merchandise plus service)	100.0	100.0	100.0	100.0	100.0	100.0	100.0	100.0	100.0	100.0	100.0	100.0	100.0
1-a.	Net sales (merchandise only)	100.0	100.0	100.0	100.0	100.0	100.0	100.0	100.0	100.0	100.0	100.0	100.0	100.0
2.	Cost of goods sold (merchandise plus service)[1]	64.6	64.5	66.1	67.7	65.7	66.0	67.1	68.0	68.8	69.2	67.2	68.7	67.0
2-a.	Cost of goods sold (merchandise only)	70.4	69.7	70.4	69.3	68.4	68.8	70.2	69.8	70.3	69.7	68.8	70.2	67.8
3.	Gross margin (merchandise plus service) (Line 1 minus Line 2)	35.4	35.5	33.9	32.3	34.3	34.0	32.9	32.0	31.2	30.8	32.8	31.2	33.0
3-a.	Gross margin (merchandise only) (Line 1-a minus Line 2-a)	29.6	30.3	29.6	30.7	31.6	31.2	29.8	30.2	29.7	30.3	31.2	29.8	32.2
4.	Total operating costs (A through E below)	34.4	34.4	32.3	31.1	30.9	31.4	30.6	28.8	28.3	24.8	27.6	26.7	26.2
	A. Administrative	24.8	24.4	23.1	22.1	22.2	22.3	21.2	20.6	20.4	16.9	19.1	18.6	18.2
	(1) Owners and executive remuneration	3.3	3.1	3.5	3.7	3.2	3.8	3.4	3.6	4.1	3.6	3.5	3.5	NS[2]
	(2) Office salaries	3.2	2.6	2.7	2.8	2.4	2.2	2.2	2.1	1.6	1.5	2.0	1.8	NS[2]
	(3) Salesmen's pay	6.6	7.1	6.4	6.0	7.2	6.0	5.6	5.7	5.6	4.8	5.5	5.5	4.8
	(4) Servicemen's wages and expenses	7.4	7.0	6.5	5.5	5.2	5.5	6.0	5.1	5.7	4.5	4.7	4.7	4.1
	(5) Vehicle expense	2.1	2.5	2.4	2.5	2.7	2.9	2.4	2.4	1.8	1.4	1.7	1.7	NS[2]
	(6) Other administrative expense	2.2	2.1	1.6	1.6	1.5	1.9	1.6	1.7	1.6	1.1	1.7	1.4	NS[2]
	B. Occupancy expense	2.5	2.5	2.9	2.6	2.8	2.9	2.5	2.5	2.5	2.6	2.6	2.8	3.0
	C. Advertising expense	2.8	2.8	2.4	2.6	2.5	2.5	2.5	2.6	2.7	2.2	2.5	2.6	2.1
	D. Bad debt losses	0.6	0.7	0.6	0.4	0.4	0.3	0.4	0.2	0.1	0.3	0.2	0.2	0.2
	E. All other expenses	3.7	4.0	3.3	3.4	3.0	3.4	4.0	2.9	2.6	2.8	3.2	2.5	2.7
5.	Net operating profit[3] (Line 3 minus Line 4)	1.0	1.1	1.6	1.2	3.4	2.6	2.3	3.2	2.9	6.0	5.2	4.6	6.8

[1] Does not include Servicemen's wages and expenses.
[2] NS means not segregated.
[3] This is Net operating profit after all taxes. Other income is not considered in this schedule.

SOURCE: Compiled by NARDA (National Appliance and Radio Dealers Association) and published in Mart magazine, July, 1963.

the questions asked revolved around a comparison of a dealer's costs for television set sales with cost of other items carried. Although hardly conclusive, the results of these interviews suggest that the dealer's costs to sell television sets, as he perceives them, are not significantly different from the average for all appliances carried.

TABLE 18
OPERATING COSTS OF A SMALL CHAIN OF TELEVISION SET DEALERS, 1962

	Percentage
Gross margin	21.0
Total operating costs	18.8
Labor	7.0
Occupancy costs	2.5
Advertising (net)	2.5
Service	1.2
Delivery	.8
Miscellaneous	4.8
Net profit	2.2

Internal Distribution Activities of Dealers

One class of internal distribution activities must be distinguished from all the rest: these are termed "physical distribution" and concern the movement and storage of merchandise. They differ from other types of distribution activities, for they are largely dictated by the state of technology and available resources and institutions. Indeed, they may be regarded as the "production side" of distributing enterprises. The other internal distribution activities consist mainly of planning and decision-making by top management. In these activities such circumstances as the severity of competition, rivals' advertising and pricing policies, the level of consumer demand, etc, are of chief concern to the business executive.

PHYSICAL DISTRIBUTION

In the retailing of bulky consumer products one finds a growing tendency to separate the sale from the possession of merchandise. That is, retailers increasingly sell merchandise that they do not have in stock. The merchandise is delivered from the retailer's supplier directly to the customer's premises, thereby reducing the amount of product handling and transportation. In addition, the chance of damaging merchandise in transit is lowered, further reducing cost and contributing substantially to customer satisfaction. Despite this trend, an important part of the average television set dealer's costs go to cover transportation and storage expenses. This amounts to about three percent of sales. Interestingly, most dealers' costs apparently have not been reduced by direct shipment from the distributor's warehouse. Distributors ordinarily do not charge dealers for transportation to their premises; and the dealer generally pays a lower transportation charge to an independent trucker than the distributor would charge him for delivery from the warehouse. Apparently, if he takes delivery, the costs to the dealer of storage, depreciation, interest, and the like are offset, or more than offset, by the savings he makes on delivery cost.

As is to be expected, this item of a dealer's cost has been profoundly affected by the growing popularity of portable sets, which usually are transported by consumers from the retailer's premises. (Like other estimates presented earlier and subsequently, these figures suffer greatly from being hopelessly interrelated with the costs of handling the many other kinds of items sold by dealers that sell television sets. They should be regarded as what the average dealer believes his transportation costs to be, rather than what they actually are.)

As already implied, the storage costs incurred by television set dealers depend heavily upon their mode of operation. Those that can obtain direct delivery from the distributor to the customer have nominal storage costs; those chains that operate large warehouses have larger, but still quite small, storage costs. The heaviest storage costs are borne by small independent retailers who must accept merchandise and hold it until purchased by their customers. Dealers located in small cities and towns are usually in this class. Although it is more folly than bravery to attempt to estimate their storage costs, they surely average well below one-half percent of the retailer's total revenue from television set sales.

The development of the cooperative buyer group has helped the medium-size metropolitan appliance dealer to reduce his transportation and storage costs. As their name implies, these groups are cooperatives that are owned and controlled by a group of independent dealers. They buy in quantity and operate local warehouses, from which they make delivery directly to consumers. In short, they manage the physical distribution activities of appliance dealers just as if they were members of a chain, securing essentially chain-store quantity discounts for their members.

INTERNAL MANAGEMENT ACTIVITIES

Many manufacturers and distributors sneer when questions are raised about the internal management of appliance dealers. In effect, they say that most dealers either do not manage at all or they only mismanage. The retailer in the appliance business, as in many others, is regarded as a primitive type of business executive by those who sell through him. With the growth of large chains of appliance stores, the emergence of the huge discount-house operation and the professionally managed cooperative buying group, there has been substantial improvement in the caliber of management in certain spheres of retailing. It remains low compared to what one finds in manufacturing and even in appliance distribution. Some of the largest and most successful appliance chains and discount houses are dominated by a single individual; these are run on a "seat-of-the-pants" basis by one man possessing great intelligence and energy. They succeed despite a basic lack of organizational skills and managerial procedures. (Perhaps these skills and procedures are most vital when firms are either very large or are run by non-owner managers with limited authority or by persons of modest ability.)

The foregoing remarks all add up to the conclusion that one finds only crude types of internal management among appliance dealers and in the case of the "momma and poppa" stores (those extremely small businesses in which the owner and his wife *are* the sales force) there is virtually no conscious management at all. Consequently, one cannot say much about the internal management activities of appliance dealers unless he discusses the few enterprises that are run on a businesslike basis. To do that is to speak about an unrepresentative segment of the retail appliance trade, however.

Skillful management and the utilization of refined business procedures would appear to have about as much value for retailers as for manufacturers and distributors. Most retailers may get by without them primarily because they compete with others who also do not employ them; but as professionalism is expanding among retailers, the nonprofessional is being forced out of business.

Forecasting and ordering. The forecasting and merchandise ordering activities of appliance dealers are enmeshed in the process usually known as "inventory management." For most small appliance dealers the availability of credit is critically important in determining *how much* they order. The determination of *what particular models* to buy involves forecasting on the dealer's part—though his decision usually is vastly simplified by "special deals" on particular models. In short, for many retailers the problem of how much and what models to order is extremely simple. They order as much as their funds and credit will get from their distributors. Typically they buy most heavily the models that are being offered on a special promotion.

Their purchase decisions actually are more complicated than this. They must remain alert to the fact that certain models have proved to be "dogs" either mechanically or esthetically, judged by customer reactions. Also, they must take account of the buying patterns in their own neighborhoods, including the proportions in which customers buy portables as opposed to tables and consoles, etc. In addition, certain cabinet styles and colors are preferred, and the retailer can get into deep trouble if he ignores them. However, the average medium- and small-size appliance retailer is aware of these preferences from his direct contact with customers and his salesmen. Moreover, he is partly protected from injury due to mistaken ordering because of his considerable ability to influence his customers' choices—as is explained subsequently. Above all, his purchase decisions are influenced by the things that are selling. In its simplest form, he follows the rule of replacing what he has sold.

Of course, the large retail chain does have a set of procedures for keeping a record of sales and inventory, which is used for the purpose of determining how much and what to order. These methods of inventory control and sales analysis vary in minute detail, but essentially consist of daily records of the number and model of sets sold on each day in individual stores. As a rough rule, retailers reorder individual items they sell when their stocks run low—but each one interprets the rule somewhat differently.

One important factor that has improved the quality of sales forecasting by dealers has been the pressure exerted by the manufacturer to obtain accurate and speedy sales information. (The great damage to price stability resulting from gluts—even of isolated models—has made manufacturers anxious to prevent inventory errors.)

Selection of items to offer. Among the most critical decisions retailers make is what items to offer for sale. These decisions include from *what products* to carry (which represent a definition of the business in which the retailer will engage), to *which* and *how many brands* of each product to offer, to *which models* of each suppliers' line to carry in stock. Dealers that are superficially in the same line of business are found to differ upon a close inspection of the individual items they carry. In some cases the differences are substantial. Some will carry a very narrow line of television sets—both in number of brands and models—while others will offer many brands and include substantial numbers of elaborate and costly combination sets. Even greater differences exist in the companion lines they carry, with some featuring lines of phonograph records or sporting goods, while others do a substantial share of their business in automobile accessories or hi-fi. An appliance store is not homogeneous, by any means.

The offerings of a television dealer rarely reflect a basic decision about the line of business he is in. He is ready to try and generally is on the lookout for "good items." Some retailers of major appliances are prepared to go far afield from the core of their main offerings if they see an opportunity either to attract more traffic or to add an item that would yield a high margin of profit. When space becomes cramped, products may be dropped to make room for new ones, but ordinarily this is not done until the new item is given a trial on a limited scale.

Television dealers are visited by many vendors who hope to get a window on the market for their products. Often they offer the dealer strong inducements to carry their item—ranging from extremely high margins, to strong advertising aid, to sale on consignment. Most dealers try different items from time to time, and their offerings shift gradually in the process.

Most retailers are in an excellent position to experiment with shifts in their offerings at little cost and risk. Given the intense competition for retail exposure, suppliers generally are willing to assume the costs and risks of a trial. They operate on the principle subscribed to by many retailers that "the best way to sell something is to have it out where customers can see it." Since a dealer might try any of a large number of items at any time, any individual supplier who seeks a trial for his product has only a small chance of having it accepted unless his item is either novel or unusually profitable.

Selection of sources of merchandise. Even after a dealer has decided what products, brands and models to carry, he generally has some choice as to how to make his purchases. If he is a very large seller who can buy in truck or carloads, he might buy directly from the manufacturer. If he is a small or medium-size retailer, he generally could join a buying cooperative.

(1) The large TV dealer. We have already discussed "direct sales" to large retailers from the standpoint of the manufacturer and, to a lesser extent, of the distributor. How does the large retailer view "direct purchase"? As already indicated, the retailer is attracted to dealing directly with the factory mainly by the prospect of paying lower prices. To effect such savings, however, he generally is forced to "stretch" when he places orders if he is to earn the largest quantity discounts. Consequently, he increases his risks of loss through mistaken purchases, ties up funds (ordinarily limited even for large retailers) in inventory, and requires the maintenance of storage facilities. For the very largest retailers, the balance of these considerations generally is in favor of the direct purchase of television sets. Some large television dealers prefer to patronize the distributor for the reasons suggested, plus the desire for some of the services provided by the distributor—such as salesman training, special credit accommodation, advertising counsel and materials, and an opportunity to get "specials" when the distributor is overstocked.

Apart from the "real" factors that influence dealers' choices of sources to patronize, there is an emotional element that is readily apparent: like many consumers, dealers want to pay the lowest price possible "on principle" and as an end in itself. The lure of a lower invoice price—whatever the other costs that do not appear on the invoice—is more than many of them can resist.

(2) The small retailer. The "buying cooperative" is a venerable

institution in the food field. Although a relatively recent development in the major appliance business, its has grown rapidly. As the name implies, it is a cooperative organization formed for the purpose of buying merchandise on terms advantageous to its members. Often managed by officers who are themselves dealers (frequently without compensation), financed by modest initial investments by the members and liberal credit terms from suppliers (the largest cooperative requires a $15,000 investment), buying cooperatives often control sufficient volume to buy on the terms obtained by the largest chains. In addition, they will store merchandise at a central warehouse and deliver directly to the ultimate consumer. Also, they sometimes provide management guidance, some product and management training, and disseminate operating cost information among their members.

Buying cooperatives account for a small proportion of television set sales, albeit one that is growing. A large majority of small and medium-size television dealers make their purchases from distributors in the manner described in the preceding chapters. The buying cooperative represents a recent development that is not welcomed by either manufacturers or distributors of television sets. Traditional channels of distribution—manufacturers selling to distributors, who resell to retailers, who then sell to the ultimate consumer—are being eroded by both direct sales to large retailers and to cooperative organizations of smaller ones.

Appliance dealer pricing. Earlier discussions of the pricing activities of television set manufacturers and distributors made allusions to the pricing methods and attitudes of appliance dealers. Far more than is the case with manufacturers and distributors, dealers' pricing policies and methods are diverse. One might say—indeed, many people in the industry do—that retail appliance pricing is chaotic. It is not surprising that foreign visitors to the United States often ask, among their very first questions, "How does it happen that prices for the same or similar items sold on the same street vary so much?"

The answer to this question is to be found both in the thinking and behavior of appliance dealers and in the viewpoint and attitudes of customers. It takes two parties to make a price. The paradoxical pattern (or lack of pattern) in retail prices for television sets requires an analysis of both the buyer and seller.

As was described, one finds distinct types of appliance dealers and appliance customers; also, particular types of buyers tend to patronize particular dealer types. The matching up of a television set customer and dealer is mainly explainable by considerations of price and partly by the services that the dealer offers and the customer desires.

What different types of price behavior and thinking can be identified among appliance dealers? At one extreme is a shrinking group (already very small) of appliance dealers that ask for and get "full list" price. These dealers should not be confused with the larger group which starts by naming list price and ends up by maiming it. These dealers cut price at the first sign of customer resistance. Appliance dealers that charge list price can be divided, in turn, into a few subgroups. One group consists of small-town dealers who may be the only dealer in their area; a second group represents high-prestige and "plush service" outlets, mainly in medium-size and small cities. The third group includes dealers who have an exclusive franchise in their area, which they understand will be withdrawn if they depart from list price.

Most of the customers who patronize these list-price dealers also represent distinct types. One group has close personal ties to the dealer; often he himself sells something to the appliance dealer at "full list" price. A second group is made up of extremely store-loyal shoppers. They ordinarily identify themselves with the store, take pride in being recognized by name and treated as a "friend" of the store owners. A third group relishes lavish attention and enjoys having others know what they are "regular shoppers" at a "prestige" store.

At the opposite extreme from the "full list" dealer is the discount house. This type of dealer owes his name and existence to selling "off list." He bids for patronage with cryptic advertisements or signs in his windows saying, "X percent off." The customer completes the sentence with the words "list price." Discount houses have diverse pricing policies; some give far bigger discounts than others; almost all of them give far larger discounts on some items than on others, and at some times than at others. Consequently, any brief summary of the way that discount houses establish price for television sets is necessarily incomplete. However, some general observations will help to explain their pricing methods in broad outline.

Perhaps the most important feature of a discount house's pricing methods to be identified is whether or not the salesmen have price discretion. In some discount house chains, the single price system is returning. It had become almost routine for senior salesmen selling major appliances in chains to be given price discretion, allowing them to vary price within designated limits. With the growing size and geographic dispersion of appliance and discount house chains top management is becoming more remote from the sales floor. Not knowing their salesmen, some chains apparently are beginning to operate on a one-price basis. Most discount houses, on the other hand, still permit their salesmen to negotiate over price—or ask them to call over a member of top management or a senior salesman when they "cannot get together on price" with a customer.

Even though there generally is some negotiation over the price of major appliances in most discount houses, they do mark their merchandise and also advertise prices on some of their promotional items. What policies underlie their "marked prices"?

Discount houses almost always will have some promotional offerings which are designed to build store traffic. When their promotional items are television sets, these will ordinarily carry a price that is low in absolute size. For example, a discount chain may offer a portable set with a 17-inch screen, brand unnamed, for $87. That kind of offering is designed to attract the attention of persons who have only a slight intention of purchasing a set. The specific $87 price (rather than $85 or $92) in turn is to be explained by both the dealer's goals and the manufacturer's or distributor's initiative. Commonly the dealer will decide in planning a promotion what would be a strong and feasible attention-attracting offering. It might then ask various sources if they could provide merchandise to meet those requirements. Conversely, manufacturers and distributors know that large retail chains and discount house chains are eager for "specials" and items that they might feature. Consequently when they are hurting for volume or are overstocked with certain models, they often seek out a large chain and offer it the merchandise. They prefer to liquidate overstocks through a single outlet for reasons of economy, as well as to minimize possible complications under the Robinson-Patman Act.

Most appliance dealers' pricing policies lie between the two extremes described. Few seek full list price on any of their models, and most do run promotions of some type. Their discounts are likely to be roughly half as great as those offered by the most aggressive discount houses. As distributors suggest minimum prices, retailers of major appliances increasingly set the suggested minimum and stick to it. The sales of the so-called "intermediate type of dealer" are composed overwhelmingly of "regular" merchandise, while those of discount houses typically are composed largely of "special" merchandise—sets bought on "deals" of one kind or another, or exclusive models.

When these three main types of dealer are combined in a single market, one finds price confusion, if not chaos. A store in any of the three categories listed will itself charge higher margins on its sets at some times than at others. Almost all dealers run sales and cut margins substantially at such times. And, when not running sales, they will often have a few promotional items. Moreover, they routinely charge higher margins on certain models than on others, varying with manufacturers' list prices or distributors' suggested minimums. The diversity within any single dealer is multiplied enormously when one combines the offerings of different types of dealer. A dealer would experience great difficulty in comparing his prices with those of his rivals because it would be necessary to process such a huge flood of data. The typical consumer has even greater difficulty in comparing prices charged by individual stores, unless they have narrowed down their choice to one or two models. Both dealers and consumers operate on the basis of general impressions, and it is difficult to find a substitute for them that is more valid.

Manufacturers have become increasingly "price shy" in the television set industry. Increasingly, they decline to exercise as much power over price as they had and as they still could, if they desired. Some manufacturers establish no list prices; others establish a list on fewer items. Most of the suggested list prices or minimum prices are being set by distributors these days. Many retailers depart from them, which indicates that they exercise consderable power over price.

Advertising by appliance dealers. Only a small proportion of all appliance dealers advertise regularly and on a significant scale. Apparently most believe that they are known to a large proportion of their potential customers without special and costly communication efforts, or they believe that advertising would not be worth its cost to them, or they would like to advertise but lack the funds to do so.

Whatever their reasons, their communications mainly consist of window banners and displays.

Even the largest retailers of appliances include few regular advertisers. Large appliance chains advertise quite heavily when they run special promotions—which is most of the time, for some of them. But even these will permit weeks to pass without a newspaper spread from time to time. Department stores advertise regularly but only very infrequently do they feature television sets. As a rough general rule, department stores advertise sets either when the *full* cost of the advertisement is borne by the manufacturer and distributor, generally under the co-op program, or when they are able to offer a very special price promotion, or when both conditions obtain. Their eligibility for co-op funds at such times depends upon whether the distributor or manufacturer (depending upon the channels through which they buy) endorses the price promotion and hopes to move large amounts of merchandise. Usually advertising monies will be discussed explicitly when a large department store or appliance chain orders large quantities of merchandise with the expressed intention of running a big and widely publicized sale. Discount houses increasingly advertise, and television sets are quite frequently among the items they feature.

Space considerations do not permit an extended treatment of what is essentially a technical and specialized subject. Therefore we shall merely list the salient points.

1. Advertising by appliance dealers is overwhelmingly done in newspapers. Radio and television are used very little and account for only a fraction—less than 20 percent—of the total outlays by appliance dealers for advertising. Dealers will sometimes advertise in circulars.

2. Advertising by retailers of appliances stress price appeals predominantly. Manufacturers therefore have mixed feelings about dealer advertising, since their stress on price tends to offset manufacturer and distributor advertising which emphasizes quality and product features.

3. Some large appliance dealers operate an advertising department of their own. A few have even established advertising agencies which handle the advertising work of the one retail chain. These agencies are essentially supported by the commissions they receive from the media.

Distributive Activities of Dealers

4. Until fairly recently all newspapers had different rates for national (manufacturer and distributor) and local advertising. Local advertisers paid little more than half the national rate, giving manufacturers a strong incentive to establish co-op advertising programs that allowed them to buy advertising indirectly at low local rates. The gap between local and national rates is narrowing and in a few cases has been eliminated altogether.

5. The advertising rates of many newspapers are nonstandard. Individual retailers are able to negotiate special deals—generally large-quantity rates—that are well below the "regular" rates. Some newspapers are notorious for charging advertisers different rates and for billing dealers at a much higher rate than they actually pay.

6. By various subterfuges, including the foregoing, some dealers have been able to overstate their outlays for advertising and thereby to tap co-op funds for larger contributions than the manufacturer and distributor intended to make. For some dealers, such profits on co-op advertising represent a large proportion of their total profits.

7. The proportion of local advertising cost borne by manufacturers and distributors has increased over the years. From the early division of costs, which was manufacturer, 25 percent; distributor, 25 percent; and dealer, 50 percent, it is now closer to retailer, 25 percent, and the balance split evenly between the manufacturer and the distributor.

8. Manufacturers try to influence retailer advertising and especially to prevent advertising of price cuts—which hurt other dealers that handle that manufacturer's line. They do so mainly in the requirements they set down for eligibility for co-op funds. However, retailers can advertise cut prices at their own expense when they are determined to run a "hot price promotion." Also, they sometimes are able to be reimbursed for advertising of cut-price offerings.

9. Manufacturers and distributors stand ready to provide most of the art work and copy themes for dealer advertising of television sets. Of course, dealers ordinarily will advertise many lines of product in the same advertisement and require advertising specialists to put together advertisements for a variety of products.

10. Increased concern by the Federal Trade Commission with co-op advertising programs—and especially their determination to insure equal availability of co-op funds—has turned those programs

back into advertising programs rather than ill-disguised price discounts.

11. The sums that large appliance dealers obtain from co-op funds are discussed most guardedly. The large dealers have the impression that special arrangements are being made all the time with other large dealers about advertising money and believe that some arrangements are far better than others. Suspicion of distributors and manufacturers on this score continues, despite an apparent marked change in actual behavior.

12. Advertising is critically important to the large appliance dealer. Most dealers feel that their business would fall off sharply if they were to stop all advertising for as little as a few weeks. One president of a suburban appliance chain said, "There is no such thing as enough advertising. Our survival depends on ads."

13. The dealer-owned advertising agency offers several benefits. Among the greatest are speed and flexibility. They can make changes in their program and take measures to counter competitors' advertising much more quickly through their own agency than through an outside agency.

14. Large appliance chains sometimes spend as much as 4 percent of sales for advertising—a very large proportion of their gross margin.

15. Apparently the feeling is growing among appliance dealers that the effectiveness of retail advertising is declining because there is so much of it. This fear causes some to shift their emphasis to merchandising programs and away from advertising.

16. Almost all dealers tend to measure the effectiveness of their advertising by the immediate impact on sales.

External Distribution Activities of Dealers

The television set dealer's chief outside contacts are with customers and his suppliers (distributors and manufacturers or both). His contacts with consumers take place chiefly through personal contacts on his premises either directly or indirectly through his salesmen.

PERSONAL SELLING

Apart from merchandise costs, which tower far above all others, the television retailer's main cost is his salesmen's salaries. (See Table

18) A salesman performs several distinct functions, though often concurrently, that should be distinguished to understand his contribution to the distribution process. First, he communicates product information and frequently demonstrates and displays merchandise in the process. Second, he is a persuader, and persuasion also mainly takes the form of communication. Third, he participates in record-keeping. Finally, he helps to manage merchandise, including the floor arrangement of merchandise, some movement from rear spaces to the sales floor and occasional participation in arranging window displays.

Communication of product information. Some distribution specialists would describe retail salesmen as purveyors of misinformation rather than as sources of information. This observation partly is a slur on the honesty of the average salesman when he has reason to believe that a fib (whether small, medium or large; white, grey or black) would mean the difference between a sale and a lost customer. It also attests to the very limited amount of product information that the salesman possesses and the dubious sources from which he draws it. Especially retail salesmen who sell a wide variety of technical products of varied brands, all of which change frequently, cannot keep informed about all the products they sell even if they have had some technical product training. For the usual kinds of people who are engaged in retail selling, the task is overwhelming. Consequently, salesmen of appliances tend to substitute glibness for solid fact. Most of them get by because of the even greater ignorance of the customer and their ability to deceive themselves (and most others) into believing that they really know what they are talking about.

The retail salesman's communication function has altered greatly in recent years. This change has affected the major appliance salesman almost as much as most others. Although self-service and self-selection date far back to the early Woolworth stores, if not before, arrangements for reducing the participation of the salesman in the purchase transaction have been so extended that they have created a new species of salesman–customer relationship. The salesman's communication function has been changed as customers have been brought in direct contact with merchandise. The merchandise itself, plus point-of-sale printed materials, packages, etc., communicate some of the product information formerly supplied by the salesman. (Sears-Roebuck, perhaps the largest seller of appliances in the United States, is an exception to these statements. Sears relies heavily on the considerable skills of its well-trained salesmen and assigns them a big role on the sales floor.)

Television set dealers vary widely in the communication duties they assign to their salesmen. Some relegate their salesmen to the role of the salesman in a food supermarket—to virtual nonexistence. At the opposite extreme, other appliance retailers assign a salesman to each customer as he enters the store who accompanies the customer as he inspects merchandise. Most retailers fall between these two extremes, displaying their merchandise so that customers can inspect it and narrow down the range of alternatives without assistance from a salesman. At some point, a salesman is summoned or volunteers his services.

Retail salesmen have been criticized very, very harshly by some retailing specialists on grounds of incompetence, low effort and limited intelligence. Some salesmen no doubt merit this harsh assessment. On the other hand, most of the retail salesmen of major appliances who were studied by the author over an extended period deserve the highest praise for skill, effort and intelligence. The proportions of salesmen that belong in these two opposing classes cannot be assessed reliably on the basis of available information. The author's investigations, which were intensive rather than extensive, suggest that talented appliance salesmen represent a large majority in large metropolitan centers, and particularly in the appliance chains. There does appear to be enormous variation in the caliber of individual salesmen, sometimes in the same store.

The retail salesman as a persuader. Although the retail television set salesman performs functions other than pure salesmanship, this function overshadows all the rest. The salesman judges himself and is judged by both his supervisors and his peers by his ability to make sales. Proprietors of retail shops are willing to forego almost any other shortcoming in a salesman in order to gain the services of someone who is a "good salesman." And there is unanimous agreement that some people are better salesmen of television sets than others. It is further agreed that the range of sales skills is extremely wide, with some salesmen able to outperform others consistently by a ratio of three or four to one over substantial periods of time.

A salesman is pretty much the same person when he is acting as a persuader as when he is the communicator of information. Indeed, the retail salesman provides information (combined with puffery allegation, falsehood, implication and innuendo) mainly in an effort to persuade. He also discusses product attributes when customers ask questions of him. The salesman uses the communication process mainly in order to persuade. He relies almost entirely upon words and gestures, combined with occasional demonstration of product, to achieve the result he desires. Consequently, persuasion and edification are inextricably intertwined, even though in intent and effect they are quite different. (One can raise serious questions about the "right" or "ethics" of any individual's persuading others to do things for the persuader's own interest, whereas the provision of accurate information about alternative products is clearly a valuable distribution function.)

Retail salesmen use many techniques to persuade customers to purchase a television set. These are common to retail salesmanship in virtually all trades. Beyond these, some sales techniques are employed primarily by sellers of major appliances that are intended to do more sell. They aim to sell a *particular item*. That item usually is not the one that the customer originally asked to see; he probably would not have purchased it if the salesman had not made a special effort to persuade him to do so. The nature of these sales tactics and a consideration of their potency and implications warrants close examination.

(1) The "bait and switch" stratagem. The appliance dealer generally sees his main objective—to make sales at a profit—as having two distinct stages: first, he must lure potential customers into his premises; second, he must induce them to make a purchase. In addition, he recognizes that his ability to prosper is profoundly affected by the nature of the items that he manages to sell. Some of his offerings yield him a much greater profit than others.

Retailers have long recognized that there is an no necessary connection between the item that is used to lure customers into the store and the items that they ultimately sell. On the contrary, the items that work best as lures for customers usually are poor profit-builders. Consequently, a strategy that is widely used by television set dealers is to offer items—and advertise them widely—that will attract customers to their store and then persuade the customer to buy other items that yield a greater profit. Retailers are also willing to settle for a partial success, wherein they sell both the item offered as a lure, plus unpromoted items which yield at least a reasonable profit. The retailer is prepared to sell the lure for a chance to employ his sales skills to persuade customers to buy items they had not intended to purchase on that shopping trip. This general sales tactic is widely known (and deplored) under the name of "bait and switch." Even some of the largest and most reputable retail establishments in the country employ it—and with success. In the sale of major appliances, even moderately talented salesmen are able to "switch" customers most of the time.

In its extreme form "bait and switch" involves "loss-leading"—actually offering lure items for less than the dealer's direct cost (whether defined to include only his payments for merchandise or those costs plus some of his operating expenses). The size of the lure can be effective even if it does not involve sales below cost; it need only be large enough to attract attention and draw traffic.

An intrinsic part of the tactic just described is "switching," which consists of diverting customers from their original intent and persuading them to buy something else or something in addition. In the usual case, the customer is persuaded to purchase a model or version of the product that offers the retailer a larger margin than the item he came to the store to examine.

"Switching" should not be confused with the related sales tactic of "trading-up." This tactic is planned for by the manufacturer at the time the line of products is designed for the market. Specifically, "stepping-up the consumer" consists of leading the customer from the model in the line in which he showed original interest to more costly models by pointing step-by-step to the features that he could obtain for "modest" added cost. (These added charges seem even more modest when expressed in terms of payments per month.) As explained earlier in Chapter III, each feature added to a set ordinarily commands a price that is very substantially above the added cost of the feature to the retailer (and to the distributor and manufacturer as well). Consequently, the manufacturer, and the various middlemen through whom he sells, have a financial inducement to "step-up" the customer to more expensive models. And, the number and magnitude of the "step-ups" as well as "switches" he engineers is a major measure of a salesman's skill.

This is not the proper place to make a detailed evaluation of these sales tactics. They can be evaluated readily on the basis of effectiveness. On that score they must be rated very high: Salesmen (with the conscious or unconscious collaboration of consumers) do succeed in "switching" or "trading-up" a very large proportion of their customers when they make the effort. No exact estimate of their number is possible, but the author would estimate that it exceeds 65 percent of television set sales at present—and it was even higher in previous years.

Evaluated briefly by its social effects, "bait-switch" selling is more puzzling than it may first appear. Although the salesman's motives clearly are not admirable, we must not overlook the benefits that might nevertheless result from this practice. Judged from the standpoint of consumers who seek merchandise at minimum *price* (which may mean high *cost* because it represents poor *value*); the "bait-switch" stratagem increases the supply of goods available that they find attractive. In rare cases, a customer literally cannot buy the lure merchandise from the retailer no matter how strong his determination to do so; these usually are called "nailed-down models." Some consumers cannot be switched. They know their own minds, are not easily intimidated or persuaded by salesmen, and will not buy an item unless they believe its worth to them exceeds its cost. On the other hand, bait merchandise will often lead consumers to make an unproductive visit to a store to purchase items that are not available or were misrepresented in the store's advertising. (Frequently, the bait item is advertised in a manner that conveys a false impression to the customer; it often does so by withholding information from the prospective customer—such as the fact that it does not include some essential feature or that it is a model about to be superseded or even a model from a previous year.) Occasionally, the bait item is made in a style so unattractive that the consumer would feel that his home had been disfigured by its presence. (The large, black, square box type of table model set is a relatively familiar example from the recent past.) It is when there is misrepresentation or nondisclosure about the lures that induce the consumer to make a shopping trip that he would not have made otherwise that the bait-switch tactic hurts even the consumer who knows what he wants and will not be diverted to something else. Not only has he made a futile shopping trip; he will, in addition, generally be subjected to sales pressure—often of an unpleasant and embarrassing sort. Many consumers end by making purchases they will regret.

The "bait-switch" syndrome raises serious questions that we shall not try to answer here. First, does the doctrine of *caveat emptor* apply under the present circumstances? Can one expect most customers for many kinds of technical products to protect themselves against injury once they have been lured onto the retailer's premises? Second, is it possible and desirable to construe, for legal purposes, the withholding of certain types of information as equivalent to outright misrepresentation? For example, if a retailer does not disclose that he is selling television sets that are "new" but were introduced three years ago, is he guilty of misrepresentation? Third, should manufacturers design their lines of product in ways that reduce the possibility of step-up, switch, and misrepresentation? It is not clear how they might do so, even if they tried, for the switch generally involves shifting the customer to another brand altogether. The manufacturer already wants to prevent this from happening.

The Salesman as Record Keeper

Salesmen are expected to give their employers and their suppliers information as well as to inform their customers. They want market information on such matters as customer reactions to individual brands and models (and specifically to particular product features, general product performance and esthetic appeal) and customers' apparent impressions of the value of the guarantees and service facilities offered by different manufacturers. Many retailers ask their salesmen to make a written record of such observations, which they collect and analyze and then transmit to their suppliers. The vast majority of retailers do not systematically gather such data, however. They only require their salesmen to do the paper work involved in effecting a sale. Especially when the transaction involves installment credit, this element of salesmen's duties can be burdensome. If the salesmen carry it out inefficiently or ungraciously it can moreover become an important source of lost sales.

CREATION AND MANAGEMENT OF RETAIL SALESMEN IN TELEVISION

We have discussed the functions performed by retail salesmen of television sets but have not mentioned the activities of the proprietor of the retail store or the top management of an appliance chain involved in managing a retail sales force. Perhaps that is appropriate, for there is very little to be said. Most retailers do not consider it to be their responsibility to train their salesmen; apparently they feel their job is done when they hire someone who seems to be a good salesman. If they find by examining actual sales records that they were mistaken, they usually hire a replacement. What training salesmen get comes primarily from manufacturer's or distributor's representatives and is concerned mainly with product, rather than sales technique.

There are some exceptions to the foregoing, of course. A few appliance chains describe themselves as "fanatics" on the subject of sales training. Inspection of what they actually do suggests neglect more than fanaticism. The retail salesman in most stores selling television sets is one of a very small group. Perhaps it is the smallness of their numbers that discourages the owner (or top management) from designing and carrying out a program of training The most common method of preparing a new retail salesman for his assignment is to put him under the wing of a senior salesman for a few days. Just what senior salesmen do at such times is difficult to determine. Although the guidance they give new salesmen can scarcely qualify as rigorous sales training administered by a training specialist, it does familiarize the new salesman with the way that store handles its paper work and with the sales approaches of at least one experienced salesman.

The substantial number of capable salesmen one finds in appliance stores is much more to be explained by the selective process—self-selection by individuals who undertake this work—and by managers and owners who generally are quick to drop persons who have little talent. Very little credit can be given to training programs for the effectiveness of the best retail appliance salesmen.

Consequences Resulting from Dealers Offering More than One Brand

As in most of retailing, appliance dealers generally carry more than one brand of an appliance. In so doing, they both perform a service for their customers and also reduce the likelihood that customers will feel obliged to look elsewhere before making a purchase. Most consumers will not buy the first brand of an appliance that they see.

In television retailing, a relatively small proportion of dealers carry a single brand of set. Although distributors do avoid selling to stores that are close to one another, both to reduce their distribution costs and to mitigate price competition at retail, almost any appliance dealer can sell several different brands of sets if he so desires.

Since the dealer and his salesmen exert very great influence over the particular brand of set that the consumer buys, a manufacturer must assure himself of retail sales support. Otherwise, virtually all consumers who enter retail stores with a preference for his merchandise will leave with some other manufacturer's goods. The retailer can and does play favorites.

The appliance dealer has several important favors to offer to distributors and manufacturers. The most important of them are: (1) exposure—in store window, on floor, via catalogues, etc.; (2) sales support—the transmission of information and persuasion via advertising and personal sales effort; and (3) capital investment to perform functions that distributors and manufacturers would otherwise be forced to perform for themselves. These favors are scarce and valuable; manufacturers and distributors pursue them zealously. They seek the best exposure and sales support obtainable for their merchandise. (The dealer's contribution is measured mainly by quantities that can be sold, price that the retailer would pay and the prices that would be charged to consumers.) They obtain them when they win the support of dealers who are highly skilled and possess large financial resources. They try to win the support of choice dealers by offering them "values"—consisting primarily of customer acceptance for their brand and relative insulation from price competition by other sellers of the *same* brand.

When a distributor has arranged for a retailer to carry his line, he has *not* assured himself of either exposure or sales support. Distributors must gain, sustain and regain dealer support in competition with the other distributors who likewise seek the dealer's favors and are also regular suppliers to him.

It is a demonstrated fact that dealers who sell different lines are fickle, to varying degrees, in the manner in which they distribute favors. One hears frequently that "dealers are just dirty prostitutes who will push any manufacturer's line for an extra buck." The distributor who offers the best deal or sales promotion program will gain most retailers' support. Just as soon as the special incentive is withdrawn—or when another distributor comes along and offers him a stronger incentive—the special support won from the retailer will be withdrawn.

The foregoing paragraphs simply restate and elaborate what was indicated earlier: retailers have great power to influence consumer purchases; they exercise this power in support of the manufacturer that gives them the strongest financial incentives to do so. Dealer loyalty, while far from nonexistent, is relatively weak in most areas of the nation. Most persons in the industry believe it is strongest in towns and small cities.

The chief effects of this condition are: (1) higher distribution costs, because distributors (and manufacturers, in the case of large retailers who buy direct) must make constant and costly efforts to win and rewin their dealer's sales support; (2) intensified price competition among distributors; and (3) sometimes strong and expensive measures taken by distributors to win the support of the dealer's salesmen.

This situation can be linked to what is a most portentous development in food retailing. The food retailer has something that manufacturer's and distributors desperately want—exposure. In supermarkets it is shelf space, because personal selling is almost totally absent. Food retailers are able to sell this valuable resource to the highest bidder, directly or indirectly. Many supermarkets, indeed, now charge some vendors—mainly cigarette vendors—for shelf space by the foot. Appliance dealers do not set a flat price for exposure of a dealer's merchandise, as do these supermarkets. They simply sell it to the highest bidder of the moment. The distributor has no assurance that he has purchased the dealer's help for long.

The coin in which appliance distributors pay for exposure and sales support from dealers is a combination of consumer acceptance, local advertising support (mainly designed to gain consumer attention and acceptance), financial accommodation, low price, special promotions, and occasionally a little personal loyalty. Even the most highly valued brand names in this industry have not succeeded in developing so strong a consumer demand that dealers cannot switch customers to some other. That fact, plus the fact that most retailers always seem to be urgently in need of funds means that the most highly prized form of payment for the dealer's favors is immediate cash.

Distributors do hold one major trump card, when their brand is among the most highly prized. They can withdraw the line altogether and offer it to a neighboring dealer. This possibility makes it almost impossible for a dealer to neglect one line completely for long periods.

The vulnerability of the distributor to dealer disloyalty has caused much thinking about and some experimentation with alternative arrangements. Since the source of the difficulty is mainly in multiple-brand retail representation, some experimentation with exclusive retail distribution is taking place which gives a wide geographical franchise in exchange for restricting the retailer to only one line of sets. Some thought has also been given to vertical integration by manufacturers into appliance retailing.

Shifts in Relative Bargaining Power of Retailers, Distributors and Manufacturers

It is almost as difficult to define "bargaining power" as to measure it. The meaning attached to the phrase here is similar to its implicit definition in discussions of labor relations. Bargaining power is composed of more than the relative ability of contesting parties to gain their objectives; beyond the actual relative strength of the opposing parties, bargaining power includes perceptual elements (i.e., how the parties assess their power) and bargaining skills (i.e., how fully they exploit their power).

It is far easier to assess changes in bargaining power than to measure it in absolute terms. Accordingly, one would find general agreement among persons engaged in this industry that the bargaining power of television set manufacturers as a group is lower in 1963 than it was in 1950. Similarly, the consensus holds that very large retailers have enjoyed a substantial increase in relative bargaining power—though it would not mean much to say that they possess greater (or less) bargaining power than, say, R.C.A. or Zenith.

The facts about changes in relative bargaining power fortunately are not highly controversial, even though they can be established only on the basis of consensus rather than direct observation. The consensus of these shifts in bargaining power for the efficiency of distribution are somewhat unclear. We shall first review the apparent changes in bargaining power and then probe their major consequences.

1. Large appliance buyers, especially appliance chains, discount house chains and large dealer buying co-ops are growing substantially in relative market power.

2. A few strong distributors enjoy greater bargaining power than ever before, but the others possess relatively less.

3. As a group, manufacturers possess less bargaining power than before. Only a few franchises in this industry have much value—Magnavox, Zenith and R.C.A., primarily. The other manufacturers, which possessed considerable bargaining power when sets were in very short supply, now bargain with distributors and large retailers at a disadvantage.

These bargaining power shifts apparently have lowered several cost elements to the final consumer. Specifically, manufacturers' profit margins have been squeezed; the distributor's costs and profit margin have been compressed (or the distributor has been bypassed altogether); transportation and handling costs have been cut; and large retailers take a smaller margin to perform the retailing function than did the conventional retailer. These four sources of price reduction have improved the values available to the discriminating buyer. Not only does the large appliance dealer charge less than the small independent, but he had forced down the prices charged by other types of appliance dealer.

This squeeze on retail price partly has been the result of eliminated functions and more efficient methods. Even more, it is the result of reduced payments for performing distribution functions due to large retailers' exercising their increased bargaining power. Direct sales to the dealer has, moreover, cut the real cost of transportation and storage. The distribution costs of persuasion and communication probably are lower per unit for the large chain, which has resources and skills that permit it to use mass distribution methods at lower cost than the smaller retailer.

Important changes in distribution may flow from this shift in bargaining power. Large chains may begin to purchase on specification—possibly retaining the manufacturer's label, while obtaining special merchandise to meet their own desires and needs. Although the large retail chains are unlikely to innovate technologically, their exposure to large numbers of consumers may enable them to identify marketable features. Especially if they succeed in establishing strong customer acceptance for merchandise bearing their brand name, the large retail chain will be able to free itself from dependence on particular suppliers. In this industry, with its substantial excess capacity, large chains would probably be able to purchase private label merchandise made to their own exacting specifications at prices substantially lower than they are now paying. With the possible exception of Sears-Roebuck—and then only with a small fraction of all customers for television sets—no large retail chain has achieved enough customer acceptance to build a large television set business on its own private brand.

Chapter VIII

APPRAISAL OF INDIVIDUAL MARKETING ACTIVITIES

The foregoing chapters described in considerable detail the activities of the many parties engaged in marketing television sets. Overriding emphasis was placed on description, though occasional assessments were made of the economic effects of particular activities and structural features of the industry. Attention will now be directed specifically to evaluation, one of the objectives—though a secondary one—of this study.

This chapter is intended to prepare the ground for the one that follows. No evaluations of the industry are made here; instead, the very possibility of making a meaningful evaluation of marketing activities is considered, and alternative standards of evaluation are set forth and assessed critically. The next chapter will advance some conclusions about marketing activities in the television set industry.

Appraisal is difficult; inevitably it involves weighing the benefits and shortcomings, virtues and evils of alternatives. Rarely can the weighing be reduced to measurement. Appraisals are inevitably subjective to some degree.

Appraisal is often more unwelcome than it is difficult. No one wants to have his social worth challenged. Even highly objective evaluations of our economy generally evokes an emotional response, whether favorable or unfavorable. Moreover, one meets suspicion and hostility for having dared to question any facet of our economy—lest he give comfort to the Communists.

Appraisal of almost everything has two parts: first, an assessment as to whether the thing in question is worthwhile *in itself*—that is, is it worth the effort or the cost? Second, an appraisal involves a decision as to whether the object of the appraisal is being handled in the best possible manner under the circumstances. With one notable exception, appraisals of economic activities pass over the first of these two parts. The important exception is advertising (especially "competitive" or "noninformative" advertising), which has long been under heavy attack from economists. Few other forms of distribution activity have been subjected to critical scrutiny, however.

One might inquire why social appraisals are not made of production—indeed, of all economic activities? Why is it generally assumed that all activities performed in order to produce an item are worthwhile? Conversely, why are people ready to question the worthwhileness of most forms of distribution? How do distribution and production differ from the standpoint of social contribution?

Classification of Economic Activities for the Purpose of Social Appraisal

For many centuries, social observers and philosophers have distinguished among economic activities on grounds of their social value or "acceptability." Money lending suffered censure very early; selling was also lowly regarded during most historical time. Very recently, popular interest was awakened in advertising and motivation research.[1] Extensive press coverage of "subliminal" advertising helped to feed popular discussion of advertising, as did disclosures of television quiz show "rigging" and the "payola" among disk jockeys.

Classical economics provides one powerful criterion for distinguishing between acceptable—or desirable—economic activities and those which are not: the test is whether the activity contributes to the satisfaction of human wants. In contrast with most philosophers, economists accept virtually *all* human wants as valid—or at least they decline to pass on the validity of personal choices. It follows that "production," or legitimate activity, consists in creating "utilities"—which means to satisfy human wants or to satisfy them better than before. The classical economist attacked the traditional division of occupations and trades into productive and nonproductive types,

---

[1] *The Hidden Persuaders*, by Vance Packard, was the main trigger for popular discussion of that subject, and it was kept alive and deepened by Martin Mayer's *Madison Avenue, U.S.A.*

which were based on the *nature of the activity* itself (that is, whether it was agriculture, mining, money lending, selling, hand manufacture, manufacture with the assistance of machinery) and substituted a test based on the *effects of the activity* (that is, whether it contributed to the satisfaction of wants.)

The tendency to separate economic activities into "good" and "evil" continues—though with the exception of popular agitation about advertising, interest in this subject is slight. Most of these efforts still rest on the nature, rather than the effects, of economic activities. For this type of distinction to be valid, all activities of a kind must have essentially the same effects, which is not at all the case. The manufacture of worthless patent medicines is not to be lumped with the manufacture of precious antibiotics.

This study of the distribution of television sets itself rests upon the distinction between "production" and "distribution." For decades, farmers and intellectuals have been intensely interested in whether "distribution costs too much" (which is the title of a book published in 1936 and now under extensive revision by Professor Reavis Cox). Apparently, there is general confidence that production does *not* cost too much. Although the division of economic activities into production and distribution is not usually intended to separate the "good" from the "evil," the general impression prevails that these activities are not *equally* valuable to the community.

DISTRIBUTION COMPARED WITH PRODUCTION,
FROM SOCIAL WELFARE STANDPOINT

According to the logic underlying our economic system, the customer is the final judge of what is worthwhile. What he purchases is, *per se*, worth the price he will pay; all activities required to make it are likewise worthwhile. If some processes are performed that have no value to the customer, or cost more than he believes them to be worth, the customer will refuse to pay what they cost and thereby penalize the producers who authorized these unnecessary activities. That penalty will ordinarily bring about quick improvement. Thus, markets are said to permit the customer to record his wishes and to pass on the relative merits of different products; in that way, he also passes on the value of the activities performed.

This rationale unfortunately does not describe the existing situation accurately. Customers actually are offered limited choices; these reflect prior selections by businessmen based on their forecasts of customer reaction. Many possible alternatives are never offered to customers, with the result that they cannot express their preferences for them. Indeed, since many products represent a large bundle of product features, it is rarely practical to offer nearly all possible combinations of these features for customer selection. More important, customers frequently lack the technical competence or experience to assess many product features; consequently, their preferences often represent mere guesses about the relative value of alternatives.

Despite the foregoing qualifications, there is a strong presumption that businessmen will not carry out activities that are unnecessary. Their economic self-interest presses them to avoid any activity that does not help to make the product that they offer to customers; also, self-interest dictates that they forego any expenditures and activities that would not increase sales or enable them to charge a higher price. Thus, the customer passes on the merits and value of different product features; the businessman strives to avoid activities that are not "worth their cost" to him and the consumer.

A similar situation does not hold for distribution. Large distribution outlays are incurred for the sole purpose of persuading customers to buy. Few customers want to pay to have their purchase plans altered; they would not accept the service if offered free. If they desired guidance in how to spend their money, they would scarcely choose persons who have a financial interest in the outcome. To be specific, many consumers do not want the usual type of advertising and they certainly do not want to pay for it. This example suggests that the interests of producers and consumers may conflict regarding some distribution outlays: the businessman is willing to pay substantial sums to persuade consumer to buy his product; the consumer wants to be informed but not persuaded or manipulated.

Moreover, the market does not provide an automatic check on distribution activities—not nearly to the extent that it does in production. A "smart" advertiser can spend large sums on advertising and persuade the customer to spend enough more for the product to cover his expenditures on advertising. Essentially, he achieves this result by altering customers' judgments. In the process, he may employ methods that reduce the ability of customers to guard their self-interest and assess the merits of rival product.

Social appraisal of production activities seems far less necessary than for distribution, for other reasons as well. Production consists of processing, refining, fabricating and altering material resources. Most results of production are tangible and recognizable, and if they do not "improve" the product for many customers, the item will not be purchased in large quantity. Most distribution activities result in intangibles; even when they provide extremely valuable services, these are not easy to measure and describe.

In addition, distribution services—such as delivery, sales assistance, gift wrapping, return privileges, etc.—are not accepted equally by all customers. Some customers have little desire for the services rendered, whereas production features yield their benefits to almost all customers.[2]

The arguments presented in earlier paragraphs indicate that there may be fundamental differences between some production and distribution activities in their intrinsic worthwhileness. Even so, a close analysis of all production activities would also uncover activities that are not worthwhile. An appraisal of production in any industry would, no less than of distribution, require an investigation of the worthwhileness of the activities performed. One cannot use value added to measure the social contribution of *any* activity until he has assured himself of the benefits provided. Accordingly, the distinction between production and distribution does not provide a firm line that separates socially useful from unuseful activities.

DISTINCTION BETWEEN "DEMAND-SATISFYING" AND "DEMAND-CREATING" ACTIVITIES

Neoclassical economics provides another basis for classifying forms of economic activity according to their social worth. That is the distinction between producing goods or services to meet *existing de-*

[2] Some marketing specialists maintain that the economic value of distribution activities can be measured by "value added" just as is the contribution of production. Several simply *assert* that there is no difference between production and distribution; a few maintain that there is no justification for a social appraisal of any economic activity, because it must necessarily be arbitrary.

mands—which might include both production and distribution activities—and *shifting the demands* of individuals for goods. This distinction is made by those who regard the expansion of desire as a social disservice, for they see it as consisting of desires for trivial products or things that merely denote the possession of wealth. On the other hand, they view the satisfaction of existing wants as the reduction of suffering caused by ungratified basic needs.

Although helpful, this distinction also produces blurred divisions of business activities. In particular, it does not distinguish between the creation or satisfaction of trivial or harmful desires and the creation of demand for vital new products. Effective efforts to induce parents to have their children vaccinated with Salk Vaccine would be considered socially valuable by almost everyone, but creating a craving for cigarettes would be deplored by many. Similarly to satisfy an existing desire for ostentatious consumption is considered of doubtful merit, while meeting the desire for cultural facilities would be applauded by almost all.

Activities intended to give consumers what they already want are, moreover, difficult to distinguish from those which produce "gimmicks" designed to create the impression of product improvement but which are made for the sole purpose of facilitating sales. Both represent changes in the physical product, but only the first type anticipates or meets existing or latent desires of consumers—that is, they are given features they would want without any persuasion once they knew of them; the second class really does not satisfy any desires—other than the desire to own the latest models and therefore demonstrate affluence. Of course, some people buy products that allegedly have been improved in the expectation that the new version will meet their needs far better than the old.

Thus one cannot readily distinguish between economic activities on the basis of whether they cater to existing demands rather than change the established pattern of demand. Nevertheless, this distinction is one that inevitably arises in the appraisal of such distribution activities as advertising and product development. Also, this distinction helps to understand another one that is used in this study: that between providing substantive services and persuasion.

DISTINCTION BETWEEN PROVISION OF SUBSTANTIVE SERVICES AND PERSUASION

The provision of substantive services consists of offering the buyer improved product features and service, which he can ordinarily see and evaluate for himself, whereas persuasion consists of advancing reasons or creating pressures to buy. The rationale for this distinction is fairly clear: it separates those economic activities that give the consumer something additional *that he wants* from those that induce the consumer to buy, without giving him anything extra.

This distinction is beset with difficulties of its own. In the first place, one vital activity or service does not have a clear position within this broad distinction. Specifically, the provision of accurate information to buyers may have great persuasive effect and yet it certainly does not alter the product or provide added service, in the ordinary sense of the word. However, the provision of such information obviously is socially valuable, for it enables consumers to make selections that meet their desires and needs.

In the second place, this distinction requires a separation of activities that generally occur in combination. Businessmen add desirable features to a product in order to make it easier to sell. Or, advertisements include puffery and emotional appeals even while they provide accurate information. Salesmen assist customers to find the items that they desire while using their wiles to persuade them to make a purchase.

This distinction also leaves out one important group of activities that neither alter the product, provide a direct service for the buyer nor give accurate information; they do, apparently, increase the satisfaction that *some* consumers derive from the product. Martin Mayer, in his widely read *Madison Avenue, U.S.A.*, builds his economic appraisal of advertising largely around this type of activity. The following sentences, selected from his concluding chapter, explain his (by no means original nor uniquely held) position:

> Advertising, in addition to its purely informing function, *adds a new value to the existing values of the product*. This added value is most obviously apparent in the case of a soda pill, a placebo, which is advertised

as a headache cure. The pill itself has virtually no value; but it will actually cure the headache of a number of people who take it. The suggestion power of the advertising has created a value for a worthless product. . . . Whenever a benefit is promised from the use of a product, and the promise is believed, the use of the product carries with it a value not inherent in the product itself. . . . the fact that the value is fictitious as *perceived* by the consumer does not mean that it is unreal as *enjoyed* by the consumer. He finds a difference between technically identical products *because the advertising has in fact made them different*.[3]

These intermediate activities allegedly satisfy human wants largely by inducing buyers to misperceive reality. They alter the effects of a product without altering the product itself. If this "value added by advertising" actually were obtained by many consumers and were not offset by equal or greater value subtracted, one might want to set a high value on these activities. However, these values are likely to be both shortlived and accompanied by great negative effect. In the first place, if consumers were even half as astute as Mayer claims ("But the consuming public, whatever its failings in the kingdom of abstract ideas, has repeatedly shown itself to be remarkably shrewd in its evaluations of competing products") they would find that they had been deceived when they actually consumed the things they had bought. Apart from the possible waste of funds due to mistaken purchases, the typical consumer would probably suffer remorse and chagrin at having been deceived—these are extremely painful emotions for most people. Also, the mistaken belief that one has satisfied a need—cured a disease or improved his appearance, say—leaves the reality unchanged; in the first instance it may cause delay in seeking competent medical assistance, and in the second case it may postpone the acceptance of one's defects or the cultivation of personal qualities to compensate for the shortcomings that cosmetics were supposed to overcome.

Many people would oppose Mayer's line of argument purely on principle, for it defends the creation of illusion, if not outright deceit. Even if one accepts the legitimacy of deceit when it adds to human happiness, it is a dangerous policy because it requires some people to deceive others for the mutual good of both. The person practic-

[3] Mayer, *Madison Avenue, U.S.A.* (New York, Harper & Brothers, 1958), pp. 314, 315.

Individual Marketing Activities

ing deception may have only his own welfare in view and, therefore may repeatedly deceive others and injure them in the process.

It often is difficult to distinguish between persuasion and substantive benefit in specific cases. A seller may provide some illuminating accurate information, but omit highly pertinent detrimental information. If the net effect of his messages was to mislead customers, the messages presumably would be considered persuasion.

Up to this point, we have reviewed the main distinctions that might help in a social appraisal of the economic activities. As one would have supposed, they do not serve all of our needs; even an inspired set of distinctions would leave many activities unclassifiable except on the basis of personal preference and prejudice. Nevertheless, these distinctions make clear that the social effects of business activities vary widely and are not to be measured by the sums expended to carry them out. It is no more possible to measure the contribution of transportation, personal selling or advertising to national well-being by the sums expended for them than it is to measure the benefits to society from water purification, education, newspapers, baseball and cosmetics by the sums that are spent for them. One can well understand and applaud the effort by economists and statisticians to find quantitative measures by which one might study the economy. One must, however, deplore use of these measures for purposes they were not intended to serve and particularly as indicators of social contribution.

One more task remains before marketing activities in the television set industry can be evaluated: to select points from which to view those activities.

Standpoints from which Marketing Activities May Be Appraised

The balance of this chapter discusses the standards that may be invoked to appraise any marketing activity. At the outset, it sets forth the viewpoint of the businessman, then that of the consumer, and finally the social welfare viewpoint. In considering the first two standards of appraisal, we shall consider both the preferences and true interest of these groups. One may err if he assumes they are the same.

THE BUSINESSMAN'S VIEWPOINT

It is easy enough to learn what distribution activities are favored by most businessmen and which ones they oppose. In general, businessmen strongly favor established distribution arrangements. A few deplore "excesses" and occasionally call upon *other* businessmen to refrain from objectionable practices, but they almost never suggest that businessmen should be prevented from or penalized for using particular distribution methods. Possibly, the businessman's acceptance of the *status quo* results from fear and dislike of government intervention.

Some distribution activities apparently are injurious to most businessmen; yet, few favor restrictions on those activities. A few individuals do gain in the process, but these activities are harmful to a large majority. To explain this paradox, it will help to consider a specific illustration.

Consider the much-criticized activity of advertising from the businessman's viewpoint. Despite numerous exceptions, much, if not most, advertising merely offsets rivals' advertising: each seller is left essentially where he would have been had no one advertised—except that he is without the funds he spent for advertising. Especially when one examines selected industries, it is difficult to resist the conclusion that most current advertising does not increase *total* sales perceptibly; to the extent that it is effective, it only redistributes patronage among individual firms in those industries—and not necessarily on the basis of merit (the intrinsic value of the goods). Where this happens, members of the industry as a whole have carried a heavy burden and made large outlays without receiving any benefit.

Where these are the facts—and they obviously are in such cases as the sale of gasoline, sugar, soap, detergents, many food products—then one would expect businessmen to oppose advertising. Since that is not the case, how can one account for this paradox?

First, the facts may *never* be what was suggested here. Second, even though the facts are as represented, businessmen may not recognize them. Third, even if businessmen recognize that advertising is self-defeating to a large extent, they might feel that they were "traitors to their class" to seek government restrictions on business.

Fourth, those businessmen who are most skillful and powerful in influencing public opinion may believe that advertising permits them to benefit at the expense of their rivals. Fifth, most businessmen may *hope* that they will excel their competitors in the use of advertising. Sixth, most businessmen may regard advertising as a method of restricting the movement of newcomers into the business. Unfortunately, there is no basis on which one could select in the abstract among these possible explanations for the apparent paradox.

One is tempted to conclude that businessmen just do not even bother to appraise existing distribution arrangements. Businessmen rarely refrain from seeking government aid or regulation solely on grounds of "general principle" and if they became convinced that particular distribution arrangements injured them, they very likely would try to alter them—with government assistance, if necessary. At present, we must conclude that although businessmen endorse established distribution arrangements, there may be some distribution practices that apparently injure most businessmen.

One has every right to ask whether outsiders can know what is good for the businessman better than he does. If, as in connection with competitive advertising, one finds possible conflict between the businessman's views of a practice and the views of specialists in economic and industrial problems, what conclusions can one draw? Has economic understanding reached the point where one can forecast or analyze the social and economic effects of particular business practices with confidence?

Answers to the foregoing question certainly will vary; some people credit economists with great understanding of economic processes, while the business world is full of men who rate them as useless or worse. One must expect economists to be far better at explaining and understanding some things than others. No one can forecast the outcome of certain practices or proposed changes. On other matters one knows enough to take a fairly positive stand. The writer believes that failure to be completely *certain* that something is harmful—when the evidence strongly suggests that it is—should not forestall criticism and that we should not leave such things just as they are. Although economic and social change should be carefully considered, it need not await irrefutable proof that the proposed change will represent an improvement. Rarely, if ever, does one get that kind of proof in the social sciences. And, even when extremely strong proof is in hand, those who would be adversely affected by conceding the point will rarely see it—and even if they do, will almost certainly not concede it.

THE CONSUMER VIEWPOINT

As with the businessman, it is possible to view the consumer's standpoint toward distribution activities to be what he favors or what is good for him—and these may be different. By applying the first criterion, one is likely to conclude that consumers basically agree with businessmen. They may be irritated by singing commercials, the amount of advertising in the public media, the pressure exerted by sales people, but they do not disapprove of advertising or personal selling in principle. If they have any misgivings about the high cost of advertising and personal selling, it does not lead them to oppose it in and of itself.

The average consumer may underrate the influence that advertising and personal salesmen exert on him. He possibly prides himself upon being immune to the salesman's and advertiser's cunning and, if asked, would say he did not believe most of the puffing of products. That opinion, however, is inconsistent with the well-established fact that really "good" salesmen and advertising seem to increase sales of individual items markedly. Advertisements and personal selling apparently exert influence—whether or not they are believed—in specific cases.

We shall not attempt to appraise distribution activities in the television set industry from the standpoint of the consumer at this point. However, this is an appropriate place to discuss the consumer's true interests with respect to distribution activities—and in particular toward those described as "persuasion to buy." This discussion rests on the premise that the consumer is served by those things that benefit him and is injured by those that do not—regardless of the consumer's opinion on the matter.

Efforts by businessmen to persuade customers to buy can be considered a source of increased general dissatisfaction. After all, the main purpose of sales persuasion is to awaken and increase desire and induce people to want things they do not have; it creates wants rather than satisfies them. On the other hand, it can be contended that efforts to sell cause buyers to enjoy and prize more highly the things they have purchased. There is much informal testimony to the effect that consumers enjoy having certain products largely because salesmen and advertising reassured them that ownership of that product was a mark of success and good taste.

Attempts to sell probably create dissatisfaction and unhappiness on the part of most people who are not able to buy the things that are extolled. Introspection suggests that unfulfilled desires—even when there is hope that they may someday be satisfied—are mainly sources of frustration rather than eager anticipation. Also, persons who are exposed to others who own something they cannot afford, given the widespread tendency to measure personal worth by what one owns and consumes, suffer envy and self-doubt. One would suppose that for every person whose enjoyment of a product was enhanced as a result of sales effort, there were many who were unhappy because they had to go without it.

The same conclusion can be reached by another route. Economic activity, as explained earlier, is directed mainly toward the satisfaction of human wants. (It also molds those wants and creates new ones.) These wants are taken as inherent and self-generated and represent tensions that can be relieved by consumption. In other words, wants can be regarded as unfortunate concomitants of life that must be overcome—and man does so by engaging in production. Any activities that would increase man's wants would, by that very fact, aggravate rather than alleviate man's misfortunes.

Consumer injury due to sales activity might be demonstrated in yet another way. Those who attempt to persuade the customer to make purchases are attempting to influence him or to manipulate him, and the seller is guided solely by his own interest rather than the customer's. Customers can regard efforts to alter their behavior as an uninvited violation of personal rights and dignity. Their objections are all the greater if these efforts constantly interrupt their favorite forms of entertainment or allow sellers to influence the sources on which they rely for information on controversial public issues.

A large proportion of all distribution activity is not designed to increase consumers' wants but to satisfy them. As such, they are legitimate in themselves. Of course, they must meet a second set of tests: Do they provide the services that consumers want at minimum cost? Are consumers offered a sufficient variety of choice? Are innovations made with the frequency that one would desire?

Most discussions of the consumer interest place overriding if not complete emphasis upon the physical product that the consumer buys and the price he pays for it. This view ignores the very substantial service component in most consumer purchases and thus tends to undervalue distribution activities. When one buys a product, he also generally wants to buy convenience of location, speed of purchase, reliability of information, courtesy on the part of sales personnel, an opportunity to examine a wide selection, the right to return a product if reflection shows it to be a mistaken choice, etc. That these things are valuable to consumers can be demonstrated in many ways—in particular by the fact that stores that provide these services or provide them better than their competitors are able to command a higher price or attract many customers, or both.

There is no reason why consumers should not be willing to pay extra in order to get these services. An appraisal of distribution activities from the consumer's standpoint must revolve largely around the value that can be attributed to the services performed by the retailer to facilitate and make enjoyable the act of purchase. It is not valid to apply as the test of efficiency that consumers buy the product at the lowest price—though this is surely an important element in any appraisal. Account must also be taken of how wide a selection they are offered, how much time it takes to complete the purchase, whether the purchase situation is pleasant or disagreeable, and the like.

Clearly, consumers benefit if offered a broad choice of services and products. Yet, some consumers may want to forego virtually all dispensable services in order to buy products more cheaply. Others may desire strongly to obtain complete and luxurious services together with the product. Both types of buying are equally sensible—if the customers know what they are getting and the alternatives available. An efficient distribution system from the consumer standpoint provides

Individual Marketing Activities

special arrangements for different types of buyers—though it does not provide *exactly* the combination of product and service desired by every single buyer. Among consumers, as with national and religious groups in matters of state, there are many minorities which must be protected and served.

THE SOCIAL WELFARE VIEWPOINT

Reference has been made to a standard for evaluating distribution activities based on "the greatest good of the greatest number." This phrase is a handy way of referring to the viewpoints of the "nation as a whole" or "what is best for the country." This standard is not easy to define in general terms, and even more difficult to give specific content in concrete instances.

Professor Vernon Mund, following the position taken almost 200 years ago by Adam Smith, defines the public interest so that it is identical with the consumer's interest.[4] He quotes the following pertinent section from Adam Smith's *Wealth of Nations* (Book iv, Chapter 8):

Consumption is the sole end and purpose of all production; and the interest of the producer ought to be attended to, only so far as it may be necessary for promoting that of the consumer. The maxim is so perfectly self-evident, that it would be absurd to attempt to prove it. But in the mercantile system, the interest of the consumer is almost constantly sacrificed to that of the producer; and it seems to consider production, and not consumption, as the ultimate end and object of all industry and commerce.

Mund believes that this quotation applies very well today if one changes the term "the mercantile system" to "modern economic systems." In current thinking, increases in consumer desires and needs are welcomed in order to provide a stronger market for goods and thus to benefit the producer. In addition to that point, Smith was remarking on the great political power of producers, which greatly exceeds that of consumers—even though the latter group is far more numerous and casts more votes than producer groups.

If we follow Professor Mund's thinking, there is no social welfare

[4] Vernon A. Mund, *Government and Business* (New York: Harper & Brothers, 1950), p. 63.

standpoint apart from the consumer standpoint. It is difficult to agree with Mund, however, for the possibility exists that other groups—such as farmers, debtors, the aged, the unemployed, members of the armed forces, or educators—might exert a prior or higher claim and deserve to benefit at the expense of the consumer.

Let us attempt to illustrate the application of the social welfare standard to competitive advertising. The following things might be said—again, for purposes of illustration: many businessmen favor competitive advertising because they believe they can defeat their rivals with this weapon. One effect of this practice is to injure the small firms in most industries, for they lack the resources to advertise on a large scale, and another is to increase the price of the product to virtually all customers. If the foregoing statement were a reasonable summary of the effects of most competitive advertising, how would one appraise this distribution practice from the social welfare standard? A simple counting of the numbers helped and hurt would let us reach a critical verdict, yet put to a general vote competitive advertising would almost certainly win public approval. If one attached weights according to the "importance" of the interests of, say, large and small producers and to different consumer groups, the verdict would depend upon the weights assigned.

Businessmen and consumers can be grouped in a variety of ways for purposes of studying how they are affected by any distribution activity. For example, one could divide businesses according to their size, whether they are old and established firms or new and untried, whether they are growing or declining, whether they are low-cost or high-cost producers, whether they sell to price-conscious or quality-conscious (or both) kinds of customers. Similarly, customers could be divided according to their income, their age, the size and composition of their families, whether they are urban or rural, etc. The effects of competitive advertising probably are not the same on all classes of businesses and consumers. If so, then how does one determine whether it contributes to or injures social welfare? We are back again with the problem of whether we count noses, votes, or whether we attach different weights to the "interest" of different businesses of individuals.

The concept of "the greatest good for the greatest number" superficially seems to refer to the "nose-counting" standard; however, when one considers the phrase "greatest good," it seems to require that one take into account the *amount* of good or harm that is done. That is, many consumers may be injured by competitive advertising but only to a very slight degree; on the other hand, businessmen in far smaller numbers may be *seriously* injured if competitive advertising were eliminated; certainly advertising and public media would be grievously hurt if competitive advertising were terminated. In such a situation, does one approve or disapprove of competitive advertising from the social welfare standard: Professor Mund (and Adam Smith long before him) offers a standard which would have us ignore the interests of businessmen altogether. Even with his standard, the problem of weighing the interests of different classes of consumers remains, however. But is it proper to ignore the interests of business altogether?

Those who argue that business interests must weigh heavily in measuring the social welfare sometimes take the line that "what is good for business is good for the country as a whole." That is, if business prospers, then all people prosper; conversely, if you injure business, then economic progress will lag and the nation will be sapped by unemployment and low income. Critics of this position could argue that the elimination of, say, competitive advertising would not cause business to languish, but rather would eliminate an advantage now enjoyed by firms that have the special skills and resources to devote to this use. Other firms, say those who were particularly skillful in low-cost production or in product development, might become relatively more successful if competitive advertising were somehow ended.

It should be clear that one can reach a definite verdict when applying the standard of social welfare only if the effects of any activity are uniformly favorable or unfavorable. Once some groups are helped while others are injured, any evaluation must involve the use of weights, which are inevitably arbitrary.

Although there are certain rare occasions when the interest of business might be considered prior to those of consumers, for the most part we shall regard the businessman mainly as an instrument for satisfying consumers' wants and for creating new and "uplifting" wants. We shall, on the other hand, not admit of business exploitation by the consumer—that is, those arrangements which are advantageous to consumers but involve hardship, financial loss or insecurity to businessmen. Although we shall consider the consumer's interest to be paramount, he is not entitled to injure those who exist to serve him. Consumer responsibility to businessmen greatly complicates social appraisal.

The standard of pure competition as developed by economic theorists, has been put forth as a social ideal and is widely accepted as such by many academic persons and public officials. One should consider the possibility that pure competition would represent exploitation of businessmen by consumers. As economic theorists analyze the situation, it is desirable that all firms operate under conditions where slight waste will result in a major financial loss to producers and where firms have no security. Indeed, returns would be so low under conditions of pure and perfect competition that businessmen would constantly consider leaving their industry, and no firms would find a competitive industry sufficiently attractive to enter it. The economic theorist may have his own reasons for finding the concept of pure and perfect competition a valuable one and even to consider it an ideal state. On the other hand, if arrangements are to be enduring, equitable and progressive, they must give greater consideration for the welfare of the businessman.

Thus, we find that the social welfare standard is ambiguous, and, at bottom, is necessarily arbitrary except in those rare circumstances when everyone either benefits or loses from some particular arrangement. We shall follow in the tradition of considering the consumer as the party whose interests are to be served by economic activity—and all producers are to be regarded as instruments for serving him. If, however, these instruments are damaged, their ability to service the consumer is impaired and the consumer is thereby injured. Accordingly, it shall be necessary, from time to time, to explore whether possible changes in existing arrangements are so harmful to business that they could not serve the consumer well.

It is to be hoped, despite the vagueness and the complexity of the social welfare standard, that in the particular context in which we attempt social appraisal, the effects will prove to be clearly favorable or unfavorable. That would be the case if a practice under examination helped or injured an overwhelming majority. Otherwise, it is necessary to qualify any verdict based upon the social welfare standard.

Chapter IX

SUMMARY AND CONCLUSIONS

In addition to summarizing and evaluating, this chapter presents some interesting information that was collected during the investigation of the television set industry and that has not yet been discussed because it did not bear directly upon the topics covered. The reader should therefore not be surprised to find some matters treated here for the first time, though ordinarily a concluding chapter would only tie together and build upon the chapters that went before.

I wish to remind the reader that some of the things reported here about the television set industry are perhaps either totally wrong or partly so. The danger of error remains considerable, despite the tedious and time-consuming efforts made to verify the information assembled. One of the conclusions that may be drawn from this study is that investigators face overwhelming difficulties in finding out what actually happens in industry; they cannot count on wholehearted cooperation even from fairly close friends. As a researcher gets close to sensitive areas or shows that he has, inadvertently, learned more than it would be wise to have an outsider know, responses to his questions, letters and telephone calls sometimes cease altogether. My experience has helped me to understand why so many of the opinions and conclusions one finds about business activities are essentially unsupported.

Many of the matters discussed in this book bear directly upon the efficiency of existing business arrangements. These should concern anyone who wishes to evaluate existing arrangements, who hopes to eliminate defects in things as they are, and who is very anxious to contribute to a rise and improvement in business conditions in the United States. To allow these activities to pass without close scrutiny and evaluation is to endorse them by default. To await the collection of indisputable evidence before reaching a judgment would also in-

Summary and Conclusions

volve endorsement by default. Such evidence has not become available in the past, and my experience suggests that it is not possible to gather irrefutable evidence about any major business activity or about industrial arrangements. Consequently, anyone who studies business with a view toward social evaluation and comes forward with suggestions for change must do so on the basis of imperfect evidence. He should be able to demonstrate that his conclusions are supported by more and better evidence than are contrary views. Those who oppose him honestly rather than out of prejudice will try to gather evidence to refute his arguments; if they cannot, hopefully they will feel obliged to yield to the "weight of evidence."

Summary of the Preceding Chapters

The foregoing pages have mainly described the activities of a substantial number of parties to the distribution process in the television set industry. Some important participants in the industry—particularly the serviceman and government—were passed over very briefly. Nevertheless, the picture that emerged shows a very large number of organizations and individuals engaged in the physical movement of merchandise, in the design of the sets to be offered to customers, and, above all, in efforts to sell. The number of parties to the distribution process was found to vary according to the type of distribution system employed. A few manufacturers cut out an entire layer of distribution activity (though this does not necessarily reduce their costs) by selling directly to retailers rather than through distributors. No matter what distribution system it employs, a television set manufacturer consciously or unconsciously designs a system of distribution for its output. With varying degrees of efficiency, it manages that system with the object of coordinating and strengthening the efforts of the many groups involved.

Major conflicts of interest sometimes arise among members of the system. The timing of their activities usually must be controlled to achieve the desired sequence of events. Also, the actions taken by individual members of the distribution system must be nurtured by a flow of information about what is happening in the market place and what is being done by the other members of the system. All of these desiderata yield advantages to a centralized control and management of the distribution system.

In the main, management of the distribution system in the television set industry rests with the manufacturer. Individual manufacturers conduct their management efforts in somewhat unique ways, though their similarities greatly outweigh their differences. Most TV set manufacturers at times have found some members of their distribution system marching in different directions. The task of tying together into an effective system the efforts of dozens of separate distributors situated across the nation and the activities of thousands of retailers is enough to tax the administrative skills of some of the best executives—especially since distributors and retailers are essentially independent businessmen with independent opinions and goals. Beyond this, many television set manufacturers are huge business enterprises whose *internal* activities are exceedingly complex and whose parts can be coordinated with one another only by dint of enormous attention to organization and management. The need to coordinate its internal activities with the activities of independent distributors and retailers compounds the management tasks of each manufacturer. When the nature of the task is appreciated, their performance as a group is quite impressive, though some have floundered more than the average.

The number of distributive activities that are performed by parties to the television set industry is far greater than the number of parties to the process. The same job seems to be redone time and again before television sets reach the ultimate consumer. For example, the manufacturer physically moves the merchandise from the site of production to the premises occupied by distributors. They, in turn, typically move the merchandise to the retailer's floor or warehouse. Retailers, thereupon, transport the set to the ultimate consumer. Thus, every major party to the distribution process must manage transportation. Similarly, each one is engaged in sales activities: the manufacturer sells (though it is different from conventional forms of selling inasmuch as it occurs through franchised distributors) to his distributors and participates in sales to large retailers; distributors sell to retailers; in turn, they sell to consumers. In most respects it is the last sale that is the governing one, for merchandise sold to consumers ordinarily will be replaced all along the line; goods sold to distributors and retailers just clog up the distribution channels until the plug is removed by sale to the consumer.

We thus observe what appears to be extreme redundancy in a three-step type of distribution system. It does not follow from the appearance of redundancy that the process is more costly than known alternatives, however. Manufacturers have exhibited a desire and determination to reduce distribution costs that is little short of maniacal. That they continue to distribute by present methods suggests the absence of better methods available to them of which they are aware. Since some of the producers of television sets are extremely large and have access to large sums, and there are apparently no institutional obstructions to change, only the absence of known superior alternatives must persuade them to do what they are now doing.

Even though current distribution arrangements may be the best known, the need for each party to the distribution system to develop proficiency in materials handling, transportation management, inventory planning, selling, pricing, advertising, record keeping, etc., places heavy burdens upon executives and reduces the number of qualified persons who can fill those positions in the distribution system with proficiency. (It could be argued that the supply of businessmen with these skills is so great that these demands do not reduce significantly the amount available. The typical manufacturer's critical evaluation of the caliber of management in distribution and retailing suggests that such a conclusion would be mistaken.)

Studies of distribution ordinarily are oriented around the costs incurred to carry out all nonproduction activities. Relatively little space and attention has been devoted to this subject here for several reasons. First, my interviews uncovered very substantial inter-firm differences that minimize the value of any single figure and make the range too wide to be of great significance. (Averages were presented, nevertheless.) Second, the cost information generally applied to somewhat different things, so that they should not really be averaged. (The violence done was relatively small only because of conscientious efforts to have the data represent costs of the same activity.) Third, the executives interviewed were willing to discuss costs but not to reveal their companies' detailed cost information. Finally, it is difficult to interpret cost data unless one possesses pertinent points of reference. Specifically, distribution cost data gain meaning primarily if they are compared to: (1) costs of *production* for the same period; (2) costs of distributing other products at the same time (Preferably those other products should be comparable in some sense.); and (3) the industry's (or the individual's firm's) own costs of distribution in the past. In this latter connection, one must examine both absolute and percentage changes in cost; neither alone is sufficient.

Available data are insufficient to support such comparisons and do not even reveal the magnitude or direction of change in the cost of distributing sets. The following succinct statements summarize the author's conclusions and indicate the basis upon which they rest.

1. Measured as a proportion of sales, the costs of distribution incurred all along the line in the television set industry have increased over the last decade or so. Measured in dollars and cents amounts, they have declined substantially, however, as the average price of sets has dropped. These conclusions are based upon answers to explicit questions but are not supported by an analysis of cost records.

2. When compared with the costs of distributing roughly comparable products, such as automatic washing machines, radios and high fidelity systems, the costs of distributing television sets appear to be very much "in line." The distribution costs for these products vary, and television sets are pretty much in the middle. The products involving the lowest distribution costs apparently are washing machines; next come radio sets. Television sets would be somewhat more costly to distribute; hi-fi, apparently, is a more costly product to distribute than the others. Compared to the traditional margins on appliances, television sets carry thin margins. Margins vary among models, but range between 30 and 40 percent to cover the costs of operations of distributors and dealers and to provide some profit for both of them. Out of this 30-40 percent must also come the discount to consumers, which is a regular feature of the major appliance business.

3. Compared with costs of production, distribution costs have declined slowly over the last decade. The shift in sales from consoles to table models and portables, and the drop in average price

Summary and Conclusions

of sets within all categories, reduced substantially the number of dollars obtained by distributors and retailers for their services over, say, the last decade or so. (On top of this, consumers' patronage shifted from the relatively high to the low margin type of retail outlet, reinforcing the decline in payments for the performance of distribution functions.) During this period, the proportion of sales revenue devoted to distribution by television set manufacturers increased; their outlays per set seem to have declined slightly.

The preceding chapters have told time and again of the variations among firms in their distribution methods, activities and concepts. It is the author's impression that if one were to study their activities one or two levels lower in the organizational hierarchy, the differences among firms might be even greater than those reported here. That is, the amount and methods of marketing research, inventory control policies, data systems, salesmen's training, etc., probably differ more than the distribution activities that were described. But even those treated in the preceding chapters show considerable variation and the causes for the observed differences invite an explanation.

In the first place, individual firms vary substantially in their opportunities, resources and basic approach to marketing. As one studies each television set company's situation and personnel closely, it is the differences rather than the similarities that are most striking. One would expect Sears-Roebuck to adopt different distribution arrangements than R.C.A.; it is scarcely surprising that small manufacturers like Packard-Bell and Emerson use somewhat different methods for reaching the consumer than Zenith and Motorola.

Apart from the foregoing differences, which derive primarily from differences in resources and opportunities, there are alternatives arising from diverse convictions and policies. Motorola saw a distinction between different kinds of large retail customers and devised two separate systems to handle them. Magnavox was among the first to see the advantages of direct selling combined with exclusivity. General Electric apparently has a view of distribution arrangements in the future that causes it to favor factory branches over independently owned distributorships. Owing partly to historical accidents and personal friendships, individual manufacturers have substantially different numbers of distributors and dissimilar distributor territories.

These variations in distribution arrangements arise partly because of differences in top management's conclusions about the best way to design a distribution system.

The main forces dictating the choice of distribution system may be listed. One important consideration is that of limiting the severity of competition at retail (which might explain Magnavox's and Sears's decisions and also account for the direction in which General Electric is moving); the desire to be selective among retailers and to command the highest quality retailers surely is dominant in the Magnavox system; a desire to gain cost economies and to become more "competitive" underlies the special arrangements of all firms for sales to large retailers; the desire to obtain the strong sales support that comes from using resellers that have a personal financial stake in the outcome accounts for the decision by some managements to utilize independent distributors rather than factory branches. (The decision of Packard-Bell to rely upon essentially one-man distributor operations takes advantage of the relative shortness of the firm's product line, its substantial volume in most Western regions and the availability of a considerable supply of individuals with the necessary skills and the limited financial means required. A consideration that may weigh fairly heavily with manufacturers is that the power of decision should be placed where it would be most adapted to the market's needs. In areas where they would otherwise be beholden to distributors (where large volume is essential but must be taken at extremely slim profit margins) they accordingly establish factory branches, as a rule.

One would like to compare the costs of different systems of distribution, but it is impossible to do so. Each system provides the manufacturer with dissimilar things, so that direct cost comparisons would be illegitimate. It is not surprising or significant to find that their costs are different. Independent and factory distributors perform different functions for manufacturers, and the value of a large retailer who is an aggressive merchandiser is not to be compared with those who are smaller, less skilled and less aggressive. Cost comparisons, when the product or service obtained cannot be measured or held uniform, can be badly misleading.

Is there a best system of distribution for a product such as tele-

Summary and Conclusions 239

vision sets? Can a brilliant analyst discover the single best way to distribute this product? The answer is almost obvious: the best system of distribution will vary according to the firm's opportunities and resources. Beyond that, the best system will almost always represent a combination of subsystems. The great disparity in bargaining power of large chain retailers and small "momma and poppa" stores as well as other differences among them will almost certainly require different methods for handling these classes of businesses. Large manufacturers will not, for a very long time, be able to sell directly to the considerable number of small appliance stores located in outlying communities; the independent distributor cannot, on the other hand, expect the manufacturer to stand aside and allow him to compete for the large orders to be obtained from the biggest retailers without lending all possible assistance. Sears-Roebuck, with one of the nation's most powerful retail distribution systems, cannot be expected to tolerate competitive brands of television sets on its floor. Consequently, there is no single best distribution system for an industry as a whole; possibly, there is not even a single best combination of different systems for an individual firm at a particular time—several combinations may be just about equally good. Moreover, any distribution system has a time dimension. With the rapid changes in product, service needs, and in retailing institutions, modification of distribution systems are likely to occur fairly rapidly.

The foregoing chapters suggested some of the critical distribution problems that manufacturers face. Perhaps the most important is how to handle the large retailer. Does the associate distributor arrangement (or the equivalent) make sense for all large retailers, or are important differences among large retailers unrecognized under such a system? The geographic dispersion of large retailers must also be taken into account. Continuity of purchases, the number of competing brands handled, effectiveness of sales support, degree of sales training of salesmen, etc., could represent significant considerations beyond quantities purchased. (The reactions of the regulatory agencies to these factors must also be taken into account, of course.)

Similarly, the best method of using established distributors to serve the large retail accounts and to reduce costs and gain greater sales effectiveness represents a related problem. Part of this problem involves a sharing of costs and income from so-called direct sales. In addition, the allocation of responsibility and the division of effort between the factory and the distributor poses problems that are either unresolved or have been resolved in some cases by having the manufacturer do far more than is either necessary, effective or economical.

On another front, the industry faces problems that will probably intensify in maintaining its exclusive distributor arrangements. The regulatory agencies are opposed to exclusive distributors if exclusivity is clearly spelled out. Inasmuch as relationships between distributors and manufacturers are conducted largely through regional salesmen —most of whom are not sophisticated in the intricacies of antitrust law—manufacturers are likely to get into difficulties constantly. This problem could become very vexing and even bring about a basic change in existing arrangements if the regulatory agencies move further to oppose exclusive distributors.

A significant finding of this study is that multiple-brand representation at retail imposes very heavy costs and places retailers in a fiduciary position relative to distributors and manufacturers. Where the product they sell, as in the case of television sets, is one in which consumers rely upon retailers for guidance, the retailer possesses great power over the sales fortunes of different brands. Increasingly, the retailer is selling his sales support to the highest bidder—regardless of its effect on the consumer or upon other manufacturers and distributors. As a result, heavy costs are incurred to win the support of retailers, which, once won, often is quickly lost. In the major appliance business, manufacturers may be impelled to insure themselves market exposure at retail by establishing their outlets or by developing new types of contractual relationships (giving exclusive franchises, purchasing part-ownership, etc.) in order to overcome this major source of insecurity. All of the good work that a manufacturer may do to design a strong line of sets, to advertise and price effectively, and to provide good services for distributors, servicemen, and retailers can lose almost all of its value if the retailer decides to push other manufacturers' brands. This problem of manufacturers' subservience to the retailers arises when two conditions prevail: the retailer offers several brands of the same product, and he possesses considerable power to divert consumers from the brand of their first choice.

Manufacturers' market power will be limited as long as retailers continue to sell several different brands. The great power that retailers exert over consumer choice is attested by the enormous differences between the brands that consumers ask for upon entering the store and the brand they ultimately purchase. Also, salesmen of appliances boast, with good reason, about their ability to switch consumers to brands that the salesmen want to sell them. Consequently, retailers may undo manufacturers' costly efforts to establish brand preference. Manufacturers can be expected to struggle and strain to devise measures that would free them from such great dependence upon retailers. One, at least, has explored the use of factory-owned retail outlets. Especially those manufacturers with a broad product line may find that such arrangements would offer, among other things, excellent opportunities to obtain reliable information from the market place speedily and accurately—information that now is extremely costly to gather.

In considering the critical distribution problems that television set manufacturers face, one should consider whether any lessons can be learned from foreign experience and the recent experience of other industries. In foreign countries, television sets pass through a two-step distribution system. No use is made of distributors at all. However, manufacturers in the United States are not likely to emulate foreign arrangements; in most commercial matters—and especially in distribution matters—American businessmen tend to be out ahead of their European counterparts.

Other major appliance industries—most of them older and better established than television—employ methods of distribution similar to those employed to sell television sets. Indeed, as noted frequently, the television set industry merely assimilated the distribution systems that had been created for radios and for big-ticket "white goods." As a result, it has learned and applied the lessons learned in the distribution of several other major appliances.

Manufacturers of major appliances may learn from producers of men's shoes, hardware, etc., the benefits of vertical integration. They may learn from a variety of trades about the benefits of mechanical vending. Applied to major appliances, automatic vending may take the form of customer's ordering on the basis of large, realistic photographic slides which present detailed product information. Viewing arrangements might be installed in a variety of retail outlets, mainly supermarkets, and provide for delivery directly to the home from distributors' warehouses.

Much of what was said in the preceding chapters can be summarized by discussing who exerts preponderant power over the design of the present distribution system. Current arrangements are mainly manufacturer-dominated. However, only a few manufacturers command a franchise that is so valuable that they possess overwhelming bargaining power in their relations with distributors or retailers. Perhaps the largest companies, such as Zenith, R.C.A., Motorola, Admiral, General Electric and Magnavox, possess enough bargaining power to establish arrangements that mainly favor themselves. Other manufacturers apparently adopt distribution arrangements that are as similar to those arrangements as they can attain. The distribution arrangements established by these manufacturers represent a compromise with distributors and retailers. Their dependence is, if anything, greater than that of the distributors and retailers.

The large retail customers clearly exert great bargaining power, even *vis à vis* the most powerful manufacturers. They have done considerable already and probably will do more to alter existing arrangements to meet their own needs and desires. If the current trend toward the elimination of the small appliance retailer and the growth of chains and large discount operations continues, their bargaining power will increase further. With greater power, they will be able to modify current distribution arrangements (in delivery, warehousing, special models, exclusivity, return privileges, servicing, margins, etc.) to better suit their needs. Market power seems to be shifting from even the most powerful manufacturers toward the large retail chains, though a few manufacturers may possess preponderant bargaining power still.

The case of Sears-Roebuck represents a retailer-dominated distribution system. As large retail appliance chains become larger, this pattern may be repeated. Major economies result when distribution is dominated by the retailer; the costs and efforts devoted to selling declines sharply, for the procurement relationships established by such firms is very similar to those of a vertically integrated company. When set quality becomes even more assured than it is at present, the development of private label television sets for major appliance and discount chains may spread substantially. If so, then some of the major manufacturers will become partly—and possibly mainly—sources of private label merchandise. (Large retailers would not need to actually acquire their own production facilities, as Sears did.)

The foregoing paragraphs certainly do not summarize all of the findings contained in the preceding chapters and were not intended to do so. Hopefully, they have reinterpreted and presented information discussed earlier in a manner that makes it clear and meaningful. The balance of this chapter will be devoted to conclusions drawn from the research that has been summarized.

Conclusions

I cannot claim to have established any of the following conclusions "beyond a reasonable doubt." Some conclusions are set forth as hypotheses that may direct and encourage work by others; other conclusions represent generalizations that appear to be far more likely to be true than false, but their validity is questionable. There are a few conclusions—still not conclusively established—that I regard as almost certainly valid. Conclusions of all these types will be presented, for some of the most shaky hypotheses deal with matters far more important than those which can be established with greater certainty.

HOW COMPETITIVE IS THE TELEVISION SET INDUSTRY?

It is extremely hazardous to appraise the competitiveness of an industry in a few paragraphs, let alone a few words. Especially is this so when the inferences are drawn directly from the theoretical conditions that must be met to have a state of "pure and perfect competition." As was first emphasized by Professor John Maurice Clark,[1] factors ordinarily conducive to monopoly may have precisely the opposite effect in particular contexts. Conversely, conditions required for

[1] J. M. Clark, "Toward a Concept of Workable Competition," *American Economic Review*, June 1940, pp. 241–56.

pure and perfect competition (like complete knowledge about price on the part of buyers and sellers) may increase the degree of monopoly power if embedded in a market structure composed of a few sellers who offer products and services that consumers regard as equally acceptable for their purpose. In short, the consequences and the competitiveness of industrial circumstances vary according to the other conditions with which they are combined. No market circumstance or business practice leads to the same consequences in all types of market contexts. A forecast of the consequences of any practice or condition requires that account be taken of the other circumstances present and the manner in which they interact.

This crucial fact will be set aside for a moment. An outline is presented here of the aspects of the industry that would, in most settings, reflect or contribute to competition or to monopoly. The competitiveness of the television set industry cannot be measured by the length of the different lists, of course. Moreover, the severity of competition may differ at the various levels of this industry; one level may be extremely competitive, while another may be much less so.

CHART 4
COMPETITION IN THE TELEVISION SET INDUSTRY

I. Indicators of competition
  A. In manufacturing
    1. A fairly high rate of failure among firms
    2. A low average rate of profit, as a percentage of sales
    3. Numerous price changes (especially when account is taken of promotions and special co-op arrangements)
    4. Differences in prices charged for comparable models by individual firms at any time
    5. Variations in differentials among individual items in different manufacturers' lines of sets
    6. Differences in product features in various firm's offerings
    7. Instability of the market penetration positions of individual firms
    8. Diversity of distribution systems employed by individual firms
    9. Existence of product "dumps"—drastic price reductions
    10. Preoccupation of top management with price and near-price developments
    11. Great diversity of market conditions and individual manufacturers' market shares from market to market

Summary and Conclusions

   B. In distribution
      1. High turnover—many firms dropping franchises or being dropped plus a substantial number of failures
      2. Low average rate of profit, whether figured on sales or on investment
      3. Frequent price changes and special promotions
      4. Inter-firm price differences at any time—both on average and on individual items in the line
      5. Relative instability of market penetration in the local markets served by individual distributors
      6. Enormous preoccupation with price on part of top management
      7. Intensive efforts to take away retail accounts from rival brands
      8. Substantial number of distributors operating within a given area relative to the volume of business available
   C. In retailing
      1. Very large numbers of sellers
      2. Heavy failure rate among sellers of appliances
      3. Rapid decline in the share of market served by medium- and small-size firms
      4. Low rate of profits, however measured
      5. Frequency of price promotions
      6. Heavy emphasis on price by most retailers in advertising, display, etc.
      7. Lack of locational monopoly owing to very large numbers of retailers offering sets for sale
II. Indicators of monopoly
   A. In manufacturing
      1. Very large size of the few firms that enjoy strong market position
      2. Ability of large and successful manufacturers to get strong distributors to represent them while others cannot obtain distributors of good quality
      3. Existence of exclusive distribution system
      4. Difficulty of entering the industry on a national scale
      5. Barriers to the entry of new firms as a result of the existence of brands that have won a strong consumer acceptance
      6. Close interaction among top executives in the industry through the trade association and otherwise
      7. List price increases that sometimes move up across almost the entire industry during a short time
   B. In distribution
      1. Freedom from competition from other distributors carrying the same brand due to exclusive franchises—in fact, if not in law
      2. Small number of "dominant" distributors in any market

CHART 4 (*continued*)

C. In retailing
1. Great power of a few retailers in many small- and medium-size markets
2. Fairly rapid elimination of small appliance retailers who characteristically have been the chief source of pressure on price

No effort will be made to establish the validity of the foregoing items. Even if valid, no acceptable method exists for combining them into a summary assessment of the industry's competitiveness. Nevertheless, the author wishes to record his conclusion that this industry is, all things considered, "highly competitive"—though not in the strict technical sense in which that term is used by academic economists. Indeed, this industry bears very little resemblance to a highly competitive industry, as defined in price theory. Yet, it probably is far more competitive than the average industry in this and other nations, in the sense in which laymen, businessmen, government officials and marketing specialists use the term.

As emphasised repeatedly, the complexity of almost every industry's structure and behavior makes any short-hand summary evaluation of its competitiveness highly misleading. To confuse matters more, a few aspects of the industry may be incompatible with the spirit of the antitrust laws, even while others seem to be excessively competitive. When one examines a particular industry in depth, he finds it very difficult to determine when competition is just severe enough.

No group would gain and many might lose if the industry were somehow made more competitive than it is now. This conclusion can be drawn from the analysis, presented below, of the way that intensive market rivalry has worked in this industry. Although competition probably has quite similar effects elsewhere in the economy, the following discussion is confined to this industry alone. At the start, the chief benefits expected to flow from competition will be matched against the actual experience of this industry. Thereupon the main perverse effects of competition—"wastes of competition," in common parlance —that have been exhibited in the television set industry will be reviewed briefly.

Perhaps the chief benefit attributed to competition is that it eliminates inefficiency and passes along the fruits of efficiency to consumers. Has competition had such effects in the television set industry? This industry witnessed the passing of almost a hundred firms that sought success as manufacturers of television sets. As indicated, numerous failures have also occurred in major appliance distribution and among appliance dealers. Thus, it can be recorded that many firms have been eliminated in all phases of this industry. However, it is not possible to state unequivocally that the firms eliminated from the industry were inefficient, in the usual meaning of the term. What, indeed, does "efficiency" mean when applied to an entrepreneur or a business enterprise? The term can be equated with financial success, so that an efficient firm is defined as one that prospers. If so, then those that fail are necessarily inefficient, by definition. By reasoning thus, we insure the conclusion that competition weeds out the inefficient.

To equate business failure with inefficiency is to ignore the circumstances that surround success and failure. A few of the most successful and innovative firms, executives and entrepreneurs in this industry have experienced bankruptcy proceedings or years of losses at times when other firms were earning profits. Conversely, many firms are prosperous despite what others in the industry regard as mediocre management. Certainly, many mediocre businessmen have made a success in major appliance distribution by virtue of having entered the business at a good time, having gotten a good franchise and having been "carried" by the manufacturer in many ways. Others who were far more efficient but lacked these "breaks" left or were driven from the business. Thus luck as well as efficiency can cause business success.

The experience of the television set industry suggests that the most important single ingredient of success is the ability to create, win and hold customers. (The same would seem to hold true for most other industries also.) Success sometimes comes to firms that are relatively inefficient in production, offer shoddy products and employ wasteful methods of handling and moving merchandise. In short, success requires mainly efficiency in marketing rather than in production, engineering, management, etc. A firm that can win a large sales volume for itself generally can endure relative inefficiencies in its other functions; indeed, it may never recognize these inefficiencies because of the important advantages that accompany large sales volume.

It would appear (data are lacking to prove either one side or the other) that success in business has increasingly shifted from those who can create what customers want and produce it at a low cost while maintaining reliable quality to those possessing skill in advertising, styling, pricing, promoting, merchandising, motivating salesmen and winning the loyalty and cooperation of distributors. The traditional skills—manufacturing and engineering—still figure in business success of course, but far less than before. A business that does not rise above some threshhold in all facets of business—production cost, styling, performance of products, breadth of distribution, etc.—would be killed in time by the lack of even a single one of them. But a firm that is mediocre in these respects but outstanding in market-creation frequently will rise to the top of the heap; its weaknesses will be obscured by its high capacity utilization and the ability to spread a swollen overhead over a large number of units. Moreover, it will, as a consequence of its large sales, generally attract executives of high talent and win the best distributors and retailers. Business also seems to be governed by the regressive rule that "to those that have shall be given."

The possession of large financial resources also contributes heavily to business success, it would appear. Firms with large resources can weather their inevitable mistakes, while others may be fatally crippled by a single major error. They can make use of the most modern production techniques promptly, can hire proved executives and can, by sheer weight of dollars, overcome firms with lesser financial strength in a struggle for a particular markets. The experience of the television set industry suggests that sheer resources are not enough, however. Such a mighty firm as C.B.S.-Columbia was forced to retire from the industry, as were Stewart-Warner and Stromberg-Carlson. Philco, after a period of heavy losses, elected to sell out to the Ford Motor Company.

The foregoing line of argument suggests that success and failure in business are only very crude indicators of "efficiency." It leaves open for consideration the hypothesis that competition often eliminates firms that are efficient in manufacturing, engineering, financing, management, handling materials, etc., and bestows success upon firms

Summary and Conclusions

mediocre in these departments if they are especially skilled in persuading customers to buy their wares.

I do not feel competent to assess the relative efficiency of present and past television set producers in their various activities. Consequently I cannot offer even a tentative opinion as to what kinds of firms have been eliminated from the industry by competition. I do believe that success in this industry has come to many whose skills and virtues are very different from those which competition is expected to foster.

Competition is expected to offer important benefits beyond the elimination of the inefficient. It is also expected to provide customers with many alternatives and thereby to free them from dependence upon a single supplier. This benefit certainly has been reaped in the television set industry to a considerable degree. Customers are offered many different brands to choose among—as well as many choices within any brand. A carping critic might argue that customers really are offered choices between Tweedledee and Tweedledum—that there really are so few differences in either the basic quality or features or styling of different brands that the consumer really has little substantive choice. Nevertheless, it certainly can be established that consumers are not dependent upon a single supplier. If they do not like some manufacturer, or distributor or dealer, they can get essentially equal value from another without great effort or sacrifice.

Another important benefit expected from competition is that it drives off the market or chastens the seller of low-quality products and rewards the firms offering high quality. If one has in mind fairly extreme differences in quality, the television industry does provide numerous examples of poor products being rejected by consumers. (In this industry, the quickest and most effective rejections of products are those made by resellers rather than by the ultimate consumer. Frequently they are initiated by servicemen who are employed by distributors and dealers.) However, if one has in mind the modest differences in product quality that are found at present among brands of television sets, the penalties that competition inflicts upon sellers of below-average quality are not discernible. The consumer is not capable of judging modest differences in set quality and has generally been willing to take almost any nationally advertised brand that a skilled salesman sets out to sell. Moreover, competition has not—here one can speak with considerable conviction—compelled producers to improve their product quality in order to win greater patronage. It has worked in reverse to a considerable extent by creating intense pressure to reduce cost even at the expense of quality in order to reduce price and thereby increase sales. In other words, both a reduction and an improvement in quality may increase sales and profits. In the television set industry—as in most others—producers have followed both routes.

Finally, another major benefit expected from intense competition is pressure upon all persons engaged in business to exert their greatest efforts. Since conditions of manufacture were not investigated, none of the following comments applies to what happens on the production lines in the television set industry. But with specific reference to distributional efforts I was struck by the strong exertions made by the individuals I met or saw at work. Businessmen and executives in this industry are characterized by high levels of activity and "pressure." The men engaged in distribution and marketing are doers and appear determined to get ahead. They apparently are confident that they will get ahead if they show that they are skilled. If manufacturers, distributors or dealers in this business fall short of the ultimate efficiency possible, it is rarely because of lack of effort. And competition—the presence of a rival who is obviously trying to win your customers away, or to win the next job promotion, or even to take away your job—seems to be responsible for this condition to a high degree. Beyond the effect of competition, however, business apparently attracts persons who are activists and who are ambitious for financial success to a far greater extent than the average. The combination of competition and the self-selection of persons anxious to achieve financial success does result, in this industry and others, in having a corps of executives outstanding in the efforts they put forward to succeed.

So much then for the benefits that competition is expected to yield and how, in fact, competition seems to have worked out in the television set industry. What are the alleged wastes of competition? Have they been in evidence in the television set industry? The chief criticisms of competition are: it causes needless redundancy of productive capacity, results in costly and unnecessary competitive sales effort and gives rise to duplicated distribution facilities.

It is impossible to measure precisely the capacity of the industry to produce sets. To make such a measurement would require a determination of the "bottleneck" and an investigation of how much that bottleneck could turn out at maximum effort. Superficial investigation suggests that the bottleneck in this industry is in the production of viewing tubes. Especially if one takes account of the existing facilities for the rebuilding of such tubes, the industry's ability to produce viewing tubes might well be double or more the highest level of unit sales attained by this industry to date. As implied, the industry could—given urgent customer demands to do so—turn out the other components needed to double output and assemble them in a relatively short time. Clearly, output could not be doubled in a day or two, but the facilities to do so are in place.

It is difficult to argue that an industry "needs" capacity to produce twice as much as it sells. On the other hand, it would be equally mistaken to maintain that it needs only enough capacity to make what it is currently able to sell. As the market fortunes of individual firms vary, their utilization of capacity fluctuates also. Possession of idle facilities provides both the opportunity and the spur to increase sales. Just how great a spur is economically justifiable cannot be stated precisely. Nevertheless, it would appear that competition has resulted in excessive production facilities in the industry with resultant waste of indeterminate amount.

Much the same thing can be said about distribution facilities. These exist in far greater quantity than is required to serve the existing level of customers with essentially the amount of comfort, speed and convenience that customers obtain at present. However, the precise amount of the excess and its cost cannot be measured, and only an extremely brave or foolish investigator would even offer a quantitative estimate. But it would be safe to assert that criticism of competition on grounds that it produces excessive distribution facilities has been borne out by the television set industry's experience.

The third usual criticism of competition—that it gives rise to costly and unnecessary competitive sales effort—is both more difficult to appraise and more likely to stir controversy. (Executives in the television set industry would not quarrel with the conclusion that both production and physical distribution facilities are excessive.) As explained, executives in this industry complain bitterly about their competitors' excessive preoccupation with price—or, intensity of price competition. However, they rarely complain about the other forms that competition takes, even though they are very costly. The main forms that competition takes in this industry, other than price, are advertising, personal selling and product change. These three forms of rivalry involve expenditures that are substantial but, again, cannot be measured precisely. And, more to the point at hand, the proportion of those expenditures that can be considered "purely competitive"—designed solely to win customers away from rivals and not offering any service of substantive value to customers—can only be conjectured.

How would one evaluate an advertisement that extols a product feature of a given brand from the standpoint of whether or not it is "purely competitive"? Certainly most advertisements are partly informational and direct the customer's attention to some aspect of the product and, hopefully, tell him something of value about that aspect. Ordinarily the advertisement will tell what stores are selling the product and sometimes will indicate the price they are charging. These "services" cannot be considered purely competitive advertising. On the other hand, the seller's chief goal in running the advertisement is to assert and imply product superiority over rivals and to offset their advertising. The main ingredient of advertising by manufacturers in the television set industry, and some admit it privately, is "competitive." Whether determined by intent or effect, a large but indeterminate proportion of all television set advertising outlays must be considered purely competitive and therefore a cost or "waste" for which competition is responsible. These outlays do *not* have the goal or the effect of increasing total sales or of providing information but only cancel out the advertising of rival firms.

The same line of analysis, when applied to personal sales efforts and to product changes, leads to a similar conclusion. Both types of activity do yield minor substantive benefit to customers but are motivated primarily by the desire to win customers away from competitors

Summary and Conclusions

—rather than to render a better service to customers or to expand the total market for sets. Moreover, if judged by the actual effects of these activities, they would almost certainly involve far greater cost than the benefits to customers would justify. Stated differently, if the costs of having present numbers of manufacturer and distributor salesmen were set against what these salesman offer to their customers, the customers might prefer half as much sales attention if they could pocket the resultant savings.

The same result would probably hold in the case of product change. Given accurate information about the changes made and about their cost, most consumers probably would prefer to forego them and take the resultant saving in lower prices. Of course, when the combined effect of advertising and personal sales influence make trifling modifications appear to be dramatic improvements, consumers are persuaded to place a high value on these modifications. But one would scarcely defend competition on grounds that it induces sellers to fool customers into regarding minor product improvements as major innovations.

Another criticism that has been made of competition is that it creates many "unnecessary" risks for businesses that inflate costs and make the conduct of business unnecessarily arduous and insecure. Surely, anyone who studies the industry must be impressed with the extent to which chance, accident, luck and uncertainty bedevil business decisions and policies. Executives just accept and assume that the most carefully researched and considered plans will fail in a considerable proportion of cases and that successes sometimes will occur inexplicably.

The hazards that surround the decisions and actions of executives in this industry are similar to those one finds in most other industries. One can distinguish three broad classes of risk: (1) Changes (whether or not predictable) in circumstances outside the television set industry itself—such as variations in general economic activity, changes in interest rates, availability of capital, variations in export markets for whatever reason, changes in volume of imports of television sets, etc.; (2) Changed conditions in the industry—including shifts in consumer demand, changes in competitors' products and prices and policies, availability of distributors, technological changes, variations in quality and number of television programs, possible availability of "pay television," additions to or reductions in the number of producers, changes in form and severity of government regulation, etc.; and (3) Changes in conditions within the firm—including shifts in consumer favor among brands, development of particular product features, the addition or loss of individual distributors, growth of local competitors, changes in cost conditions, threat of labor stoppages, changes in morale of labor force or distributor organization, and personnel shifts among top management. The foregoing list is very long, though far from complete. Most of the items on this list have nothing whatsoever to do with competition. However, those that have the greatest effect on a firm's fortunes and that principally occupy the thoughts of top executives result from rivals' actions—whether they are predictable or not. The constant striving of dozens of competitors to gain an advantage over him creates the largest single class of risk that confronts the business executive in the television set industry.

The presence of such great uncertainty surely affects what businessmen do, how they do it and the consequences of their actions. It also affects their costs and determines what kinds of executives and firms will succeed.

An almost universal reaction to a discussion of the nature and costs or risk in business resulting from competition is, "That is the nature of our economic system," or, "That is what businessmen are paid profit to put up with." Both of these reactions are basically valid. We should, however, ask whether risk on this scale is either unavoidable or desirable in the light of alternative feasible arrangements.

It is difficult to argue in defense of chaos, at least as an underlying principle for an economic system. The amount of risk and uncertainty that must inevitably surround business operations is considerable; climate, international relations, general business activity, technological changes, etc. cannot be controlled fully or predicted precisely. As a result, wastes will occur, and luck and accident inevitably will affect the fortunes of every individual and firm. Just as any other painful and wasteful condition, avoidable risk should be eliminated to the fullest extent possible.

The stress placed on the amount and cost of risk and uncertainty comes close to the argument advanced by reformers and radicals in favor of "economic planning." Partly because this line of argument is similar to views expressed by some radicals, one rarely hears it even discussed. Indeed, businessmen in this industry appear to be resigned to risk and uncertainty on a grand scale as a routine way of life, even though they despise it. Is there no escape, within the framework of a free enterprise economy?

The foregoing discussion of the effects of market competition in the television set industry was only sketchy and not intended to exhaust this big subject. It should have succeeded in its chief objective: to indicate that competition takes various forms, some of which are not particularly laudable, and exists to varying degrees. Excesses of competition may cause as much misery as an insufficiency. Economic theory does not help much to understand and appraise competition; the layman's general endorsement of competition as the "best kind" of control mechanism for industry speaks from prejudice rather than from conviction based on knowledge of the way that competition works. Until we know more about competition's effects, in its various forms and degrees, maybe we should have a moratorium on broad generalizations about the virtues and wastes of competition. Moreover, any generalizations about competition have meaning only if expressed in terms of feasible alternatives to competition. If competition is wasteful by some ideal or absolute standards, that fact is of slight interest if other arrangements are even more wasteful.

THE CHIEF GOALS OF EXECUTIVES IN THE TELEVISION SET INDUSTRY

One of the strongest impressions gained from this investigation is that top and middle management in the television set industry is overwhelmingly preoccupied with sales. It is true that management does suffer frequently from "product problems," constantly seeks product improvements and cost reductions, and recognizes the important contribution that these make to business success. Yet far more than with these matters, management thinks, plans, schemes and talks about sales. Concern with sales permeates every department of every business in the industry.

Preoccupation with sales could easily be confused with what marketing specialists call "consumer orientation," which designates the view that businessmen will prosper most by offering consumers the kinds of things they desire rather than what businessmen find it easy to provide. Preoccupation with sales in the television set industry is not symptomatic of consumer orientation as a path to success but as concern with *results*. It appears that many executives in this and other industries are not terribly fastidious about the methods by which sales are obtained.

Similarly, preoccupation with sales should not be mistaken for "profit orientation" or with a striving for growth, as an end in itself. Many businessmen assume that increased sales mean greater profits. However, they sometimes pursue greater sales even when they conflict with short-term and at other times with long-term profits for the firm. "Sales preoccupation" thus is not to be equated with either consumer orientation or profit orientation, though it includes them in part. Sales preoccupation makes sales the absolute measure of success both for executives and for their firms. Most executives apparently perceive themselves as successful and rank their colleagues mainly by their contribution to sales.

This observed preoccupation of top and middle management with sales raises the problems of business goals that was touched on, but lightly, at several points in the preceding chapters. To understand and appraise the performance of an organization or an industry it is necessary to examine the goals its members seek. In discussing business goals, a distinction must be made among what eexcutives say, what they actually believe, what they want others to believe and what they actually do. It is not uncommon for people to believe sincerely that they are moved by pure motives and yet behave in a manner that is consistent only with base motives. The problems of uncovering the true motives of individuals are enormous—yet many discuss them with great confidence but without knowledge. The following discussion is based upon detailed study—though the reader should question, as I have questioned, the validity of both my method of study and its results. One should be especially critical of the discussions of business goals, which are based on virtually no research and are invariably consistent with the public relations statements by top executives and with the preconceptions of the persons expressing them.

Although the following conclusions are tentative, some are quite obvious. First, businessmen in the television set industry pursue a variety of goals. Some of these goals are personal and contribute toward the individual's personal success and achievement. Many goals doubtless are unconscious and reflect the fulfillment of personal—and possibly idiosyncratic—needs. Many of the goals are those of the business enterprise itself, with which top executives in this industry "identify" very strongly. A clear finding of the study was that top executives form a strong emotional link with their enterprise and find it difficult to think of joining a rival manufacturing firm. (Under pressure to obtain income or needing activity and the feeling of "belonging" that is satisfied by holding a job, most of those who resign or are fired do go to work for another manufacturer in this industry.)

The following discussion is concerned with the objectives attributed to the firm. Obviously a business, as such, has no objectives other than those attributed to it by human beings—the stockholders and the management in unclear proportion. We shall not deal here with the motives of individuals that are personal and individual, except to report that in some respects they seem to conflict with those of the firm. (One case in the industry is so outstanding that it cannot be discussed without disclosing the individual's identity to many people in the industry. There is considerable gossip to the effect that this person responds primarily to personal ego drives rather than to his firm's goals.)

Second, the goals of television set manufacturers and distributors rarely are stated explicitly. Consequently, there is some disagreement as well as puzzlement about what those ends are and what they imply in specific cases. It is rare that management will, in the course of reaching an operating decision, cite the stated objectives of the firm —if any exist. They apparently make their decisions and plans on the basis of unspoken assumptions about corporate goals. (A highly fertile field for research—by someone who is not easily discouraged and who has the ingenuity of ten geniuses—would be to discover what these assumptions are in specific corporations.)

Executives in the television set industry display great interest in, and more than a little concern with, problems of "business ethics," "the public responsibility of business" and "consumer problems." These and related problems all relate to the goals of business. To deal with these matters, as they relate to the industry, we will discuss separately executive concern with the consumer interest and with the public interest. (We shall pass over problems involving labor relations, into which no systematic inquiry was made.) Specific sensitive issues will be discussed as they arise in fairly common situations rather than in exceptional cases. Interest will be centered on the goals and ethics of firms with a reputation for integrity rather than with firms whose ethics are below the average for the industry.

Businessmen's concern with the customer's welfare. A variety of situations arise which call forth an expression of businessmen's concern with the customer's interest. Occasionally, a decision that serves their firm's and their own goals would also be in the customer's interest. It is crucial to know what proportion of business decisions that possibly involve the customer are in this category. The rationale of competition holds that businessmen are compelled to act as if they were defenders of the customer's welfare in order to survive, and thus their interests should coincide.

The discussion of retailing in an earlier chapter made it clear that such often is not the case. Television set buyers as a group are not discriminating and wise judges of their own self-interest in the purchase of sets and thereofore frequently are swayed by skillful sellers. Appliance salesmen have developed and acquired mastery over sales techniques that enable them to induce customers to buy rather than not buy, to select one brand rather than others, to perceive differences in quality that do not exist, and even to misperceive the level of price. As a consequence, businessmen sometimes must choose between what is best for their firm or for their own advancement on one hand, and what is best for the customer on the other. How frequently and in what kinds of situations do such choices arise, and how do businessmen decide?

Within the broad class of executive decisions in the television set industry involving possible conflict between the businessman's and the customer's interest, it is useful to separate decisions whose full effects work themselves out over a short period from those whose full effects are felt only over a fairly long period. The time dimension of executives' goals may affect their choices in any specific case. Reward systems established by most firms typically induce them to select the course that yields the greatest benefits in the short run, even though that course may be less advantageous than some other to the firm over a longer period. Similarly, they might be willing to make a personal sacrifice and reduce the firm's profits for a short period in order to provide *immediate* and noticeable benefit for consumers and to provide near term gains for the firm. But they might be unwilling to do so if the benefits would accrue to the firm only in the distant future—when the connection between their efforts and sacrifices on the one hand and consumer benefit on the other might not be recognized.

Under what fairly common conditions might an executive decide for his firm and against the buyer of the set? In what situations might he decide for the customer and against the television set producer? When might he decide to help the customer now, hurt his firm for a while, but in several years end up by helping his firm? To be even more realistic, when might he help the customer now at the firm's short-run expense with a fairly good chance of helping his firm in the future? The farther away in time that the effects of any action are felt, the greater the uncertainty of their realization, as a general rule.

Below are three common types of situations in which executives' decisions reflect their concern with the buyer's welfare. It might be helpful to explore them if one wishes to understand businessmen's goals involving the consumer.

1. Profit margins are ample, and management is asked to consider a reduction in price. Customers would gain increased purchasing power and the firm's unit sales might rise almost immediately. On the other hand, rivals might match their price reduction and cancel most of their possible sales gains; or, if sales do increase, they might not rise nearly enough to compensate for the price decline. The firm might, on the other hand, gain in the future because of consumer appreciation for the price reduction and the impression that this company gives good value.

2. Engineers come forward with a method of improving the quality of television sets in a way that is not visible or demonstrable. Because of the nature of the quality improvement and the market situation, the firm would not be able to increase price, even though costs would rise somewhat. All executives agree that sales would not rise as a result

of the change, at least for some time. It is expected that a few consumers would recognize the improvement or learn about it from servicemen and would be influenced to purchase this brand rather than some other. On the other hand, it is recognized that all other manufacturers would have to make equal improvements in quality to match this company's improvement in quality and no sales benefits would rebound to the seller—but costs would remain at a higher level than before the change.

3. A retailer faces a customer who is interested in buying a set from him. New lines of sets have already been announced by manufacturers, and the retailer has seen them; he is quite certain that the consumer would much prefer some of the new sets to the present model he is willing to buy. Faced with the clear opportunity to make a sale now and the risk that the customer would make his purchase elsewhere if encouraged to wait for the new line, what would the typical retailer do? He would doubtless recognize that he might gain the customer's appreciation and loyalty from such advice and thereby, through word-of-mouth praise, gain more customers.

In plain fact, we do not know how businessmen in this industry decide in such situations, even though they frequently find themselves in such conflict situations. The considerations that would dictate specific choice will vary, of course, but some are common to almost all executives, and these will be sketched briefly.

Executives recognize that television sets are purchased very infrequently. Consequently, a satisfied customer today does not mean "repeat business" in the near future. Indeed, data on this point suggest that even consumers who have been highly satisfied with their previous set purchase will often buy another brand to get a special deal or to get a particular product feature or just because they like the styling of that brand best. Consequently, in this industry the gains from consumer goodwill are far less than in products that are repurchased frequently. Businessmen's self-interest would dictate that they concentrate on the current sale and not worry much about the customer's next purchase.

The consequences of any business decision or policy are difficult to assess. These decisions and policies exert their effects in combination with market conditions that change rapidly and markedly. A wise decision may, if other circumstances worsen, be perceived as mistaken. An action that was of benefit to the firm might be judged to have been harmful. The longer the time interval between the making of the decision and the reaping of the rewards, the smaller the likelihood that the gains will be attributed to the true source. Despite the enormous and costly efforts made to measure the effectiveness of advertising, for example, the goal has not been achieved. The effects of other business actions are no easier to measure. Consequently, a firm that made minor improvements in quality might never know whether they resulted in greater profits—or even in higher sales.

In decisions about product quality executives are overwhelmingly concerned with what the customer is able to see for himself. They start with the premise that the set must perform adequately when it is in the customer's home without early breakdown. Given that basic constraint, they distinguish sharply between features that the customer can recognize readily and those that are "inside the set." They find that legitimate claims that the quality of the set was improved have not been believed by consumers unless accompanied by some visible evidence of improvement.

In short, experience in this industry teaches businessmen that even if they could significantly improve the durability of their sets or provide more reliable tuning or a slightly sharper picture, virtually no consumers would be able to recognize the changes. Moreover, customers would not believe the manufacturer's claims to have made such changes, unless they could be demonstrated. Many executives in this industry, especially those engaged in product planning, feel extremely frustrated because many product improvements in the customer's interest they might make generally would involve cost penalties for the firm and would go unappreciated by the customer. It is easy for them to feel that the "customer gets what he deserves," and, "If the consumer is concerned mainly with gimmicks, trivial features or appearance, we must give him what he wants," and, "If we spent an extra ten dollars to make a substantially more reliable set and one that gave a less distorted picture, the consumer would not pay an extra nickel unless he could actually see the difference for himself."

Thus major obstacles exist to the industry's taking actions that would benefit the consumer. The rewards of so doing are uncertain, and frequently they can serve the consumer only at the expense of the firm they serve. We know of no firm in any industry that tells its executives that it is more important to do what is good for the customer than to make money for the firm.

Businessmen in this industry will, in conversation, frequently speak of giving the customer a better set or of providing better value, and they boast that the industry has improved quality substantially over the years, even while reducing prices. However, the consumer interest is not, in my opinion, given any consideration by executives in this industry when it conflicts with the firm's interests. (I know of no industry that is different in this regard.) Consumer's welfare is served *only* when it is consistent with the company's. Although consistent to a considerable degree, they are not identical. When the interests of business and its customers are in conflict, the customer's interest is the one to be sacrificed, even by "honorable" firms in the television set industry.

The foregoing account of businessmen's goals should not offend any business executive's sensibilities. No one could expect or ask him to act differently. On the other hand, it is clear that he is not a protector of the consumer. Competitive pressures and fear of government prosecution prevent him from abusing the consumer except in relatively minor ways. But, given the technical complexity of television sets, the consumer does need protection. He has not acquired the knowledge necessary to buy sets wisely, and it is unreasonable to expect that he will ever do so. Mainly, the consumer assumes that the businessman (partly under the threat of government prosecution) will look after his interests or that competition will bring about the equivalent result. Such is not the case, especially in matters involving invisible product quality.

The television set buyer depends upon the businessman to safeguard his interest in many matters, but it is unreasonable to expect businessmen to do so under existing conditions. The fault is neither the customer's nor the businessman's. However, something is wrong. We will not get around to setting it right until we face the fact that, whatever they say in public pronouncements, businessmen do not include the protection of the consumer's interest among their goals.

This statement applies to the television set industry *as now con-*

stituted. A balanced picture of businessmen's goals requires consideration of how they might behave under quite different circumstances. How would present executives in the industry behave if they possessed very great market power and were consequently able to abuse the consumer if they wished—and could get away with it? Would they grab all they could get?

Conjecture about such questions is extremely dangerous. It is even difficult to select a basis on which to build a guess. Under the situation postulated, the author believes that most business executives would not forego their own and their firm's goals to serve the consumer interest. (Some managements in the industry are more likely to do so than others.) However, since no firm enjoys certain freedom from government prosecution, potential competition, consumer resentment and adverse public opinion, extreme abuse is very unlikely. When it does occur, it is almost always short-lived. But it is *not* ended by any solicitude of executives for the consumer's welfare.

Businessmen's concern with the public interest. It has already been indicated that some people identify the consumer's interest with the public interest. This view is rejected, because some important groups besides consumers make up the nation, and their interests are no less meritorious than those of consumers. The consumer is a minority interest for any single product if one simply counts heads. What, then, is the public interest, and to what extent are businessmen in this industry concerned with it?

The public interest has already been defined as "what is best for the country as a whole, taking account of the degree of benefit and sacrifice as well as the number of persons gaining and losing." Here we will assemble observations dealing with the extent to which television set executives are, as businessmen, moved in their policies and in their behavior by considerations of public interest. Even more specifically, we want to know under what circumstances they will knowingly sacrifice their firm's goals or their personal aspirations to serve the public interest.

A few observations may serve to narrow this broad and controversial subject to a point where fruitful discussion of this industry's experience becomes possible. First, it is difficult to define the public interest even in specific instances in a way that will obtain unanimous agreement; consequently, almost any action and policy might be construed to be compatible with the public interest. Given the great ingenuity of public relations specialists, it is difficult even to imagine any business action that cannot be defended partly on grounds of serving the public at large. Second, the only convincing test of devotion to the public interest is that a sacrifice must be made to serve it. In other words, one must reject any action and policy that furthers a firm's or an executive's interest as one that is not motivated by concern with public welfare; the public interest can only be identified in conflict situations. Third, virtually no group—including public representatives in local, state and federal legislatures, and possibly even judges—puts the public interest above its own. Certainly one cannot argue that labor unions or laborers in general or farmers or even teachers or clergymen are devoted to the public welfare above all else and without regard to personal sacrifices or the sacrifices of their organizations. Fourth, it has become fashionable for businessmen to state that they attempt to balance the competing interests of consumers, labor, management and stockholders, and the public. They deny that the achievement of purely business goals is their sole concern and claim to give weight to public welfare where it is affected by their actions. In that sense, they seem to accept the obligation to do so—at least in principle. Fifth, often there is consistency between what is in the public interest and what best serves the firm's goals—at least in the long run. Clearly, to take actions that are immoral will expose a firm to public censure and customer resentment. With many alternative sources of roughly equal values, a firm might suffer a very large loss of patronage if it openly flouted the public interest. After all, businessmen have themselves fostered the notion that they are obliged to serve the public interest.

The following discussion does not review specific actions of members of the television set industry to determine when their behavior has been inconsistent with the public interest. As indicated, any single instances would be open to conflicting interpretations. Instead, a few questions will be discussed that should illuminate—though they will hardly settle—this vexing problem. Are top executives in the television set industry (or must others) capable of defining the public interest in a way that would be acceptable to most of the public? Is it necessary or desirable that we depend upon businessmen to protect the public interest? If not, how can it be protected?

When we say "define the public interest" we obviously are not asking whether top executives can master a textbook definition but whether they have the objectivity, experience, frame of reference, etc. to understand what is best for the nation as a whole. Relatively few persons do have this ability. On the other hand, some occupational groups are better able than others to understand the problem and to overcome their personal biases well enough to grant due weight to the claims of other members of the nation. How do television set businessmen rate in this regard? One can only venture a personal opinion that is necessarily based upon weak evidence. (It is difficult to know what would be strong evidence on this point.)

I conclude that top television set executives—or executives in other industries—are not likely to understand and be objective with regard to the public interest. (I have observed considerable improvement over the last 20 years or so, however.) I question the ability of any group to define the public interest when it conflicts with its own. The hierarchy of groups ranked according to their ability to define the public interest objectively might have at the top social scientists, members of the higher courts, legislators and well-educated housewives. Close to the bottom of the list are union leaders, representatives of business groups in general and individual business executives.

One might ask why this should be so. That question raises interesting issues that need not be discussed at length in a study of the television set industry. There are reasons, and they are not that certain groups are "nicer" than others or "more public spirited" than others. Rather, they relate to the forces within the organization that account for success. Business executives rarely rise to the top because of awareness of and concern with the public interest. Contributions to the firm's progress and goals are the main bases for advancement within the firm. I met no executive in this industry who was so strongly moved by the desire to render public service that he would do so at his firm's expense. Such a man would surely be considered unreliable, if not a menace, by almost every board of directors. Indeed, labor union officials probably would be very worried about working for such a management.

No one apparently has studied top executives to learn their own views on this subject. My impression is that most of the executives in the industry do not consider themselves particularly well qualified to define the public interest (and certainly would not trust their competitors to do so) and do not want the responsibility of safeguarding it. They recognize that their public pronouncements must show them and their firms to be public spirited and basically fair, and they are developing skills in the public relations phase of their duties. But they are basically business executives who have the heavy burdens of running highly complex organizations. The top executives in the television set industry give the author the impression of wishing to be left alone to do their jobs and not be bothered with such extraneous and vague and essentially meaningless matters as "the public interest."

The foregoing discussion leads directly to the question, must we depend upon businessmen to protect the public interest? Although not particularly germane to the study of the television set industry, this question merits brief discussion at this point.

The logic of a free enterprise system does not require businessmen —or any other group—to serve the public interest when that conflicts with its own. Indeed, the rationale of our economic system—and perhaps its greatest strength—is that it only requires individuals and groups to look out for themselves. Naked self-interest, combined with competition, is believed to serve the public better than any other arrangement that can be devised. If we do not need businessmen to safeguard the public interest, are we then dealing with a trivial question?

Regrettably not. The actions of certain businesses frequently have repercussions on the public—and they generally do have a choice in those matters. That is to say, many large firms generally possess several feasible alternatives and their specific choices exert a significant influence on what happens to the public. Would we be wise to depend upon businessmen to protect the public interest in instances in which the public would be injured if they did not do so? If we do not wish to depend upon businessmen to protect the public interest, what alternatives do we have?

In the case of the television set industry, the severity of competition provides great (though not necessarily sufficient) protection for the

Summary and Conclusions 267

public. Clearly, business executives in this industry are not free to do what they wish with respect to product quality, price, payments to labor and the like. Their discretion in matters affecting the public interest is very small. At some times and in subtle ways they can cut corners and "get away with something" while injuring the public in the process—though concrete examples of this are hard to find. Given the number of firms that left the television set manufacturing industry during the last five years, this situation may not prove to be permanent. If individual manufacturers did acquire strong market power, on whom must we depend for protection of the public interest? On the manufacturers themselves?

The answer would appear to be obvious. It is not the function of business executives, and not one of their talents, to understand and to feel dedicated to the public interest. We actually depend upon duly constituted regulatory authorities—mainly legislatures, regulatory agencies and the judiciary—to protect the general public. When businessmen abuse excessive power, these authorities must curb and punish them. Reliance on self-control and self-regulation by business is not idealistic or naive; usually it is a cynical policy advanced by those seeking to capitalize on public gullibility and the widespread reverence for businessmen. These forms of control scarcely make sense as national policy. As a nation, we rarely invoke self-regulation as a safeguard of the public interest in other spheres; it is no more likely to be effective where business is concerned than elsewhere.

On occasion, businessmen have the legal right to do things in their own interest that might injure the public badly—though these situations rarely are obvious and noncontroversial. Matters involving national defense, vital work stoppages, even major spurs to inflation might fall in this category. At such times, we *must* depend upon businessmen to sacrifice their self interest to serve the public interest— simply because *we lack the time to invoke the usual regulatory processes*. We can scarcely justify reliance on self-regulation in such cases because we consider it more effective than government regulation. Perhaps in compensation for this very occasional dependence upon businessmen to make voluntary sacrifices for the public interest, the public (through government or spontaneous community efforts) is equally obliged to give extra-legal assistance to them when their interest is threatened and time is lacking for the usual regulatory processes to be invoked. In the absence of such reciprocal obligations on the part of the public, it is difficult to require sacrifices from business that are extra-legal. Moreover, it would clearly be dangerous to oblige business management as a matter of law to heed the pleading of all men in public office.

We can be grateful, but we should be greatly surprised when any organization voluntarily sacrifices its goals for the welfare of others. The study of the television set industry convinced me that businessmen in this and other industries can neither define public interest accurately nor be depended upon to make sacrifices to serve it. They will, on the other hand, obey the letter of the law even when they regard it as unfair and unwise. In no sense of the term do they regard themselves as public officials who have a loyalty to public welfare "beyond the call of duty to their corporation." If they could grievously injure the public within the scope of the law, some would do so without hesitation, though others doubtless would cooperate in closing opportunities for such abuse. But, once the law is enacted, that becomes public policy for the typical business executive in the television set industry. And, in my opinion, that is how it should be.

THE CALIBER OF BUSINESS EXECUTIVES IN THE TELEVISION SET INDUSTRY

Business executives vary in intelligence, personality, integrity, perseverance and in other human qualities, much as any other group of people. To generalize about them implies uniformity where substantial variation is the rule. Nevertheless a few generalizations can be advanced about the executives who were interviewed and observed in connection with this study.

Top and near-top executives with whom I came in contact are natively as intelligent as successful doctors, lawyers, dentists and accountants that I know. Also, they appear to be quite as intelligent as college professors (and more intelligent than some). Criticism of executives' intelligence comes from two sources: the group that is most critical of executives is other executives. Business executives are as critical of one another as are Ph.D. candidates, who characteristically deal harshly with authorities in their field. The second group of

Summary and Conclusions

critics are academic specialists in business. These apparently are upset by the fact that many executives do not know all that they could easily learn about their jobs or their industry. These critics confuse knowledge for the capacity to learn or understand. It is scarcely surprising that business executives are less scholarly and less familiar with the vast literature about business than university folk. (Of course, executives are no less critical of university people for equally unsupportable reasons; they imply that professors should know as much about what actually happens in business as they do.)

In part, businessmen are less studious about their jobs than they should be—in their own interest. As a result, some employ outmoded methods and frustrate their subordinates and fail to command the full respect they require to secure their full contribution to the firm. For the most part, businessmen appear to be victims of a mistaken "image" of a successful executive, which is almost incompatible with studiousness. The prevailing notion about what constitutes a "good executive" includes the following elements: decisiveness, activity, self-sacrifice for the business, social adeptness, affability and ability to inspire respect and fear. The bookish and meditative type is almost at the opposite pole from this image. Many executives appear to be mystics when they talk about the qualities that make for success in business. They imply that it is an indefinable quality of personality and mind that basically cannot be learned and is not easily identified. (This view of the skills an executive requires may well explain the great insecurity that most top executives are said to feel. If success depends upon such an intangible ability, it is hardly surprising that executives often wonder whether they have it, or whether they lost what they once had.)

Business executives place a relatively low value on the basic skills that could be brought into play in the conduct of business. They stress personality factors. It is therefore not surprising that they accord relatively little respect to the well-informed academic specialist and get quite little in return. Judged as a business executive—as a leader of men, source of new ideas, energizer and organizer—the average executive in the television set industry seems first-rate to me. I have no fears, however, that many of them could—or would be foolish enough to want to—win my job from me.

Many unkind words have been spoken about the ethics of businessmen. The public has damned them, even as an old, buccaneer-type businessman proclaimed, "Let the public be damned!" With regard to integrity, it is essential to distinguish personal integrity from business ethics. They may be interconnected to a degree, but they mainly appear to be quite separate. As individuals, business executives seem no more or less honorable than other men. Perhaps they stand up well in comparisons with other groups because other groups are so tainted, rather than because of their exemplary nature. Whatever the explanation, an individual could expect to receive as humane treatment, sincere consideration, and mercy from a business executive acting as an individual as from members of the professional groups mentioned before, including college professors.

If businessmen act like rogues, it is in their capacity as businessmen and not when acting as individuals. Business actions and decisions take place within a special role and within a subculture that is fashioned out of different goals, values, symbols and standards than exist outside business. When a business executive makes a business decision, he is essentially a different person—much as a prize-fighter is completely different in the ring than with his family. It would not be mistaken to say that executives have different codes of ethics as businessmen and as individuals. There does not seem to be any connection between these facets of their lives. Moreover, most executive decisions are impersonal, concerning prices, advertisements, margins, product features, etc. In a vital sense, these decisions do not really involve the executive's emotions very intimately. They have little relationship with his personal relationships either in or outside the firm.

Some executives do appear hard and unfeeling in their relations with associates, and there was slight evidence that this carried over into the home in a few instances. At work, top executives are treated by their subordinates as if they were despots—even when the supervisor neither acts nor feels like one. The power of his position, and in particular his power over subordinates, is close to being absolute. Some subordinates consequently relate to him as if he were an absolute despot. Some executives act like martinets and invoke all of the power of their position to demean and humble their associates. Their

Summary and Conclusions

behavior to subordinates carried over to their behavior with me and my associates. In all probability, these attitudes toward others pervade all of their personal relations—in the home and elsewhere. But these men may not have been changed by their careers as business executives but rather may have purposely selected a career that would give them an opportunity to express these attitudes without incurring severe penalties.

Concern is sometimes expressed that top executives of today have an excessive craving for security and the easy life as compared with the business leaders of an earlier time. Driving energy, a neurotic desire to succeed for the sake of success, a single-minded devotion to business and a willingness to sacrifice anything or anyone that stood in their way have been attributed to the famous entrepreneurs of the late 1800s and early 1900s. Certainly, one finds none of this type left at the head of firms in the television set industry—or at the head of any of the nation's largest enterprises. (Large numbers may still be found running small- and medium-size businesses and in the professions; a few also are engaged primarily in financial pursuits, mainly acquiring and merging enterprises.) The largest manufacturing and industrial firms are run today by men whose devotion to business success seems more moderate and whose lives are far better balanced than were those of Rockefeller, Carnegie, Hill, Vanderbilt, Swift, etc. Is our economic effort any the less efficient and productive and innovative as a result?

It is difficult to imagine the results of placing a hard-hitting buccaneer at the head of, say, R.C.A. or U.S. Steel. The image conjured up by that supposition is that of an enterprise out of step with the times that dissipates its energies in futile conflict with government, labor and rivals. To operate successfully with the limited power possessed by business owners today within an undefined power structure takes skills, diplomacy and patience, which executives neither possessed nor needed 75 years ago.

The top executives in the television set industry are as devoted to their jobs and to success as could possibly serve any purpose. In most cases, their "drive" does not stop short of a neurotic striving for success. No gain in efficiency or creativity could be expected from an intensification of the drive; the contrary is more likely in television set manufacturing. At the top and short of the top, one finds heavy emphasis on change and innovation—perhaps too much, if one counts its cost. The top executive who expects to move ahead or to have his firm prosper by delaying change markedly is a rarity in the industry. Much as they might welcome a less hectic life (though theirs is less hectic than some earlier generation enterpreneurs faced), the top executives in the television set industry have little security, and their enterprises are always in danger of suffering heavy losses with little or no warning. They seem to live with and cope with this insecurity and somehow manage to guide their firms with tolerable financial success.

Worry about the future of our economy should not be on grounds of the lack of competence or drive of the nation's top executives. They are intelligent, active and aggressive and possess a huge desire to succeed, unless executives in the television set industry are a rare exception. What I know of other industries confirms my conclusion that firms in the United States are headed by men of talent, drive and skill who are able to function effectively within situations such as the television set industry, which are extremely lacking in information, constantly changing, risky and chaotic.

Although not studied in depth, methods and attitudes with respect to executive development were investigated. In no company is there evidence of any carefully organized and concerted effort to train executives for higher level posts or to up-date their skills. Moreover, no emphasis seems to be attached to the training of subordinates by the industry's top executives. In these respects, the firms in the television set industry do seem to differ from many with which I have familiarity. When men in this industry are promoted to higher posts, they must learn their new responsibilities on the job and learn them quickly. There is little patience with failure, no matter what the cause, and no inclination to wait for a man to master his new responsibilities. As one would expect under such circumstances, there is considerable turnover among top-level executives; moreover, few men in top management have assimilated the new management and research techniques that have been developed in recent years. Most of the men at or near the top in the television set industry are much too busy doing their present job to acquire new skills and techniques. The climate of management is not conducive to an investment in oneself—let alone in the training of one's subordinates. Executives seem to have an extremely short time horizon, aimed at showing results now so that they can move further up the ladder when the next opening arises.

THE INSTABILITY OF MARKET DOMINANCE

There appear to be several powerful market forces which limit a firm's ability to remain the number one company in the industry or even in any one major market area. First, the most widely purchased brand becomes the most widely "shopped" brand by consumers (as well as by comparison shoppers) for retailers. As a result, both prospective customers and retailers become extremely well informed about competitors' prices and know the lowest prices in the market. Prospective customers even are sophisticated about different model numbers in the best-selling brand line. As a result, competitive price pressure becomes extremely severe and tends to drive prices down quickly whenever any retailer makes a price cut. On less popular brands, the contagion of a price cut is far smaller and slower.

Second, there seems to be an irresistible temptation to the manufacturer who has achieved first position to use his new market power in a variety of ways that ultimately alienate some of his retailers. Also, his distributors, sometimes without his knowledge or blessing, frequently will exert pressure on dealers when their brand is in active demand. Moreover, a distributor's salesmen in violation of his wishes, will use the dominant position of that brand to pressure retailers in ways that may ultimately weaken their position in the market.

The distributor handling the "hottest" brand in the market has an understandable desire to add the strongest retailers as his accounts. When he does so (for many will want to carry his line when it reaches the top who refused to do so formerly) he is intensifying the competition for his "regular" retailers and reducing the value of their franchise. As one executive put it, "Every time you add another retailer you are adding a carbuncle." The combination of additional retailers (reducing the volume available for each one, on average) plus stronger price pressure makes the best-selling line a less profitable line to carry. Retailers, who carry multiple lines, therefore push it less vigorously or actually sell against it.

Instances have been reported, and they are said to be numerous, in which distributors whose line has grown in popular favor have pressured their dealers to drop other lines and to devote more floor space to their line. They sometimes even threaten dealers with the loss of their franchise if they do not place sizable orders at that particular time. It seems to be accurate that the distributors who have a brand that has grown in popularity to a dominant position become extremely arrogant and alienate retailers. The same types of pressure may be exerted by the salesmen representing distributors without their employers' knowing about it. The dealer, however, would assume that the salesman was carrying out the distributor's wishes.

Intensified competition, distributor arrogance and pressure, and a reduction in profit margins all combine to lessen the retailer's support for the best-selling line. After a while, it may cease to be the best-selling line for that very reason.

Conclusions about Methodology

This study represents an experiment with a method of academic research that rarely is used by marketing specialists and economists. Social scientists in other fields are more familiar with this method and dignify it by the name of "ethnography." They even set forth some moderately convincing arguments to show that this method is superior *in some respects* to the use of statistics and formal market surveys.

Ethnographic investigations do get behind the surface of what happens and can be focused on the processes that go on and the thinking behind observed behavior. Business as a process and as a series of interrelated decisions can be studied effectively by this method alone. But, as has been constantly stressed, such studies lack breadth of coverage and are beset by errors resulting from the imperfections of personal interviews as a research tool. But, for many business and economic problems, statistical and formal survey data are even less reliable.

Summary and Conclusions 275

If so little is known about the nature of our business system, as the foregoing chapter suggests, how can we learn more? Has this research project established the workability and value of the method that was employed?

The reader should judge what, if anything, has been gained by using this method. I can only testify to the time and costs that it involves. Both are very great. Without some substantial financial assistance, no researcher will be able to afford the numerous trips to distant places, often to stay for a week or more, the frequent long-distance calls, research assistants and secretarial help that the use of this method entails.

If there is a single methodological lesson that I learned from this project, it was the value and necessity of interviewing many different parties to the same situation. Even the most perceptive, frank and cooperative business executive cannot describe what he does, his company's policies and the results of his actions and policies with a high degree of accuracy. It is only by speaking to his colleagues, his secretary, his subordinates, customers and suppliers, and members of the trade press and trade associations that one arrives at a picture of the man, his business, his approach and the company that rings true and corresponds with available information. The difference between what one would believe if he took the statements of an executive at face value and the final picture one forms by speaking to many persons associated with him often is great. In some cases, there is no resemblance between the two pictures. Moreover, in order to get all that an executive could tell you that is of value, it is necessary to speak to him several times so that he comes to know and trust you. The first interview generally yields something that the public relations department would have been willing to release. On a third or fourth interview, one learns many highly confidential things.

Fortunately, an executive's associates and subordinates tend to observe him very closely—if not wholly objectively. After one has visited a company several times, one generally can obtain some frank and critical—as well as adulatory—statements about its top executives in confidence. The many conflicting stories one gets require sifting, and often one ends in serious doubt about the true situation. The method used here does not always lead to clear, unmistakable conclusions; the people who hold high posts in industry, their methods and the effects of their actions are not clear, and any method used to study these matters must capture the amorphous nature of business personalities, methods and influence.

I would pronounce this method a success and capable of uncovering the essential nature of business. Other methods less costly and cumbersome must be developed, however, for this method has many limitations—beyond cost and time and effort. It requires special kinds of skills that are not ordinarily developed in academic scholars. To be successful, researchers using this method must be experienced and natively equipped to do personal interviewing with people who are very busy and wary; they must command enough respect so that the person interviewed does not brush them off with a few polite words or give answers that are superficial or untrue. They must, in some way, elicit a desire on the part of the respondent to help—even though the respondent is usually terribly pressed with other things and recognizes that there are some risks in being frank. Even a researcher with unusual interviewing talents might well fail at such an undertaking unless he begins with at least a few close personal contacts in the industry he is studying.

It is not difficult to understand why studies of this kind have not been made of many industries. The difference between what one learns from such a study and what one believes otherwise suggests that such studies are urgently needed. Otherwise, our picture of the American business system will continue to be built upon a foundation of falsehood and exaggeration. Although the prevailing picture of American business and American businessmen is highly flattering, it does hold dangers. Clearly we should know the truth, even if only for its own sake. More important, unless we understand, we cannot improve. And it is difficult to read the foregoing pages—or to have lived through the collection of the information on which they are based —without concluding that there is much room for improvement.

INDEX

Admiral, 13, 25-26, 39, 60, 62, 71, 242
Advertising, 17, 36, 39-40, 60-72, 67, 113, 135, 151, 160-64, 197-200, 222-25; merits of, 1; competitive, 16, 251-52; cooperative, 17, 46, 61-63, 67, 113, 135, 161-62; direct to consumer, 40, 151; national, 46, 61-62, 68-69; trade, 132
Alteration, 16
American Management Association, 4
American Television Corp., 10-11
Andrea Radio Corp., 10-11
Assembly function, 15
Associate Distributors, 57, 112-13
"Authorized servicing dealer," 177-78

Baird, John L., 8
Bait and switch stratagem, 203
Bargaining power, 210-12; distributors', 210-11; retailers', 211; manufacturers', 211-12
Billing, 116
British Broadcasting System, 9
Bruno Distributing Co., 156
Budget, 16, 44, 50-52; manufacturer's, 44, 50-52
Business executives, caliber of, 268-73
Business practice materials, 4

Campbell-Swinton, A. A., 8
Clark, John Maurice, 243
Collection, 116
Columbia Broadcasting System, 9, 14, 248
Commercial Finance Companies, 99-100
Communications, 70, 120-23; media, 70
Competition, 3, 54-55, 244, 252-55; among firms, 3; various forms of, 3, 244-46; price, 54-55

Consumers, 33-36; function of, 33-34
Corning Glass, 20n
Cost accounting, distribution, 16
Costs, 150-52, 186-88; advertising, 150; direct, 150; expense, 150; overhead, 150; provisions (bad debt), 150; salaries, 150; selling expense, 150; service, 150; shipping, 150; total selling compensation, 150; warehouse, 150; general and administrative, 150-51; interest, 150-51; sales, 150-52; dealers', 186-88
Credit, 15, 98-100, 106, 116, 132-34; risks, 106; manufacturers' extension to dealers, 132-34
Crosley, 11
Curtis Mathes, 25
Customer classification, by retail salesmen, 184-86

Dealer organizations, 169-72
de Forest, Lee, 8
Delivery, 15
Delivery costs, distributors', 153; retail, 189
Department stores, 113
Discount houses, 34, 113, 182-83, 196, 211
Discrimination, in co-op advertising allowances, 162
Display, 15, 36, 134-35; window, 134-35
Distribution, 1, 15-16, 24, 27, 32, 38-88, 89, 123-27, 143, 152-55, 222-31, 235-37; by manufacturers, 24; exclusive, 27, 123-27, 143; selection of, 39; physical activities, 152-55; costs, 235-37
Distributors, 27-31, 39, 90, 91-109, 143, 147-78; factory owned, 27-30, 90, 109-15; independent, 27-31, 90-

Index

Distributors (*Continued*)
109; functions of, 29-30; development of, 39; management of factory branches, 39; financial accommodation, 39; servicing, 39, 98-101; performance, 39, 101-9; high turnover, 93; costs of changing, 93-95; selection of, 95-97; economic functions, 143, 147-49; activities, 143, 149-78; experience, 143-47
DuMont, 10-14
DuMont, Allan B., 8

Economic activities, 214-31; nature of, 214-15; social appraisal, 214-21; effect of, 215; "demand-creating," 217-18; "demand-satisfying," 217-18
Electrical Merchandising Weekly, 132
Electronic Marketing Directory, 19
Emerson-DuMont, 25, 26, 237; *see also* DuMont
Excise Tax, *see* Federal Excise Tax

Factory branch managers, 110
Farnsworth, 11
Fedders, 148
Federal Communications Commission, 9
Federal Excise Tax, 17-18, 37, 56
Federal Trade Commission, 162
Franchises, 27-29, 101-2, 105-6; cancellation clause, 101

General Electric, 10-11, 13, 18, 23, 25-27, 39, 62, 71, 74-76, 79, 99, 141, 148, 237-38, 242
General Electric Acceptance Corporation, 99
Government, 36-37; role of, 36
G. I. Bill of Rights, 140
Guarantees, 16, 40

Hoffman Electronics, 14
Home Furnishings Daily, 132

Information, 15-16, 29, 39, 130-31; provision of, 15, 29, 130-31; collection of cost and sales, 16
Insurance, 15
International Television, 11

Jenkins, C. Francis, 8

Kefauver, Senator Estes, 4

Madison Avenue, U.S.A., 219-20
Magnavox, 25, 112, 117-18, 137, 211, 237-38, 242; system of distribution, 117-18, 237-38
Majestic (Kit), 11
Management, 190-206, 255-68; internal activities, 190-200; external activities, 200-6; chief goals of, 255-68
Market dominance, instability of, 273-74
Marketing, 1, 39, 41-53, 84, 128-42, 156-57; arrangements and practices, 1, 3; activities, 1, 128-42; programs and policies, 39, 41-53, 84, 156-57; plans, 47-48, 52, 53
Market research, 16, 78
Market shares, 48-50
Mart, 132, 180
Materials handling, 15, 22
Mayer, Martin, 219-20
Merchandising, 17; trends, 46
Methodology, 274-76; models used in industry studies, 5-7; ethnography, 274
Motorola, 13, 25-27, 39, 60, 71, 75-76, 237, 242
Mund, Vernon, 227-28
Muntz, 25, 112, 119-20, 137; system of distribution, 119-20

National Appliance and Radio Dealers Association, 186
National Broadcasting System, 9, 62
National Credit Office, 18
National Industrial Conference Board, 4
"New Marketing Concept," 41
"New Year's Resolution Syndrome," 49
Nipkow, Paul, 8
Norge, 148

"Objectives and goals," 45, 46
"Open house," 131
Outlets, 179-86, 187-90, 194-200, 207-8, 210-11, 241-42; department and other general stores, 181; furniture stores, 181; household appliance stores, 181, 183-90, 194-200, 207-8, 210-11, 241-42; radio and television stores, 181; other, 181

Pacific Mercury, 25; *see also* Sears Roebuck

Index

Package deals, 164-65
Packard-Bell, 25-26, 112-19, 237-38; system of distribution, 118-19, 237-38
Parts warranty, 17
Philco (Ford), 11, 13, 25-26, 39, 62, 71, 75, 148, 248
Pilot, 11
Piser's Furniture Store, Bronx, 9
Planning, 16, 45, 46-48, 52, 53; product, 46-48, 52, 53
Premiums, 165-66
Prices, minimum, 159-60
Pricing, 39, 46, 53-59, 157-60, 194-97; appliance dealer, 194-97
Product design, 72-81
Product improvement, 15-17, 39-40, 76; engineering, 17; examination, 15; level of quality, 39, 76; designs, 39-40, 76
Production, 17, 81-88, 90; direct, 17; model "line" and "mix", 81-84, 90; scheduling and forecast, 84-88
Production activities, 1
Production costs, 35
"Product Manager for Television," 54
"Product Planning Section," 74
Product quality, level of, 72-81
Promotions, 164-69
Public relations, 141-42

R.C.A., 10-13, 18, 23, 25-27, 32, 39, 62, 71, 75, 79, 136-38, 141, 211, 237, 242
Refrigeration, 15
Regional sales managers, 106-9
Repair, 16
Resale price maintenance, see Prices, minimum
Research and development, 16, 17
Retailers, 31, 33, 40, 89, 115-27, 179-80, 197-202; functions of, 31-32; financial accommodations, 40; physical distribution by, 188-90; forecasting and ordering, 191-92; selection of merchandise, 192-93; selection of sources, 193-94; advertising, 197-200; product information, 201-2; salesmen, 202
Retailing, 179-212, 240-41; structure of, 179-86; nature of, 183-86; consequences of offering more than one brand, 208-10, 240-41

Returns, privileges, 15
Robinson-Patman Act, 113
Rosing, Boris, 8

Sales, 16, 35, 84, 88, 106-9, 155-56, 255-56; forecasting, 16, 84, 88, 155-56; force, 106-9; management preoccupation with, 255-56
Salesmen, retail, 129-32, 206-8; performance, 129-32; record keeping, 206-8; merchandise manager, 206-8; creating and management of, 207-8
Sales promotion, 29, 46, 96, 102-6, 111-12; quotas, 102-6, 111-12
Sears-Roebuck, 14, 25, 31, 112, 116-17, 212, 237-39, 242-43; system of distribution, 116-17, 37-39, 242-43
Second World War, 5, 9-10, 32, 140, 145, 180, 182
Selling, personal, 16; direct, 17
Service effort, 17, 36
Servicemen, 32, 137-40, 176-77; "authorized," 139; independent, 137-40
Silvertone, 117
Singer Manufacturing Company, 118
Smith, Adam, 227
Stewart-Warner, 11, 14, 248
Stromberg-Carlson, 11, 14, 248
Sylvania, 18, 25, 39, 75

Television, development of, 8
"Television Product Sales Manager," 54
Television set industry, production, 12
Temporary National Economic Committee, 4; hearings, 4
The Organization Man, 3
Trade press, 3
Training, 40, 100-1
Transportation, 15, 92, 152
Tubes, 46; size of, 46

Warehousing, 15
Warwick, 25; see also Sears-Roebuck
Wealth of Nations, The, 227
Westinghouse, 10-11, 25-26, 62, 75, 87-88, 141, 148
Whyte, William, 3

Zenith, 11, 13, 23, 25, 26, 32, 39, 60, 68, 69, 71, 136, 138, 141, 211, 237, 242
Zworykin, Vladimir, 8